This book is due for return not later than the last
date stamped below, unless recalled sooner.

HOMICIDE LAW IN COMPARATIVE PERSPECTIVE

A number of jurisdictions world-wide have changed or are considering changing their homicide laws. Important changes have now been recommended for England and Wales, and these changes are an important focus in the book, which brings together leading experts from jurisdictions across the globe (England and Wales; France; Germany; Scotland; Australia; The United States of America; Canada; Singapore and Malaysia) to examine key aspects of the law of homicide.

Key areas examined include the structure of the law of homicide and the meaning of fault elements. For example, the definition of murder, or its equivalent, is very different in France and Germany from the definition used in England and Wales. French law, like the law in a number of American states, ties the definition of murder to the presence or absence of premeditation, unlike the law in England and Wales. Unlike most other jurisdictions, German law makes the killer's motive, such as a sadistic sexual motive, relevant to whether or not he or she committed the worst kind of homicide. England and Wales is in a minority of English-speaking jurisdictions in that it does not employ the concept of 'wicked' recklessness, or of extreme indifference, as a fault element in homicide.

Understanding these often subtle differences between the approaches of different jurisdictions to the definition of homicide is an essential aspect of the law reform process, and of legal study and scholarship in the criminal law. Every jurisdiction tries to learn from the experience of others, and this book seeks to make a contribution to that process, as well as providing a lively and informative resource for scholars and students.

Volume 6 in the Criminal Law Library series

Criminal Law Library

Volume 1: Self-Defence in Criminal Law
Boaz Sangero

Volume 2: Evidence of Bad Character
John Spencer

Homicide Law in Comparative Perspective

Edited by

JEREMY HORDER

·HART·
PUBLISHING

OXFORD AND PORTLAND, OREGON
2007

Published in North America (US and Canada) by
Hart Publishing
c/o International Specialized Book Services
920 NE 58th Avenue, Suite 300
Portland, OR 97213–3786
USA
Tel: +1 503 287 3093 or toll-free: (1) 800 944 6190
Fax: +1 503 280 8832
E-mail: orders@isbs.com
Website: www.isbs.com

Hart Publishing, 16C Worcester Place, OX1 2JW
Telephone: +44 (0)1865 517530 Fax: +44 (0)1865 510710
E-mail: mail@hartpub.co.uk
Website: http://www.hartpub.co.uk

British Library Cataloguing in Publication Data
Data Available

ISBN: 978–1-84113–696–7 (hardback)

Typeset by Columns Design Ltd, Reading
Printed and bound in Great Britain by
TJ International Ltd, Padstow, Cornwall

Preface

THIS VOLUME EMERGES from the work that was done by the contributors towards the writing of the Law Commission's final report on the law of homicide in England and Wales, *Murder, Manslaughter and Infanticide*.[1] A number of jurisdictions world-wide have been reviewing or revising their homicide laws, and each has engaged in comparative analysis. An important new contribution to this process can be made by compiling a detailed scholarly analysis of the law in a range of jurisdictions (both recently reformed and unreformed). In addition, Chapter 2 provides an overview of how the Law Commission for England and Wales justified its conclusions as to how the law of homicide should be reformed.

Key questions, answered in different ways in different jurisdictions, confront would-be reformers of the law of homicide. For example:

1. Should 'murder' be the most serious homicide offence? Alternatively, should there be aggravated versions of murder, above murder itself? In England and Wales, as in a number of former common law countries, the first question is answered 'yes' whereas in France and Germany, by way of contrast, 'yes' is the answer to the second question.
2. Should murder be confined to an intention to kill? Once again (broadly speaking), in France and Germany the answer is 'yes', whereas in Scotland and in England and Wales, as in Australian states, the answer is 'no'. Although the answer is also 'no' under American state codes, under Canadian law and under the Singaporean penal code, the approach in the latter jurisdictions is more highly sophisticated (which is not necessarily to say that it is better).

These essays explore these and many other issues where different jurisdictions have taken a diverse range of approaches to key issues in the law of homicide. The essays are not so regimented as to ensure that each author explores precisely the same issues in the same depth. Authors have been given scope to develop their contributions in a way that brings out important or pressing issues within the jurisdiction under consideration. This will enable those engaged in comparative analysis, for the purposes of law reform, to gauge where they are most likely to find material and discussion more detailed and advanced in some jurisdictions than in others.

---

[1] Law Commission, *Murder, Manslaughter and Infanticide* (Law Com No 304, 2006).

When speaking of comparisons between legal systems, and of homicide trials in particular, Sir James Stephen once wrote, 'The whole temper and spirit of the French and the English differ so widely, that it would be rash for an Englishmen to speak of trials in France as they actually are'.[2] In this volume, the contributors have not taken such a gloomy view of attempts to understand 'foreign' laws of homicide. They are right not to have done so.

I would like to pay tribute to the unfailing support and encouragement that I have had from the start from all at Hart Publishing for the publication of these essays. I would also like gratefully to acknowledge the intellectual debt that those of us writing on English law in this volume owe to Lord Justice Toulson, former Chair of the Law Commission of England and Wales. His profound influence on the development of the Commission's thinking on homicide, and his encouragement of our efforts to adopt a more comparative approach, were at all times crucial.

---

[2] Sir James Stephen, *History of the Criminal Law of England* (London, 1883), i at 77.

Contents

List of Contributors

Jeremy Horder is a Law Commissioner for England and Wales, Professor of Criminal Law, University of Oxford, and Porjes Trust Fellow, Worcester College.

David Hughes is Criminal Law Team Leader, Law Commission for England and Wales.

JR Spencer is Professor of Law, University of Cambridge, and Fellow of Selwyn College.

Antje du Bois-Pedain is Lecturer in Law, University of Cambridge, and Fellow of Magdalene College.

Claire Finkelstein is Professor of Law and Philosophy, University of Pennsylvania.

Winifred Holland is Professor in the Faculty of Law, University of Western Ontario.

Ian Leader-Elliott is Senior Lecturer in Law, Adelaide University.

Victor Tadros is Professor of Law, University of Warwick.

Stanley Yeo is Professor of Law, National University of Singapore, and Southern Cross University.

Table of Cases

Table of Legislation

Commonwealth

European Union

France

Germany

India

Malaysia

New Zealand

Singapore

UK

1

Comparative Issues in the Law of Homicide

JEREMY HORDER AND DAVID HUGHES

1. Introduction

I N THE COURSE of formulating its provisional proposals and then its
recommendations for murder and manslaughter, the Law Commission has
sought to learn from comparisons with other jurisdictions. Significant critical light on the perspective from which particular proposals are seeking to
achieve reform can be shed by consideration of the way similar issues are
addressed from different perspectives elsewhere. Trying to understand how other
jurisdictions tackle similar problems, almost always from a different vantage-
point in terms of the norms of criminal procedure, is what can shed such critical
light. We go in search of this understanding without being drawn into addressing
second-order questions about the making of comparisons between jurisdictions.
It would be possible to ask, for example, whether a comparative analysis is fatally
weakened if it is insufficiently broad or insufficiently deep. Further, one might be
troubled by the question whether greater attention should be paid to the
solutions provided by the law in a jurisdiction with a similar political tradition,
or in a jurisdiction governing tens of millions of people rather than hundreds of
thousands. Important though these second-order questions often are, they may
obstruct what we regard as a simple truth that comparative analysis can be
undertaken in different ways for many different purposes. From the law-
reformer's perspective, an idea or solution crudely lifted from another jurisdiction, even if it was taken out of context or misunderstood, may eventually be
made to bear fruit in fresh soil; and if it does, that will have justified the

comparative exercise.[1] We will consider here a selection of key differences between the Law Commission's recommendations for the law of homicide and the provisions currently employed in other jurisdictions. At one time, such an exercise would almost certainly have been undertaken in order to demonstrate the supposed superiority of solutions based on the common law tradition over the solutions provided by fully codified systems in mainland Europe. A splendid example is provided by the work of the famous judge and jurist, Sir James Stephen, writing over 100 years ago. Stephen was inordinately proud of English criminal law, although fully aware of its deficiencies. For him, its development symbolised the seemingly unchallengeable moral and legal authority of the state itself:

> [English criminal law] represents … the result of the labours of the powerful legislature and the most authoritative body of judges known to history. In no other country in the world has a single legislature exercised without dispute and without rival the power of legislating over a compact and yet extensive nation for anything like approaching to so long a period as the parliament of England. In no other country has a small number of judges exercised over a country anything like so extensive and compact the undisputed power of interpreting written and declaring unwritten law, in a manner generally recognised as of conclusive authority.[2]

To bolster this claim, Stephen marred his otherwise highly learned account of French criminal law by a series of partisan claims about its deficiencies. In his view, not only was 'the spirit of French Legislation…very favourable to persons in authority' and 'a dictator like Napoleon [was] placed in such circumstances that he can practically impose his will on a great nation',[3] but also, in French homicide trials:

> the admission of unrestricted appeals to prejudice and sentiment…would appear to us to crown by feeble sentimentality a proceeding instituted secretly and carried on oppressively.[4]

Stephen did not mince words. He railed against the restriction of *meutre* in French law to intentional killings. This, he found, led to 'distinctions revolting to common sense'.[5] Further, the seemingly innocuous practice of sending a man condemned for parricide to the place of execution with his head covered by a black veil, Stephen thought, 'seems to our English taste puerile'.[6] For some reason, the English practice whereby the trial judge donned a black cap on top of his wig to pass the sentence of death escaped Stephen's censure. Almost needless to say, Stephen considered that in English law:

---

[1]   The Law Commission is, eg, borrowing the distinction between first and second degree murder from American state law, even though it is not being used for an identical purpose: see Finkelstein, ch 5 below.

[2]   Sir James Stephen, History of the Criminal Law of England (London, 1883), iii, at 355.

[3]   Ibid, ii, at 77.

[4]   Ibid, i, at 565.

[5]   Ibid, iii, at 93.

[6]   Ibid, at 95.

It is unnecessary to distinguish between the morality of the Legislator and that of the persons legislated for, for the two may be considered practically identical.[7]

For Stephen, the common law was 'formed by very slow degrees and with absolutely no conscious adaptation of means to ends', having, 'an organic unity which seems to me to be wanting in the [French] system'.[8] Distancing ourselves from this kind of bombast, our aim is not to show that the Commission is 'right' and other jurisdictions are 'wrong'; that would be absurd. The aim is to show that, whilst we realise that there may be perfectly acceptable alternative solutions to similar problems, the Commission had sound reasons for going in its chosen direction.

2. English Homicide Law: Charting the Changing Philosophies

Historically, the law of homicide in England and Wales has had a number of distinguishing marks. One mark has been that it does not build considerations of motive into the demarcation of offence categories. Another mark has been that, putting aside the anomalous case of petit treason, homicide law has not traditionally demarcated those categories according to some special status or feature of the victim.[9] This stands in contrast with English law's approach to non-fatal offences. Although consideration of motives is still very much the exception in the definition of offences,[10] amongst the non-fatal offences it is common to find distinctions drawn between offences on the basis of the victim's age,[11] gender[12] or status[13] (although there is little consistency in the law's approach). A further distinguishing mark can be found in the fact that fatal offences in English law are relatively insensitive to the way in which the homicide took place, whereas this is not true of the non-fatal offences. 'Causing death' is the keystone of the law of

---

[7] Ibid, i, at 77.

[8] Ibid, ii, at 565.

[9] Until 1828, some murders of those in positions of authority were regarded as a form of treason. As we shall see shortly, 20th century developments have made this distinguishing mark much less distinct, through the passing of, eg, the Infanticide Act 1938 (where the victim must be an infant under a year old) and the Domestic Violence Crimes and Victims Act 2004, under which the victim must be a child or vulnerable adult.

[10] The offence of female circumcision may also be thought to be in some sense motive-sensitive, attacking the conduct of those who engage in the practice for religious reasons or in order to maintain certain cultural traditions: see the Female Genital Mutilation Act 2003, s 1.

[11] An essential element of the distinctions between offences under the Sexual Offences Act 2003. See also the offence of Child Cruelty in the Children and Young Persons Act 1933, s 1.

[12] See, eg, the Sexual Offences Act 2003 and the Female Genital Mutilation Act 2003.

[13] In English law, there are offences of assaulting a police officer in the execution of duty (Police Act 1996, s 89), and ill-treating or neglecting a mental patient, where the offender is a member of staff in a relevant institution (Mental Health Act 1983, s 127).

homicide, even when (exceptionally) the offence is confined to a specific context[14] or to a specific mode of commission.[15] By way of contrast, the non-fatal offences have varied much more widely in this respect. Replacing the old distinctions between drowning, suffocating, strangling, using a loaded gun or knife, and so on[16] have come new distinctions. Examples are provided by female circumcision,[17] the tattooing of minors[18] and torture.[19] These take their place alongside older, retained offences, such as administering a noxious thing[20] or maliciously preventing a person on board (or having just quitted) a ship in distress or ship wrecked from trying to save his own life or that of another.[21] Once again, it is worth referring to Stephen's patriotic defence of the bewildering mélange of often overlapping or outdated offences that has for 150 years characterised English law:

> The history of our law upon personal injuries is certainly not creditable to the legislature, and the result at which we have presently arrived is extremely clumsy, but I think its substance is greatly superior to the corresponding provisions of the French and German codes, besides being much more complete.[22]

As we will see shortly, to some extent the old order is now changing; but what has explained the basic difference of approach as between fatal and non-fatal offences?

Allowance must be made for the fact that any reform of or innovation in the law of homicide in England and Wales is liable to be far more controversial and difficult at the Parliamentary stage, as well as more costly and drawn-out at the stage of consultation, than a reform of the non-fatal offences. So, ad hoc reform addressing the perceived evil of the moment has until relatively recently been more rare in the domain of homicide. Allowing for that, however, two considerations may well have played an important role in explaining the difference of approach. First, great respect has been paid historically by the English legislature to the judge-fashioned crimes of 'murder' and 'manslaughter'. Until the twentieth century, no serious challenge was mounted to these crimes as the basis for virtually the whole of the law of homicide. Even attempts in the nineteenth century to reform and codify these crimes in themselves failed.

Secondly, there has been a basic difference between the approach to conceptual categorisation of homicide in England and Wales and that adopted in some other jurisdictions. Other than in the road traffic context, there has never been any

---

[14]   As in the offence of causing the death of a child or vulnerable adult under the Domestic Violence, Crimes and Victims Act 2004.

[15]   As in the offence of causing death by dangerous driving under the Road Traffic Act 1988.

[16]   See Sir James Stephen, History of the Criminal Law of England (London, 1883) ii, at 113–18.

[17]   Female Genital Mutilation Act 2003.

[18]   Tattooing of Minors Act 1969.

[19]   Criminal Justice Act 1988, s 134.

[20]   Offences Against the Person Act 1861, ss 23 and 24.

[21]   Offences Against the Person Act 1961, s 17 (see also s 37).

[22]   Sir James Stephen, above n 16, iii, at 118.

inclination in England and Wales routinely to make 'causing death' an aggravating factor in what is, in essence, a discrete non-fatal offence. So, when the Legislature has created offences of female circumcision or torture, or health and safety and work offences, it has not buttressed them with an aggravated version in which death is caused in the course of the prohibited activity. By way of contrast with the approach in France, for instance, there is no offence in English law of 'causing death' by torture,[23] by rape or by the administration of substances.[24] There is simply no tradition in England and Wales of automatically giving consideration to such aggravated versions of non-fatal offences, when the latter are created.[25] So far as more general offences are concerned, the much-disputed case of so-called 'one punch' manslaughter would be treated as an aggravated form of assault in France and Germany.[26] The English lacuna could be rationalised by the suggestion that the creation of such offences would undermine the authority of murder and manslaughter; but that authority has been to a considerable degree undermined already.

Since the early twentieth century, Parliament has shown increasing willingness to challenge the moral and legal hegemony of murder and manslaughter within the law of homicide. So far as manslaughter is concerned, Parliament has created new free-standing offences to deal with perceived problems, where manslaughter has been thought unequal to the task. The main examples are infanticide,[27] causing death by dangerous driving[28] and causing the non-accidental death of a child or vulnerable adult.[29] In each case, the reasons have differed for creating a new offence rather than seeking to adapt the crime of manslaughter, but taken together the offences represent a considerable inroad on the scope of the authority of manslaughter.

So far as murder is concerned, without changing the legal definition of the crime, Parliament has recently outflanked the traditional judicial understanding that murder is essentially 'one crime (killing by malice aforethought); one

---

[23] In French law, a higher penalty for 'torture or acts of barbarity' may be given if death is unintentionally caused in the course of such acts: see John Spencer, ch 3 below. See also J Spencer and A Pedain, 'Approaches to Strict and Constructive Liability in Continental Criminal Law' in AP Simester (ed), Appraising Strict Liability (Oxford, 2005) 237 at 264–66.

[24] French Penal Code, arts 221–225. For the contrast with French law see John Spencer, ch 3 below.

[25] Such offences would not, on the face of it, seem likely to fall victim to quite the same range of criticisms that there have been of the so-called 'felony murder' rule (abolished in 1957), whereby killing in the course or furtherance of a felony was deemed to be murder. Ironically, the only exception to this 'cultural' rule has been the creation of the offence of causing death by dangerous driving, where there has historically been no non-fatal equivalent of causing non-fatal injury by dangerous driving.

[26] See Antje du Bois-Pedain, ch 4 below; John Spencer, ch 3 below; see also Spencer and Pedain, above n 23. This point was noted—perhaps surprisingly, without criticism—by Stephen: see Sir James Stephen, History of the Criminal Law of England (London, 1883), iii, at 90.

[27] Infanticide Act 1938, s 1.

[28] Road Traffic Act 1988, s 1.

[29] Domestic Violence, Crimes and Victims Act 2004, s 5.

sentence (life imprisonment)'. Parliament has done this by creating myriad differences between kinds of murder for sentencing purposes.[30] These differences have drawn on ideas hitherto foreign to English law, such as making motive, or the mode of killing, or the status of the victim relevant to the judge's decision as to the minimum initial period that the killer must serve in custody. So, for example, intentionally killing more than one victim, or a police officer on duty, or with a sadistic motive will justify a hefty minimum term (or even the rest of the offender's life) in custody. This development was designed to shore up public confidence in sentencing for murder. Ironically, it will slowly but surely undermine the traditional basis for murder's authority and even its 'mystique' as a crime, namely that it is one crime (killing by malice aforethought) and one sentence (life imprisonment; previously, of course, execution).[31]

These developments might be thought to open the way for a new approach to homicide, even if dispensing with the terms 'murder' and 'manslaughter' is, politically, not a realistic possibility. One approach would be to relegate murder and manslaughter to the legal background, the foreground being occupied by a series of offences of 'causing death by...' attached to all non-fatal offences where the causing death might foreseeably occur.[32] Another approach would be to try to restore some of the authority of murder and manslaughter as general crimes of homicide. There could be a reason to take the latter approach, even if it is accepted both that murder has irretrievably lost a good deal of its mystique or uniqueness, and that manslaughter must in some contexts yield place to more specific homicide offences. Much though there is to be said for the former approach, the Law Commission has opted for the latter. In part, the reason for this is the Commission's reliance on the view that unlawful killings are discrete wrongs, and not just deaths caused by misfortune in the course of committing some other wrong.[33] Unlawful killings should, then, be dealt with as stand-alone offences which is of course how they are dealt with in England Wales through the crimes of murder and manslaughter.

There is another reason for taking the route of seeking to restore some of the authority of murder and manslaughter. Even those jurisdictions with very different philosophies of criminal law commonly have two or more general

---

[30] Criminal Justice Act 2003, s 269, sched 21. For an analysis in these terms see A Norrie, 'Between Orthodox Subjectivism and Moral Contextualism: Intention and the Consultation Paper' [2006] Crim LR 486.

[31] Naturally, in suggesting that murder's mystique is connected with its status as 'one crime; one sentence', we do not overlook the different forms of fault element that historically have fallen within the scope of 'malice aforethought', nor the fact that the fate of a convicted murderer has always varied very considerably depending on the circumstances.

[32] A further possibility, that a single offence of unlawful killing replace all other offences of homicide, has not been seriously considered by any jurisdiction that has reformed its laws of homicide. For further discussion see Law Commission, A New Homicide Act for England and Wales?, Consultation Paper No 177 (London, 2005) at 2.32–2.38.

[33] For a general theoretical discussion see J Gardner, 'On the General Part of the Criminal Law' in RA Duff (ed), Philosophy and the Criminal Law: Principle and Critique (Cambridge, 1998) ch 5.

crimes of homicide, usually with one especially serious one. Many people are familiar with the idea of distinguishing between first degree and second degree murder, an idea at the heart of American state codes. Analogous distinctions are very common elsewhere, even if the crimes in question have somewhat different content. So, in German law, we find the basic offence of *Totschlag* (broadly, voluntary manslaughter, in English law), the more serious crime of *Mord* (the equivalent of murder), along with less serious instances of voluntary homicide, such as killing on request or killing under provocation. A separate provision deals with cases where death has been caused through an intention to cause bodily injury that has through recklessness led to death.[34] In France, there is also a basic offence of *meutre* (broadly, voluntary manslaughter in English law), and more serious versions of this crime including *assassination* (killing with premeditation, equivalent to first degree murder under most American penal codes). As noted above, French law also treats killing through assault, and through a selection of other non-fatal offences, as an aggravating feature of those crimes (warranting a higher sentence) rather than as discrete homicide offences.

This suggests that it is not wrong to continue to place murder and manslaughter at the heart of the law of homicide, as almost all criminal codes influenced by the English speaking world continue to do.[35] Murder has irretrievably lost its authority in the traditional form of 'one crime; one sentence'; but its authority can be given a fresh basis. The Commission proposes to do this by dividing murder into a more and a less grave version. The more grave version (first degree murder) is to continue to carry the mandatory life sentence, whereas the less grave version (second degree murder) will have a discretionary life maximum sentence. The Commission believes that effecting this division will do something to restore the authority of the law of murder by attending to basic distinctions, in point of culpability, between the ways in which homicide can be committed, and by making the available sentence track these distinctions.[36]

As in France and Germany, the most serious version of murder (first degree murder) will involve intentional killing, but the recommendation is that the most serious version of murder should go further. It should include instances in which the killing involved both an intention to do serious injury and an awareness that there was a serious risk of causing death.[37] The reason for this is that the two fault elements are morally indistinguishable, a point as well explained by Stephen as by anyone before or since:

> Is there anything to choose morally between the man who violently stabs another in the chest with the definite intention of killing him, and the man who stabs another in the chest with no definite intention at all as to his victim's life or death, but with a feeling of indifference whether he lives or dies? It seems to me that there is nothing to choose

---

34   See Anje du Bois-Pedain, ch 4 below.
35   See Stanley Yeo, ch 9 below.
36   For detailed analysis see Jeremy Horder, ch 2 below.
37   Ibid.

between the two men, and that cases may be put in which reckless indifference to the fate of a person intentionally subjected to deadly injury is, if possible, morally worse than an actual intent to kill.[38]

The less grave version of murder (second degree murder) is to cover one instance currently treated as murder, namely where the killing stemmed from an intention to do serious injury. Beyond that, it is also to include some instances of what is currently treated as manslaughter, namely killing by intentionally causing injury or a fear or risk of injury, in the awareness that there is a serious risk of causing death.[39] Here is a major difference from the Franco-German approach, under which (as we have seen) such instances would be treated as aggravated forms of assault,[40] although the fact that second degree murder will have a discretionary life maximum sentence—not a mandatory life sentence—diminishes the distance between the two approaches in punishment terms.

3. Premeditation, Motive and Partial Defences

As indicated at the beginning of the last section, by choosing to focus on the content or extent of intention or awareness, in point of culpability, the Commission has not taken routes favoured in some other jurisdictions. The Commission has not built a requirement of premeditation into its definition of first degree murder (by way of contrast with France and many American state codes). It has also continued the English traditions of excluding motive from the definitional element of any homicide crimes, and of refusing to discriminate between categories of homicide victim (again by way of contrast with the position in France, Germany and most American state codes[41]). Premeditation, motive and the status of the victim will remain, as at present, matters for the judge at the sentencing stage. The theoretical issues driving the Commission's approach are worth more detailed consideration.

To begin with, there will always be a question for juries about whether 'premeditation' is a state of mind (the decision to commit the crime), or is in a broader sense a reflection of what happened (planning, or setting a trap for the victim, for example) between the point at which a decision was taken to commit murder and the murder itself; or both of these.[42] A premeditated murder can be

---

[38] Sir James Stephen, History of the Criminal Law of England (London, 1883) above, iii, at 92.

[39] Second degree murder will also be the result when a partial defence to first degree murder is successfully pleaded. Second degree murder is in this sense the equivalent of the basic offence of homicide (*meutre*, *Mord*) in French and German law.

[40] Arts 222–227 of the French Penal Code.

[41] And possibly also Scotland: see Victor Tadros, ch 8 below.

[42] See the Criminal Justice Act 2003, s 269 and sched 21. Someone can begin to plan or take steps towards a 'hypothetical' murder without, as yet, having taken a decision to commit it, or vice versa. It

distinguished not only from a planned murder but also from an intentional killing. Taking a decision to commit murder (premeditating it) involves no less, but no more, than reaching a conclusion in practical reasoning that the killing will be done. It need involve no more than this, in that the decision can be acted on straight away without any element of planning. It involves no less than this (taking a decision), however, in that, as a deed, a 'killing' may be intentional under that description without necessarily being preceded by a conscious *decision* to kill in the sense just described.[43] Especially in cases where, for example, there has been a provoked loss of self-control or a spontaneous self-defensive reaction, the deed is done—and may have been done intentionally—before practical (decision-making) reasoning can become involved.[44] Is there a reason to mark out for special treatment intentional killings that are the execution of a prior decision to kill?[45]

The problem with this approach is that premeditation is not unquestionably an aggravating factor. A battered woman may understandably delay putting into effect her intention to kill her violent abuser until his back is turned. That can demonstrate premeditation; but in such a case it would be wrong to see the premeditation as aggravating the offence. A similar point could be made, in a very different context, about mentally disordered offenders. If a mentally disordered offender delays killing until the ides of March, because 'the omens are propitious at the time Caesar died', the delay should not be treated as an aggravating factor. Still less, in all such cases, should the element of premeditation be treated as, in principle, an aggravating factor, but then 'traded off' against the mitigation found in the shape of the battered woman's inability to confront her abuser directly, or in the shape of an offender's mental disorder.[46] In such cases (albeit obviously not in other kinds of instances), the particular nature of mitigation undermines the status of premeditation as in any sense an aggravating factor. No doubt there is considerable room for disagreement on this score. In the Commission's view, however, these difficulties or controversies should not have to be confronted when a jury is being instructed on how to decide of which offence an offender is guilty.

---

could be the taking of the steps towards the crime that makes the potential offender's mind up for him or her, one way or the other. See the discussion of the difficulty this has caused in American law in Claire Finkelstein, ch 5 below.

[43] See J Hornsby, 'On What's Intentionally Done' in S Shute, J Gardner and J Horder (eds), *Action and Value in Criminal Law* (Oxford, 1993).

[44] See, further, J Gardner and H Jung, 'Making Sense of *Mens Rea*: Antony Duff's Account' (1991) 11 *OJLS* 559 at 567: '[b]ut it makes no sense to think of *intention in action* as having exclusionary force. By the time one acts with a certain intention, it is too late to any excluding of considerations. The deed is done.' That is not to say, of course, that someone cannot be held responsible for provoked or spontaneous self-defensive reactions of this kind: see, further, J Horder, *Excusing Crime* (Oxford, 2004) at 11–12.

[45] In its Consultation Paper, the Commission did not find very convincing the case for saying that the spontaneity of a killing necessarily made it less grave than an identical killing undertaken with premeditation: Law Commission, above n 32 at paras 2.42–2.45.

[46] See the discussion of the position in German law by Antje du Bois-Pedain, ch 4.

So far as motive is concerned, its incorporation into the definition of (aggravated) murder is not uncommon, especially in mainland European jurisdictions. In France, an aggravated form of homicide is committed, for example, when the killing is meant to facilitate another crime, or to ensure the impunity of a criminal, or if the murder has a racist or homophobic motive.[47] Perhaps the most interesting example of the incorporation of motive into the definition of the offence is in German law, where the most serious offence (*Mord*) is committed if the offender acts:

> out of a lust for killing, [or] in order to satisfy his sexual desires, [or] motivated by greed or other despicable reasons...[or] in order to enable or to cover up the commission of the crime'.[48]

It would be hard to imagine a more wholly evaluative definition of 'murder'.[49] Why, then, did the Commission not go down this route?

When it comes to the possible incorporation of motive into the definition of murder, procedural differences at trial between England and Wales, on the one hand, and France and Germany, on the other, ought to give pause to those whose inclination is to damn the Commission for a defensive unwillingness to look beyond the local and the familiar. Underlying the different approaches in, on the one hand, England and Wales and, on the other hand, France and Germany may be a difference in the way that the presumption of innocence is interpreted.[50] By way of contrast with England and Wales, in France and Germany the defendant has no entitlement at trial to run his or her case that he or she was not the offender, whilst keeping matters relevant to sentence out of the court room until the (guilty) verdict has been brought in. No formal distinction is drawn between issues relevant to conviction and issues relevant to sentence, either at the stage of investigation or at the trial.[51] Instead, a defendant is expected at the outset to plead the whole of his or her case:[52] for example, 'I did not do it, because you have the wrong person, but if you find that I did do it, there is mitigation in the form of my mental problems and deprived background'. If the defendant thinks it would be best not to mention the evidence of mental problems or deprived background in case this undermines his or her case that he or she was not the

---

[47] See John Spencer, ch 3 below.

[48] See Antje du Bois-Pedain, ch 4 below.

[49] It can be argued that there is also a requirement of bad motive in Scottish law, in the form of a need to show that an intent to kill was 'wicked': *Drury v HMA* [2001] SCCR 583. For further discussion see Victor Tadros, ch 8.

[50] The presumption of innocence is an essential element of a fair trial under Art 6(2) of the ECHR. In France, Art 6(2) considerations have led to a refusal to permit a defendant to enter a guilty plea, a major point of contrast with modern English criminal procedure, although guilty pleas were actively discouraged in English criminal trials into the 19th century: JM Beattie, *Crime and the Criminal Courts in England 1660–1800* (Oxford, 1986) at 336.

[51] See Antje du Bois-Pedain, ch 4 below; C Elliott, *French Criminal Law* (Uffculme, Collompton, 2001) at 36.

[52] In France, a trial begins with a cross-examination of the accused.

offender, that evidence may not be considered at all by the court (the *Cour d'Assises*). When, in a homicide case the jury retires to consider its verdict, it considers both whether the accused should be convicted as charged and if so, what sentence should be imposed.[53] There is no strict division of function, in that regard, between the roles of judge and jury, as there is in England and Wales.

A system in which motives for killing, as well as the state of mind in which—or the intention with which—someone was killed, are made relevant to guilt of (a particular degree of) homicide fit very naturally into a legal system that operates in this way. Motive-based offence definitions fit much less naturally into a system such as that in England and Wales, in which a defendant may rely at trial on a presumption that he or she did not do the deed itself, let alone do the deed for a particular (wicked) reason.[54]

Having said that, of course, there are offences in which motive is relevant to guilt in English law, such as the need for the prosecution to show in a blackmail case that a demand made with menaces was 'unwarranted'.[55] Moreover, there is now a requirement in England and Wales that a defendant must provide evidence at an early stage of any defence on which he or she proposes to rely at trial.[56] That narrows the gap between the way in which the two systems operate, through bringing together their different understandings of the presumption of innocence. There is a certain irony in this, so far as defences are concerned. In Germany, for example, there is neither a legal nor an evidential burden on the accused with respect to the excusatory or justificatory defences, because the evidence for an applicable defence is something the investigating judge must look for in the course of his or her enquiries ex officio.[57] In broad terms, however, in England and Wales motive-based offence definitions would sit uneasily alongside the presumption that someone did not do the deed itself. This is because such definitions would place a tactical burden on the defendant to put forward evidence denying that there was an evil motive for the deed when in fact what is really denied is that he or she did the deed at all.

Perhaps the structural features of English law have been distorted by the expansive interpretation given to the presumption of innocence in this respect. A degree of merger between trial and sentencing issues—a return, in that respect, to early modern trial practice[58]—would mean less awkwardness in incorporating motives into the definition of offences. However, a convicted offender is already

---

[53] Jury trial was introduced in France for serious cases in 1791. See Elliott, above n 51 at 49. It is comprised of a mixture of professional judges and lay people.

[54] If D's case is that the nature of the deed *itself* is not as the prosecution claims—for example, that contact with the victim was accidental and not deliberate—that evidence can be expected to form part of the defendant's evidence at the stage of pleading.

[55] Theft Act 1968, s 21. It is also not uncommon to find offences in which behaviour is criminal only if an action is undertaken 'without lawful excuse', or the like. See also the definition of sexual assault under the Sexual Offences Act 2003.

[56] Criminal Procedure and Investigations Act 1996.

[57] See Antje du Bois-Pedain, ch 4.

[58] See J Langbein, *The Origins of Adversary Criminal Trial* (Oxford, 2003) ch 1.

reasonably well protected in English law against a mistaken finding that he or she acted out of an evil motive. In a case where the issue of motive is disputed, the prosecution must prove its case for evil motive beyond reasonable doubt, post trial, at a so-called *Newton*[59] hearing conducted before the judge. So, the existence of differing approaches to motive as between England and Wales and some major mainland European jurisdictions looks like a case where two equally valid ways of approaching the issue have been taken.

4. Partial Defences and the Adversarial Process

Two important factors have shaped English homicide law's approach to mitigating motives, as opposed to aggravating ones: a mandatory penalty for murder and the continued existence of a judicial power to shift the legal boundaries between murder and manslaughter. The existence of the mandatory penalty for murder has from time to time led judges to shield some classes of killer from that penalty by using their law-making powers to render those classes of killer in law guilty only of manslaughter (where the penalty is discretionary). Historically, the use of this power to determine who should receive the mandatory penalty has not always been uncontroversial. For example, in a mid-seventeenth century case concerning provocation by an illegal act, which at that time could reduce murder to manslaughter, Aske J argued forcefully that:

> It was the Popish power that introduced the clergy to be given for manslaughter…in diminution of the Common Law and of Regal power, yea, and of the law of God also…And by the law of God I find no difference between hot and cold blood as we do now distinguish.[60]

Be that as it may, what these two factors have bequeathed to English law— followed, in this respect, in many other jurisdictions—is a system of 'partial defences' to murder.

Partial defences centre on a limited and formally structured range of mitigating reasons for killing, put in issue at trial by the accused with a view to being convicted of manslaughter rather than of murder (and hence escaping the mandatory penalty). There may be some advantages to this 'trial-adversarial' way of dealing with mitigating reasons for killing,[61] but there are also serious

---

[59] *R v Newton* (1982) 77 Cr App R 13.

[60] *Buckner's Case* (1655) Style 467 at 469. 'The Clergy' was, of course, the right of the Church to try and to punish ordained members of the clergy for alleged crimes. Such an offender could also be tried in the King's courts and then handed over to clerical authority for punishment. Punishments were usually less drastic than those that might be imposed by the King's courts. The 'benefit' of clergy was available for those found guilty (for the first time) of manslaughter, but unavailable for murder.

[61] One arguable advantage of this system relates to trial by jury. Making partial defences an issue bearing on conviction rather solely on sentence in murder cases gives the jury a role in evaluating the

disadvantages. In relation to a partial defence it may, for example, be impossible to place before a jury the whole story of how the defendant came to kill, because of restrictions on the kind of evidence that it is in law thought safe for juries to hear. That is the 'trial' disadvantage of the English approach. So far as the admissible evidence is concerned, in so far as he or she bears any kind of burden of proof there will also be a strong temptation for the defendant to exaggerate as far as possible any element of blame that can be attached to the deceased victim for what happened, to show up the defendant's own actions in a better light. This is something understandably resented greatly by those close to the victim,[62] who may justifiably feel that the victim has been 'defamed'. It is also something the effect of which is difficult for the prosecution effectively to counter.[63] It is the 'adversarial' disadvantage of the partial defence approach of English law.

The way that English law has developed means that some alternative approaches have never become serious possibilities in the way that they might, and perhaps should, have done. One such possibility is that mitigating factors should be made more directly relevant to sentence. For example, judges could be given the discretion to depart from the mandatory sentence for murder when the mitigating circumstances are especially strong, whilst leaving the conviction for murder intact.[64] The partial defence of diminished responsibility provides an illustration of what might be a missed opportunity in this respect. When introduced in 1957, this was automatically shaped along traditional 'trial-adversarial' lines.[65] In this respect, there is a strong contrast with the approach in France and Germany.[66]

Although also defined as a matter of law in France and Germany, if diminished responsibility is found proven by the court it means in principle a lesser sentence, rather than conviction for a lesser offence. Accordingly, the court (rather than the parties) takes the lead in investigating the case for regarding the defendant as

---

defendant's conduct above and beyond their more usual fact-finding role. Almost needless to say, however, not everyone regards this as an advantage, since it may lead to great inconsistency of treatment as between very similar cases.

[62] See the evidence on the drawbacks of a system of partial defences given by Victim Support to the Law Commission, summarised in Law Commission, *A New Homicide act for England and Wales?*, (London, 2005) at para 2.33.

[63] If the defendant attacks the character of the victim, the prosecution may be able to cross-examine the defendant as to his or her own (bad) character, but in practice this is not an especially powerful weapon in the hands of the prosecution at trial.

[64] A political desire to reduce the amount of discretion that judges have over sentencing in murder cases has also made such an alternative a very remote possibility. For further discussion of a different, sentence-orientated approach see J Horder, *Excusing Crime* (Oxford, 2004) ch 4.

[65] So, it is for the defendant to show that he or she was suffering from diminished responsibility, and for the prosecution to disprove this beyond reasonable doubt.

[66] See Antje du Bois-Pedain, ch 4 below; John Spencer, ch 3 below.

having been influenced by diminished responsibility, eliminating the 'trial' disadvantage.[67] Further, the 'adversarial' disadvantage is much lessened in France, given the considerably more prominent role afforded to victims' relatives at the stages of preliminary hearing and trial, as compared with their more minor post-trial role in England and Wales.[68] In France, the victim's heirs can bring a civil action for damages (for the harm suffered by the victim) in the criminal courts, as by attaching that action to the early stages of criminal proceedings against an offender. This will give them the right to damages against the offender (and his or her heirs or parents), if he or she is convicted. Further, during the trial their own lawyer will be kept informed about the progress of the case (and the contents of the file) at all times, information that can be relayed to his or her client.[69]

So far as provocation is concerned, an interesting comparison is provided by German law. To begin with, in German law provocation is more closely defined than in England. German law puts emphasis on the need for the killer to be blameless, given the nature and degree of the physical or verbal abuse from the victim. At first blush, that might seem to give rise to the same 'adversarial' disadvantage that is so troublesome in English law.[70] Further, if established, a finding of provocation also entails conviction for a lesser offence—*Totschlag* (voluntary manslaughter) rather than *mord* (murder)—seemingly raising the 'trial' disadvantage of English law as well. The difference in German law, however, is that the existence of sufficient provocation to warrant a conviction for *Totschlag* is not properly characterised as a partial 'defence' as English lawyers understand that notion. It is not understood as something that is essentially for the defendant to raise and for the prosecution to disprove beyond doubt.[71] The sufficiency of the provocation is something for the court to investigate ex officio. This reduces considerably or even eliminates both the 'trial' and the 'adversarial' disadvantages of English law.

---

[67] See the discussion in the Law Commission's Consultation Paper, *A New Homicide Act for England and Wales?*, (London, 2005) at paras 2.86–2.88; Law Commission, *Murder, Manslaughter and Infanticide*, Law Com No 304 (London, 2006), Pt 5.

[68] Which is not to say that we regard the more active role of victims' families in trials in France as an unmixed blessing.

[69] See C Elliott, *French Criminal Law* (Uffculme, Collompton, 2001) at 32–5. For a discussion of the view that victims' relatives in England and Wales should have the right to see the file on a defendant see A Sanders, 'Victim Participation in Criminal Justice and Social Exclusion' in C Hoyle and R Young (eds), *New Visions of Crime Victims* (Oxford, 2002).

[70] See Antje du Bois-Pedain, ch 4 below. There is no provocation defence in French law.

[71] Of course, under the Homicide Act 1957 s 3, it is not strictly speaking necessary for the defence to raise provocation, as the judge must do so if there is evidence of loss of self-control. However, this is commonly regarded as an anomaly, and will disappear if the Law Commission's proposals are adopted: see Law Commission, above n 67, Pt 5.

5. The Reliance on 'Probability' in Fault Elements

One may intend, foresee or be indifferent to possible events, whatever the degree of likelihood that they may occur. However, a distinction is traditionally drawn in point of liability between, on the one hand, an intention to bring about an event and, on the other hand, foresight of or indifference to an event, where the likelihood of that event occurring is concerned. If one intends to bring about a prohibited outcome, then one's liability is the same whatever the chances one had of fulfilling one's intentions. Someone who intends to kill at point-blank range is liable for the same offence, for the same reason, as someone who intends to kill by shooting at a distance so great that they believe there is little chance of fulfilling their intention. The probability of success may influence a would-be killer's decision to try to kill; but it plays no role in determining liability consequent upon that decision, once made. The fact that killing is the *reason why* the would-be killer acts sidelines the degree of chance of his or her succeeding as a relevant moral and legal factor (most obviously, in the case where the would-killer succeeds in killing, but to a considerable extent in the case of an attempt as well).

A different approach may be taken to mental states other than intention, such as foresight or belief that a prohibited outcome (say, an unlawful killing) will or may occur if a particular action is performed. In such cases, the killing is not the reason the person acts and its occurrence would not count as in that sense a success (even if its occurrence is for some reason welcome). The person acts for some other reason, foreseeing or believing that an unlawful killing will or may come about as a side-effect. In such cases, the issue of the degree of chance that the unlawful killing will occur need never drop out of the picture, morally or legally, because it is never sidelined by the killing becoming the thing for the sake of which the person acts. The degree of chance that the unlawful killing may occur may continue to have moral, evaluative 'weight' in our moral assessment of the action the person does intend to perform. Someone who throws an unwanted brick from a high building will earn condemnation commensurate, at least in part, with the degree of likelihood in the circumstances that (they realised) the brick would strike someone down below.

So, the degree of chance that an unlawful killing will result from particular actions—actions not themselves aimed at producing the killing—matters morally. Does it follow that it should matter to criminal liability? Not necessarily. A rash action on my part that I realised risked killing you and did kill you could be approached in two ways, so far as legal liability is concerned. The simple fact that an unacceptable risk was created by the action, a foreseen risk that turned into reality, could be the basis for liability as such, with the (foreseen) *degree* of that risk left as a matter relevant to sentence.[72] Alternatively, the (foreseen) degree of probability that the killing would occur could be built into the test for liability itself. On this point, we find a difference of approach between jurisdictions.

In Singapore, the known or foreseen probability of an unlawful killing stemming from one's actions is central to liability and grading in homicide offences.[73] It is, for example, culpable homicide for someone to cause death 'with the knowledge that he is likely by such act to cause death'; and it is murder for someone to cause death 'if the person committing the act knows that it is so imminently dangerous that it must in all probability cause death…without any excuse for incurring the risk of causing death'.[74] By way of contrast, the modern English law of homicide avoids the use of the degree of a foreseen probability as a basis for liability.[75] In the murder case of *Hyam*,[76] Lord Hailsham agreed with the observation of Lord Reid in the civil case of *Southern Portland Cement v Cooper*[77] that:

> Chance probability or likelihood is always a matter of degree. It is rarely capable of precise assessment. Many different expressions are in common use. It can be said that the occurrence of a future event is very likely, more probable than not, not unlikely, not improbable, more than a mere possibility, etc. It is neither practicable nor reasonable to draw a line at extreme probability.[78]

Whether or not one agrees with this final remark where the objective possibility and probability of consequences occurring are concerned, it has considerable resonance when what is in issue is the *foreseen* possibility or (degree of) probability that consequences will occur. A jury in such a case is being asked to make a double inference from the facts as proven. First, in a homicide case, the jury is being asked to infer that the defendant foresaw the risk of killing. Secondly, the jury is being asked to infer that the defendant foresaw a certain degree of risk that a killing might occur. In some circumstances, where the risk was quite obviously certain to turn into reality, there may be no special difficulty involved for the jury in making this double inference.[79] However, when the question is whether the defendant saw the risk as 'probable' *rather than* as (say) merely 'possible', it is much harder to see how the jury can move with any confidence from the conclusion that a defendant must have been aware of 'a' risk to the conclusion that the defendant was aware that killing was to a specified degree a likely or possible outcome. A defendant might quite commonly give the

---

[72] We will not address here how the relationship between actual probability and foreseen probability should affect liability or sentence.

[73] See Stanley Yeo, ch 9 below.

[74] Cap 224, 1985 Rev Ed (Singapore), 229(3) and 300(d).

[75] Even though, as is well known, when a killing is thought to be a virtually certain result, this can be a basis for finding an intention to kill: *Woollin* [1999] AC 1.

[76] [1975] AC 55.

[77] [1974] AC 623.

[78] [1974] AC 623 at 640.

[79] See *Woollin* [1999] AC 1.

actual degree of likelihood of killing no thought at all, or have only the vaguest sense of what that degree might be. There is an unhealthy air of unreality involved in supposing that a foreseen degree of probability can be proven in the circumstances in which homicide is commonly committed, as compared, for example, with the circumstances in which an experienced gambler comes to place a particular bet. As Ian Leader-Elliott argues in his examination of the Australian courts' struggles with these issues:

> There is every reason for scepticism about the use and, indeed, the intelligibility of such a scale [of (foreseen) probability] when the difference between murder and manslaughter is in issue. Its incantatory quality is more obvious than their communicative content.[80]

The issue has become an important one in homicide cases where the question is, what test should govern the fault element for the liability of a secondary party for murder committed by a principal offender in the course of a joint criminal venture that did not have murder itself as its aim? In England and Wales the test is, did the secondary party foresee that, in the course of the joint criminal venture, a party to the venture 'might' commit murder? What must be foreseen by the secondary party is a real rather than a remote or purely hypothetical risk that another party might commit murder; but it is not necessary to show that the secondary party foresaw that another party would 'probably' or 'very probably' commit murder.[81] By way of contrast, the High Court of Australia has been driven to adopt a different test in the same area of law in construing section 8 of the Queensland Criminal Code, which stipulates that the test is whether the commission of murder by the principal offender was 'a probable consequence' of pursuing a joint criminal venture.[82] The High Court considered no fewer than four different meanings of the word 'probable', concluding (by a majority) that it is:

> ...difficult to arrive at a verbal formula for what it [probable] does mean and for what the jury may be told. The expression 'a probable consequence' means that the occurrence of the consequence need not be more probable than not, but must be probable as distinct from possible. It must be probable in the sense that it could well happen.

It is easy to sympathise with the High Court when it said that determining the meaning of 'probable' was no simple matter; and it is hard to see how the law is improved by the use of such terms, especially (as we have said) when what the jury must find beyond doubt is that the defendant him- or herself saw the risk of murder being committed in those—probabilistic—terms. We believe that, in this respect, the approach of English law is to be preferred.

---

[80] Ian Leader-Elliott, ch 7 below, text before section 10.
[81] *Chan Wing-siu v R* [1985] 1 AC 168.
[82] *Darkan v The Queen* [2006] HCA 34. See, further, Ian Leader Elliott, ch 7 below.

2

The Changing Face of the Law of Homicide

JEREMY HORDER

1. The Law Commission's Three-tier Structure for Homicide

BUILDING ON ITS Consultation Paper, the Law Commission has now published a final Report recommending a new structure for the law of homicide in England and Wales.[1] Replacing the current two-tier structure comprised of murder and manslaughter is to be a three-tier structure. The top tier in this structure will be 'first degree murder', the middle tier 'second degree murder' and the lowest tier manslaughter. The existing, familiar terminology—murder; manslaughter—is thus retained, but murder is to be sub-divided, as (but not in the same way as) in most American penal codes.[2] The structure will be comprised of the following elements:

First degree murder: (a) intentional killing; (b) killing with an intention to do serious injury in the awareness that there is a serious risk of causing death.

Second degree murder: (a) killing with the intention to do serious injury; (b) killing with the intention to cause injury or a fear or risk of injury, in the awareness that there is a serious risk of causing death; (c) the result of a successful partial defence plea to first degree murder.

Manslaughter: (a) causing death by gross negligence; (b) causing death through a criminal act intended to cause injury, or in the awareness of a serious risk that injury may be caused.

---

[1] Law Commission for England and Wales, *A New Homicide Act for England and Wales?*, Consultation Paper No 177 (London, 2005); Law Commission for England and Wales, *Murder, Manslaughter, and Infanticide*, Law Com No 304 (London, 2006).

[2] See Claire Finkelstein, ch 5 below.

Why put a three-tier structure in a place of the two-tier structure that has been in place for 500 years or more? For one simple reason. The two-tier structure is no longer able to meet the increasing demands being made of it.

First, pressure is being placed on the two-tier structure by developments in the partial defences.[3] 400 years ago, there was only one partial defence to murder, provocation (although at that time it was not clearly distinguished from excessive defence). Currently there are three partial defences—provocation, diminished responsibility and half-completed suicide pacts[4]—and the Commission is proposing to introduce a further such defence, under the aegis of provocation, namely excessive defence.[5] Practice regarding these defences varies considerably world-wide. Some jurisdictions have no defence of provocation[6] or no defence of diminished responsibility[7] (still less, one of half-completed suicide pact). By way of contrast, others regard excessive defence as a basis for complete acquittal.[8] At present in England and Wales, an offender who pleads any of these defences successfully has his or her crime reduced to manslaughter, even though he or she may admit having intended to kill. This is controversial or problematic because, as a substantive offence, manslaughter is a crime that may involve relatively low culpability. It can be committed with a fault element well short of an intention to kill. So, it is not obvious that the partial defences should have the effect of reducing murder to manslaughter, thus lumping together in the same offence category those who killed intentionally in excusing circumstances and those who may not even have intended to do someone an injury. In general terms it is, of course, not wrong to use the same offence category for a successful lack-of-intent plea as for a successful excusatory plea.[9] The question is whether better 'labelling' of offenders who may have intended to kill but have an excusatory partial defence can be achieved. An obvious solution is to place them in a new offence category with those who, whilst they lack the fault element for the highest category of homicide offence, are significantly more blameworthy than those committing manslaughter as a substantive offence.

Secondly, the existing structure must now seek to accommodate a whole variety of different fault elements without being able to rely, as in the past, on the inherent flexibility or vagueness of 'malice aforethought' as an umbrella term

---

[3] Partial defences will not, as such, be a focus of discussion in the rest of this essay.

[4] Homicide Act 1957, s 4.

[5] See n 1 above. On the Law Commission's view, roughly speaking, 'excessive' defence arises in a murder case where, whether or not the defendant lost control before killing the victim, the defendant feared being subjected to serious violence by the victim if he or she did not kill the latter.

[6] See John Spencer, ch 3 below.

[7] See Claire Finkelstein, ch 5 below.

[8] See Antje du Bois-Pedain, ch 4 below.

[9] See V Tadros, 'The Distinctiveness of Domestic Abuse: a Freedom-Based Account' in RA Duff and SP Green (eds), *Defining Crimes* (Oxford, 2005) at 136: '[a] criminal offence might quite properly reflect overlapping values, or vices, whereby two instances of behaviour that fall within that offence do not share all of the salient and distinctive elements that make any particular token of the offence wrongful.'

capable of covering them all. The Homicide Act 1957 restricted the scope of malice aforethought,[10] although it quite clearly anticipated that this term would continue to express the fault element for murder. However, since 1957 the judiciary have been increasingly uncomfortable using the term.[11] The House of Lords has now said that malice aforethought is not to be regarded as a suitable term for the fault element in murder, although it is far from clear that Parliament thought it unsuitable in 1957. 'Intention' has become the judiciary's favoured term, but this change of use has led to new set of difficulties. Intention does not have the narrowest possible meaning in English law.[12] None the less, malice aforethought was clearly capable of covering highly culpable states of mind, such as a willingness or preparedness to kill in the course of conduct, which intention, as such, is not. Cases that would have been treated as murder cases 50 years ago, when the term malice aforethought was still in use, must now be treated as cases of manslaughter because there was no actual 'intention' to kill or to inflict serious injury.[13] The policy question whether that development is desirable has never been directly addressed in the case law. That is, perhaps, understandable. An acute policy dilemma is raised by any attempt, through case law development, to change the definition of murder within the two-tier structure. As much by accident as by design, in abandoning the use of 'malice aforethought' the courts have narrowed the definition of murder from what it was when Parliament reformed the law in 1957. That has left the law with a crime of manslaughter that has an unacceptably broad scope. Manslaughter is now unable to reflect the legitimate demand that the offence label reasonably accurately reflect the nature of the wrong done (a point made above, in relation to the partial defences). However, were the courts consequently to widen the law of murder at manslaughter's expense, that would entail the broadening of the class of offenders on whom the mandatory life sentence must be passed, a matter that ought above all else to be regarded as a matter for Parliament.

There have been attempts to persuade Parliament to strike the right balance between murder and manslaughter. The last attempt to do so through provision of a full definition of murder was in the Homicide Bill of 1878–9. The relevant provision ran as follows:

---

[10] By abolishing so-called 'constructive malice' in the law of murder.

[11] See, in particular, the criticisms of Lord Bridge in *R v Moloney* [1985] 1 AC 905 at 920. In fact, immediately after the passing of the Homicide Act courts were already suggesting that malice aforethought was merely a term of art, standing in for nothing beyond 'intention': see *R v Vickers* [1957] 2 QB 664.

[12] *R v Woollin* [1999] AC 92.

[13] The classic case is setting fire to a building known to be occupied by sleeping inhabitants, where the claim is that the intention was only to frighten the occupants, but someone was killed in the conflagration. In 1975 this was treated as murder if the defendant knew it was likely that someone would die: *DPP v Hyam* [1975] AC 55. With the complete demise of malice aforethought as a term of art broader than intention, by the 1980s such cases had to treated as ones of manslaughter: see *R v Nedrick* [1986] 3 All ER 1, and the discussion of other such cases in M Wasik, 'Sentencing in Homicide' in A Ashworth and B Mitchell (eds), *Rethinking English Homicide Law* (Oxford, 2000) 177.

Culpable homicide is murder…

(a)_if the offender means to cause the death…

(b) if the offender means to cause to the person killed any bodily injury which is known to the offender to be likely to cause death, and if the offender, whether he does or does not mean to cause death, is reckless whether death ensues or not…

(c) Culpable homicide is also murder…if [the offender] means to inflict grievous bodily injury for the purpose of facilitating the commission of any of the offences hereinafter mentioned.

The provision formed the basis for the existing Canadian law of homicide,[14] and it is not far removed from the Law Commission's current recommendations for the fault element in first and second degree murder combined. The provision does succumb at the end to the temptation to retain a (watered down) version of the felony-murder rule. Although that rule has a wide currency in the English-speaking world,[15] it has been heavily criticised and was rightly consigned to legal history by Parliament through section 1 of the Homicide Act 1957. Like the overwhelming majority of its consultees, the Commission has resisted the temptation to re-introduce it (although 'criminal act' manslaughter remains). Putting this point on one side, what is the function of defining murder in the way the 1878–9 Bill does? Over 100 years later, William Wilson expresses the function thus:

> The key task, for the purposes of fair labelling, is to cut up the murder-manslaughter cake in a way which renders the two wrongs meaningfully distinct and makes it clear exactly how citizens must behave to avoid the relevant prohibition.[16]

To regard this as *the* key task is, however, to take the existing 'two-layer cake' structure for granted. The Commission no longer believes that is the right thing to do. A 'three-layer cake' structure makes it possible to distinguish between wrongs, and hence to respect principles of fair labelling, in a more sophisticated way. To achieve this, each of the three tiers within the recommended structure has two morally equivalent wrongs, each (with first degree murder at the top) being in principle lower down in the scale of severity than the wrongs in the tier above.[17]

Furthermore, a three-tier structure would enable a greater measure of justice to be brought to sentencing in homicide cases. The mandatory life penalty cannot

---

[14] See Winifred Holland, ch 6 below.

[15] See Claire Finkelstein, ch 5 below; Winifred Holland, ch 6 below; Ian Leader-Elliott, ch 7 below.

[16] W Wilson, 'Murder and the Structure of Homicide' in A Ashworth and B Mitchell (eds), *Rethinking English Homicide Law*, (Oxford, 2000)at 38. On the issue, raised at the end of the passage, of whether distinctions between offences are aimed at citizens seeking legal guidance ex ante, or at officials judging wrongdoers ex post facto, see J Horder, 'Criminal Law and Legal Positivism' [2002] 8 *Legal Theory* 221.

[17] It might be said, alternatively, that each tier has what might be thought of as a principal wrong, and a subsidiary wrong that can be regarded as morally equivalent to it. Not much hangs, however, on the characterisation.

be taken as seriously as it should be when such a diverse range of offenders as at present falls within it. Suppose D is provoked by V to lose his self-control and strikes V on the knee with a baseball bat, breaking V's kneecap. V goes to hospital, but his knee becomes infected and he dies. If the provocation was not such as might move a reasonable person to do as D did, D can be convicted of murder if his intention was to inflict an injury with the bat that the jury judges to be serious. It is murder even if in the heat of the moment D had no idea that his action would lead to V's death. In such a case, therefore, D will receive the mandatory life penalty. However, the judge is likely to impose a tariff or initial period in custody of perhaps only eight to ten years (conceivably less), given D's provoked loss of self-control and the absence of an intention to kill.[18] If he is a man in his 30s, D therefore stands to spend eight to ten years in custody, but perhaps another 30 to 40 years out on licence. Such cases, where the tariff period must inevitably be relatively short because there was both a lesser degree of culpability and some element of partial defence, form a significant proportion of the total.[19] They raise questions about the width of murder in the context of the obligation to pass a life sentence upon conviction. As Martin Wasik has argued:

> the principled development of sentencing guidelines requires the avoidance of overly broad offences. Such offences fail to make explicit the moral distinctions which should be reflected in the law, and they lump together very different forms of conduct under a single, misleading, offence label. Sentencing coherence in homicide, it seems, depends on offences being arranged hierarchically, and with gradations within those offences being clearly based upon the different degrees of offender culpability for causing death.[20]

To restore some moral authority to the mandatory sentence, it must be confined to the offence of homicide with the highest degree of fault. Further, to ensure that not only fair labelling but also justice in sentencing for homicide offences ranked below the top-tier offence, manslaughter should cease to remain an all-encompassing jumble. That means the introduction of a three-tier structure[21]; but how should the offences within it be defined? I will concentrate on the less familiar and more controversial of the offences in the three-tier structure, first and second degree murder.[22]

---

[18] Both of these are expressed to be mitigation factors in murder cases under the Criminal Justice Act 2003, s 269 and sch 21.

[19] See the analysis of such cases in the Law Commission's Consultation Paper, *A New Homicide Act for England and Wales?*,(London, 2005) App E.

[20] M Wasik, 'Sentencing in Homicide' in A Ashworth and B Mitchell (eds), *Rethinking English Homicide Law* (Oxford, 2000) at 192.

[21] The three-tier structure relates to general offences of homicide but, for the sake of completeness, it ought to be added that there is a notional fourth tier. This is comprised of specific homicide offences regarded as in principle less serious than manslaughter, such as causing death by dangerous driving, infanticide or causing the non-accidental death of a child or vulnerable adult.

[22] Considerations of space mean that I will not be dealing with the issues raised by the recommendation that partial defences should reduce first degree murder to second degree murder.

2. The Fault Element for First Degree Murder

Under the Commission's proposals, first degree murder will be committed when someone kills intentionally, or kills with an intention to do serious injury, in the awareness that there is a serious risk of causing death. This involves a change from the provisional proposals in the Consultation Paper, where the proposal was that first degree murder should be confined to intentional killing. There was considerable support amongst the Commission's consultees for confining first degree murder (and, hence, the mandatory life sentence) to intentional killing. That said, the Commission decided that to confine it so closely would have meant that some killings morally just as heinous as intentional killings would have escaped categorisation as first degree murder. An example might be the person who tortures his victim in hideous ways over a prolonged period, but the victim dies of a resulting heart attack before the torturer has forced the information from him. In such a case, the desire to continue the application of the torture is inconsistent with an intention to kill through the act of torture, as such, but there are compelling grounds for regarding the torturer as guilty of murder. The torturer has intentionally inflicted serious injury. Further, in cases of prolonged and severe torture he or she is bound to be aware of a serious risk that the victim will die in the course of the torture whether or not the information demanded has yet been revealed. Under the expanded definition of first degree murder the Law Commission is now recommending, the torturer in such cases will therefore be guilty of first degree murder. In more commonplace cases the expanded definition also gives greater reassurance that a charge of first degree murder is appropriate. If, say, D shoots or stabs V in the head or heart, then, in the absence of any special explanation about his intentions, D can readily be found to have had the fault element for first degree murder.

The recommended definition of first degree murder does little more than update the proposal made for reform of the law of murder in England and Wales in the Draft Criminal Code of 1989.[23] What are different are the recommendations for the new middle-tier offence of second degree murder. Second degree murder is made to do a great deal of work under the Commission's recommendations. It functions both as a free-standing offence in two different situations and as the crime to which first degree murder is reduced when a plea of provocation, diminished responsibility or half-completed suicide pact is successful on a first degree murder charge. I shall be concerned here with its function as a free-standing offence.

Broadly speaking, the Commission's recommendations for manslaughter follow the Home Office's own earlier recommendations: see Home Office, *Reforming the Law on Involuntary Manslaughter: the Government's Proposals* (London, 2000).

[23] Clause 54: 'A person is guilty of murder if he causes the death of another—(a) intending to cause death; or (b) intending to cause serious personal harm and being aware that he may cause death.'

3. Second Degree Murder: Cases of Intending Serious Injury

The first situation in which second degree murder is committed, as a free-standing offence, is when someone kills having intended to do serious injury, even if they were *un*aware of a serious risk of causing death (compare first degree murder, above). Under the current law, killing in these circumstances is murder. Broadly speaking, that reflects the position in jurisdictions in, or influenced by, the English-speaking world,[24] although in mainland European jurisdictions killing in such circumstances would commonly be a lesser offence.[25] The current position in English law can lead to injustice, because it means that the mandatory sentence of life imprisonment must be passed on someone who may have had no idea that his or her actions might cause death. Such a person should not fall within the highest category of homicide, as is recognised by those jurisdictions that treat it as second degree murder or as some other offence. Under the draft code of 1989, someone who killed having intended to do injury regarded as serious by the jury would have been guilty of manslaughter. The Commission does not now regard this as a satisfactory solution. Manslaughter is widely considered to be an over-broad crime even at it stands. It would have become still wider with the inclusion of killing where there was an intention to do serious injury. This would have been a serious matter, because it is likely that a large proportion of killings currently categorised as murder take place when there is an intention to do serious injury but no intention to kill. Moreover, there are sound moral reasons for thinking that killing with intent to do serious injury should be treated as a crime of murder, even if not as first degree murder. The nature of the harm intentionally done will in many cases mean that the defendant has made death a foreseeable consequence of his or her action. To launch an attack of that severity against another person demonstrates a disregard for the vital interests of others deserving of the label 'murderous', even if it would not be right to regard the crime as one of first degree murder. Liability for second degree murder is justified by the fact that when death occurs, albeit unforeseen, D is not being held responsible for harm done out of all proportion to the harm intended.[26] Consequently, there is no need to add, as the 1878–9 Bill does, the further restriction that the intentional infliction of serious injury must have been for the purpose facilitating the commission of a range of specified offences. The history of such 'felony murder' provisions has not been a happy one although, as

---

[24] See Ian Leader-Elliott, ch 7 below; Claire Finkelstein, ch 5 below. In some jurisdictions, killing with an intention to do serious injury will only be murder if an indifference to life can be inferred from the defendant's action.

[25] See the discussion in Jeremy Horder and David Hughes, ch 1 above.

[26] On this point of principle see W Wilson, 'Murder and the Structure of Homicide' in A Ashworth and B Mitchell (eds), *Rethinking English Homicide Law*, (Oxford, 2000) at 36; J Horder, 'Two Histories and Four Hidden Principles of Mens Rea' (1997) 113 *LQR* 95.

indicated above, many jurisdictions have retained them and they have a small band of spirited and ingenious contemporary defenders.[27] Such provisions lead to the drawing of arbitrary distinctions between offenders.[28] They entail secondary litigation, often leading to further complexity and arbitrariness, over the meaning of terms such as 'for the purpose of facilitating'.[29] We are better off without them.

4. Second Degree Murder: Tackling Reckless Killing

Under the Commission's recommendations, the second situation in which second degree murder is committed as a substantive offence will be when D intends to cause some injury, or a fear or risk of injury, in the awareness that he or she is posing a serious risk of causing death. This is similar to the proposal in the 1878–9 Bill (above), although I will be explaining how the extension of it in the Law Commission's recommendation to include cases where D intended to cause a *fear or risk* of injury is significant. Unlike the 1878–9 Bill, however the Commission's recommendation now eschews use of the term 'recklessness'. Here is an important change from the Consultation Paper. In that Paper, the Commission provisionally proposed that someone should be guilty of second degree murder if they killed another person through 'reckless indifference'.[30] The aim of that proposal was to ensure that two kinds of reckless killer fell within the scope of second degree murder, and that a third kind fell outside its scope (manslaughter being the appropriate crime in latter case).

The first kind of reckless killer meant to fall within second degree murder is (in general terms) the kind regarded under the old law as acting out of malice aforethought, and hence guilty of murder, but currently falling outside the scope of murder because there is no actual intent to kill or to inflict serious injury:

Recklessness Case 1: D injects V with an illegal drug, realising that the drug may amount to an overdose or contain potentially lethal impurities. The drug is an overdose or does contain such impurities, and V dies in consequence.[31]

Recklessness Case 2: D sets fire to V's house where V is asleep, intending to cause V to run in terror from the house, but knowing that V may be killed if he or she does not escape. V fails to escape and is killed.[32]

---

[27] See Wilson, n 26 above.

[28] See C Finkelstein, 'Merger and Felony Murder' in RA Duff and SP Green (eds), *Defining Crimes* (Oxford, 2005).

[29] JWC Turner (ed), *Russell on Crime*, 12th edn (London, 1964), i, at 487–8.

[30] Law Commission, *A New Homicide Act for England and Wales?* (London, 2005), pt 3.

[31] See *R v Parfini* (2003) 2 Cr App R (S) 362.

[32] See n 13 above.

In both cases, D's potentially harmful act is aimed at V in the knowledge that the act poses a risk of death. Under the Commission's provisional proposals, in both cases D could be regarded as acting with 'reckless indifference'. The question was to be whether D's attitude towards injecting V was 'if this causes V's death, so be it', or 'so what?'.[33]

The second kind of killer meant to be caught by the provisional proposal was one who, without aiming any potentially harmful act at V, none the less acted with such a high degree of recklessness that his or her attitude could be regarded as one of indifference:

> **Recklessness Case 3**: D overloads a lorry with people hoping to obtain entry to Britain illegally. Although (as D knows) there is no way of ensuring that fresh air enters the locked compartments where the people are hidden, D completes a long journey into Britain without stopping to check on the people's condition, in order more quickly to obtain his payment. A number of people in the compartments are suffocated to death.[34]

In this example, likewise, it seems plausible to suppose that D's attitude is 'if death is caused, so be it'. That would make him recklessly indifferent, and hence guilty of second degree murder even though no act of his was aimed at causing injury or the fear or risk of injury.

The insistence that a lethal act manifest reckless *indifference*, if it is to amount to second degree murder, was meant to ensure that not all killing by advertent risk-taking became second degree murder:

> **Recklessness Case 4**: D is an electrician. D has installed wiring that he or she knows does not meet official safety standards, because he or she is highly sceptical about the value of the 'officious meddling' involved in setting standards. The poor quality of the wiring leads to V being electrocuted and killed.[35]

In this case, it seems unlikely that D could fairly be said to be manifesting a callous attitude towards potential victims, although his or her conduct is reprehensible and in a basic sense 'reckless'. D's misplaced distrust in officialdom explains his or her actions better than a disregard for the safety of electricity users. D could be found guilty of manslaughter by gross negligence, but should not (at least on these facts) be guilty of second degree murder.

Commentators on the Commission's provisional proposals were sharply critical of 'reckless indifference' as a test of liability, principally on the grounds that it was too vague[36] or left too much unstructured discretion to the jury.[37] There would certainly be no improvement on the present law if a whole series of cases had to be taken to the appeal courts to determine meaning of 'reckless indifference'. Consequently, in its final recommendations, the Commission has dropped

---

[33] Law Commission, n 30 above, Pt 3.
[34] The facts are not dissimilar to those in *R v Wacker* (2002) EWCA Crim 1944.
[35] See, more generally, *R v Merrick* (1996) 1 Cr App R 130.
[36] See, eg, J Rogers, 'The Law Commission's Proposed Restructuring of Homicide' [2006] *JCL* 223 at 240–3; W Wilson, 'The Structure of Criminal Homicide' [2006] *Crim LR* 471 at 477–8.
[37] *Ibid* at 478–9.

the reckless indifference term and substituted a test with clearer language, the test of whether D 'intended to cause injury, or a fear or a risk of injury, and was aware of a serious risk of causing death'. The question is whether that test fulfils the same function as the test of reckless indifference. How does it apply to the recklessness cases 1–4 above? In case 1, D can be found guilty of second degree murder under the Law Commission's recommendations because D intended to cause injury (in the shape of the injection) and was aware of a serious risk of causing death. This would probably also have been the result under the 1878–9 Bill (above). Under that Bill, the jury would also have to have been sure that the defendant acted recklessly as to causing death, but it is unclear what that really added to the other requirement that D knew that his or her unlawful action was likely to cause death.

Unlike the 1878–9 Bill, the Law Commission's recommendations for second degree murder extend to cases in which D intends to cause a *fear or risk* of injury, in the awareness that a serious risk of death is being posed. There is good reason for extending the mental element in this way, and it is illustrated by case 2. Here, D would not have been guilty of murder in the 1878–9 Code because he or she did not intend to cause bodily injury as such. None the less, D intended that V should fear injury, and hence D falls within the scope of second degree murder because D was also aware of a serious risk that V might be killed. The Commission further extends the scope of second degree murder beyond the limits set by the 1878–9 Bill to cover cases where D intends to create a risk of injury, aware that there is a serious risk of causing death. What kinds of cases does this extension cover?

> **Recklessness Case 5**: D intends to play 'Russian roulette' with V. D puts a single bullet into a revolver, spins the barrel and points the gun at V's head while V is not looking. Without checking to see whether the gun will actually fire, D pulls the trigger. The gun goes off, killing V.[38]

Here, D intends to subject V to a risk of injury and is aware that in so doing there is a serious risk of causing V's death. If the Commission's recommendations had stopped short at intending to cause a *fear* of injury, then whether D was guilty of second degree murder in this kind of example would have turned on whether or not V was sufficiently aware of what D was about to do to fear injury. The boundary between homicide offences ought not to turn on such an issue.

That leaves the contrast between cases 3 and 4. One reason that the Commission initially proposed the reckless indifference test, as opposed to an updated version of the 1878–9 Bill, was to ensure that examples like case 3 fell within the scope of second degree murder and were not confined to manslaughter. On re-consideration, it seems quite likely that many such cases will in fact fall within the now recommended definition of second degree murder. What must be borne in mind is that foresight of a consequence that is virtually certain to occur can be

---

[38] See *Faure* [1999] VSCA 166, discussed by Ian Leader-Elliott, ch 7 below.

a basis for inferring 'intention' in law.[39] In case 3, when D continues on his long drive despite knowing the conditions that those hiding in the back must endure, it can readily be found either (a) that he foresees it as virtually certain that they will eventually fear injury, or (b) that he foresees it as virtually certain that there will be a risk of injury. That being so, the jury is free to infer that D intended to subject the victims to the fear of or to a risk of injury. If the jury does so infer, then if it is also found that D was aware of a serious risk of causing death, he or she can be found guilty of second degree murder under the recommended test almost as easily as if the reckless indifference test were being applied.

By way of contrast, it is less likely that D in case 4 foresees a risk of injury as certain to be posed. Even if he or she did, it is highly unlikely that a jury would infer from this that D intended to subject potential electricity users to a risk of injury. That being so, there are good grounds for thinking that in case 4 D will be found guilty only of manslaughter, not of second degree murder, even if he or she was aware of a risk that someone might be killed by electrocution. Allowing for variations in the facts of particular cases (clearly, it is not inconceivable that a 'corner-cutting' electrician could, and should, in some circumstances be found guilty of second degree murder), this seems to be the right result.

There are no easy or perfect solutions to be found in this hinterland between murder and lesser homicide offences. What takes some of the heat out of the debate is the three-tier structure. The Commission recommends a discretionary life maximum penalty for second degree murder, just as there is for manslaughter. So, whilst the labelling issue will continue to divide commentators, the sentencing consequences are not so stark as under a two-tier structure.[40] What might add further subtlety is the adoption of a special regime for sentencing in second degree murder cases where a fixed term of years in custody is the appropriate sentence. This could involve a change to the current, controversial system in which the judge states the maximum term of custody that may be served, but the offender can be released at the half-way point. Instead, the judge could state the minimum that must be served, and a formula (say, one quarter of that minimum) would determine the maximum. Second degree murder cases are likely to attract long determinate prison sentences, even when a life sentence is inappropriate. The longer the sentence the more anomalous it seems when someone stands to be released at the half-way point. Under the current system, if a judge wishes to ensure that an offender spends, say, 15 years in prison under a determinate prison sentence, he or she must pass a sentence of 30 years' imprisonment. Small wonder that so many life sentences are passed in such cases, inappropriate though they may be. It would make more sense in such a case for the judge to be able to say that the offender must spend at least 15 years in prison

---

[39] See *R v Woollin* [1999] AC 92.
[40] Although one can expect that sentences for second degree murder will be higher than they are for manslaughter: see Law Commission, *Murder, Manslaughter and Infanticide* (London, 2006), App A.

and allow a formula to determine what the maximum period will be. The Government has now trailed this possibility, for sentencing more generally, in its latest Consultation Paper on sentencing.[41]

5. Questioning the Aspiration for a Codified Law of Homicide

The Law Commission's Consultation Paper was entitled *A New Homicide Act for England and Wales?*. That gives an indication of the limits of the agenda given to the Commission for homicide law reform. The Homicide Act alluded to, that of 1957, was primarily concerned with aspects of the fault for murder (section 1) and with partial defences (sections 2–4). That same agenda accounts for a substantial part of the Law Commission's work in *Murder, Manslaughter and Infanticide*, although there is a broader focus, in the sense that complicity in murder, the defence of duress and the offences of infanticide and manslaughter are also considered. What the Report does not do is provide a 'codified' law of homicide in the sense in which that notion is commonly understood, namely a comprehensive, ordinary-language statement of the entire law of homicide.

The aspiration to codify the law is, of course, one of some antiquity, and is written into the Law Commission's founding statute.[42] Over 120 years ago, the then Attorney-General said to the House of Commons:

> Surely, it is a desirable thing that anybody who may want to know the law on a particular subject should be able to turn to a chapter of the Code, and there find the law he is in search of explained in a few intelligible and well-constructed sentences; nor would he have to enter upon a long examination of *Russell on Crimes*, or *Archbold*, and other text-books, because he would have a succinct and clear statement before him.[43]

This volume provides ample evidence of jurisdictions that have codified their law in its entirety, following Jeremy Bentham's famous clarion call for the abolition of 'unwritten', judge-made common law:

---

[41] Home Office, *Making Sentencing Clearer* (London, 2006), para 3.5 (The Paper is co-signed by the Home Secretary, the Lord Chancellor and the Attorney General.)

[42] Law Commissions Act 1965: 'to take and keep under review all the law with which [it is]...concerned with a view to its systematic development and reform, including in particular the codification of such law....'.

[43] H C Debs, 3 Apr 1879, vol 245 (third series), col 316, cited by Lord Bingham, 'A Criminal Code: Must We Wait Forever?' [1998] *Crim LR* 694 at 695. Bentham had already expressed a similar hope, calling for a legal system to have 'written, visible, and intelligible, and cognisable...rule[s] of action and guide[s] to human conduct', cited by P Scofield and J Harris, '"Legislator of the World": Writings on Codification, Law and Education' in P Scofield and J Harris, *The Collected Works of Jeremy Bentham* (Oxford, 1998) at 18.

so long as there remains any, the smallest scrap, of unwritten law unextirpated, it suffices to taint with its own corruption—its own inbred and incurable corruption—whatsoever portion of statute law has ever been or can ever be applied to it.[44]

Clearly, wholesale codification of the law of homicide would not, as such, be a bad thing. It is an open question, however, whether codified law necessarily equals better or even simpler law.[45] Still less would codification put an end to controversy over the structure and content of the law. It is hard to imagine that the pens of the criminal law's critics will be laid down once and for all if a criminal code for England and Wales is finally enacted; far from it. Criticism and pressures for change will begin almost from the moment of enactment. In any event, how plausible was it, or is it, to suppose that codification of any given part of the criminal law requires no more than 'a few intelligible and well-constructed sentences'?

The former Attorney-General's claim seems politically naïve because it over-looks the priority commonly given by the Legislature to the particular over the general. This political priority was acknowledged Bentham who, in addition to his relentless attacks on judge-made law, also directed his critical fire at what he called the 'two rules…in modern British legislation', namely: 'never to move a finger till your passions are inflamed, nor ever to look further than your nose'.[46] Examples of these two 'rules' in operation in the modern era abound in the law of homicide. Examples include the creation of the offence/defence of infanticide in 1922 (but no defence of diminished responsibility until 1957), the creation of the 'killing in pursuance of a suicide pact' partial defence in 1957 (before the review of the law governing suicide itself, leading to the Suicide Act 1961) and the tacking to and fro between 'recklessness' (Road Traffic Act 1988) and 'dangerous-ness' (Road Traffic Act 1991) as the wrongful element in what was, at the start, the offence of 'causing death by reckless *or* dangerous driving' (Road Traffic Act 1956), along with the ad hoc creation of allied offences such as causing death by careless driving when under the influence of drink or drugs.[47] A credible law reform policy for England and Wales has to try to make a virtue of this overriding concern with the particular. England and Wales may not have a criminal code, but it has a series of statutes concerned with particular crimes—and with some defences—that, for all their omissions, errors and other wrinkles, have stood the test of time reasonably well. Homicide is an area of law severely lacking in that respect, and the Law Commission's Report is meant to form the basis for putting that right.

The late Sir John Smith memorably declared:

---

[44] See *ibid*, at 20–1.
[45] See, eg, Winifred Holland's criticisms of the Canadian Criminal Code, ch 6 below.
[46] Cited by G Postema, *Bentham and the Common Law Tradition* (Oxford, 1986) at 264.
[47] Road Traffic Act 1988, s 3(A).

> I am in favour of codification of the criminal law because I see no other way of reducing a chaotic system to order, of eliminating irrational distinctions and of making the law reasonably comprehensible and certain.[48]

I think this over-states the case for codification. Whatever one may say in specific criticism of, for example, the Accessories and Abettors Act 1861, the Homicide Act 1957, section 3 of the Criminal Law Act 1967, section 8 of the Criminal Justice Act 1967, the Theft Acts 1968 and 1978, the Theft (Amendment) Act 1996, the Criminal Damage Act 1971, the Criminal Law Act 1977, the Criminal Attempts Act 1981, the Computer Misuse Act 1990, the Sexual Offences Act 2003, and even the Offences Against the Person Act 1861,[49] they together constitute considerably more than just legalised chaos. They are a vast improvement, for example, on the preceding criminal law that had been developed at common law, derided by Bentham as 'this impostrous law , the fruits, the perpetual fruits [of which] are…in the breast and in the hands of the judge, power everywhere arbitrary, with a semblance of a set of rules to serve as a screen to it'.[50]

Sir John's real complaint in the passage just cited is, of course, that these offences have not been gathered together in a single code and 'rationalised', so that the guidance of a single thread of principle moulds them into a univocal system. There are, for example, what he would have regarded as 'irrational distinctions' between the objective standards of liability employed in the Sexual Offences Act 2003 and the more subjective standards that run through the Criminal Damage Act 1971, distinctions he believed ought to be erased in favour of the latter. With all due deference to Sir John, his appeal for the elimination of such so-called 'irrational distinctions' seems less than compelling. It has for some time ceased to be clear that subjective standards of liability are appropriate in, say, rape cases, in the way that they may be in, say, conspiracy or criminal damage cases. The beguiling thought that it might actually be *irrational* (not just unfair, from one—contested—point of view) to distinguish between crimes by applying objective standards to some and subjective standards to others, rests on a now outdated picture of the world of criminal law reform. The image is one of an apolitical, technocratic realm in which the specialist lawyer holds sway, using what Robinson Cahill and Mohammed have called 'deliberate craftsmanship', rather than 'mere politicking'.[51] That faded image is reflected in Glanville Williams' claim that criminal law reform is best conducted through 'open Government using the best brains of the legal profession…reasoned consideration and consensual amendment'.[52] Williams claimed that statutes are 'very

---

[48] 'Codification of the Criminal Law', Child & Co Lecture 1986.
[49] See J Gardner, 'Rationality and the Rule of Law in Offences Against the Person' [1994] *CLJ* 520.
[50] See P Scofield and J Harris, '"Legislator of the World": Writings on Codification, Law and Education' in P Scofield and J Harris, *The Collected Works of Jeremy Bentham* (Oxford, 1998) at 20–1.
[51] P Robinson, MT Cahill and U Mohammed, 'The Five Worst (and Five Best) American Criminal Codes' (2000) 95 *Northwestern ULR* 1 at 64.
[52] G Williams, *Textbook of the Criminal Law,* 2nd edn (London, 1983) at 18.

inartistically drawn'[53] and 'often neglect juristic principles'.[54] In response, one might argue that criminal law statutes stand more plausibly to be judged (along with standards such as their fitness for purpose) by the moral integrity of the wrongs that they express than by whether 'the best brains of the legal profession' endorse them. To retain political credibility, codification should not be understood to mean, as it seems at times to have meant to Williams and to Smith, the privileging of the expert criminal lawyers' perspective (c.1965) on the principles of criminal liability over the perspective of, say, victims' family groups, faith groups, groups representing women's interests or non-specialist MPs concerned with law reform.

Perhaps I am being too harsh by taking this line of criticism of the aims of would-be codifiers of the criminal law in general. So let me turn to the specific question of how high a priority we should give the embodiment of the entirety of the law of homicide in a single Homicide Act.

6. Plural Values and the Virtues of Piecemeal Reform

It is commonly assumed that there are advantages in wholesale codification of the law of homicide, as compared with more piecemeal reform aimed at making particular parts of the law of homicide more just, accessible and humane, as the Homicide Act 1957 so successfully did (for all its flaws). I have doubts about whether the Law Commission should give wholesale codification a high priority, even though its statutory duty is to move towards codification of the law. Quite simply, it is unclear how much intellectual or moral coherence there would be to an Act that sought to address all homicide-related law. As I shall now suggest, such an Act might fail to recognise the pluralistic basis on which legislation on particular homicide-related issues comes to be 'nested' in a variety of different social and political contexts.

At present, England and Wales has many different statutes dealing, directly or indirectly, with the preservation of life or with the ending of life. Examples include: the Treason Act 1351, the Offences against the Person Act 1861, the Infant Life Preservation Act 1936, Article 2 of the European Convention on Human Rights 1950, the Homicide Act 1957, the Abortion Act 1961, the Suicide Act 1961, the Internationally Protected Persons Act 1978, the Road Traffic Act 1988, the Law Reform (Year and a Day Rule) Act 1996, the UN Personnel Act 1997 and the Terrorism Act 2000. To these, of course, must be added judicial decisions concerning the meaning of life (for the purposes of the law of

---

[53] *Ibid*, at 17.
[54] *Ibid*, at 18.

homicide[55]) and on when it is acceptable to end life, such as *Airedale NHS Trust v Bland*[56] (patients in a persistent vegetative state), and *Re A* (conjoined twins).[57] The case for an all-embracing 'Homicide' Act rests on the assumption that it would be beneficial legislatively to integrate under the rubric of 'homicide' all of the instances – addressed by such laws – in which death has been unlawfully caused. In other jurisdictions, some steps have been taken towards this end. So, for example, the Californian Penal Code includes the following provisions:

> 187.(a) Murder is the unlawful killing of a human being, or a foetus, with malice aforethought.

> (b) This section shall not apply to any person who commits an act that results in the death of a foetus if...the act complied with the Therapeutic Abortion Act...

> 191.5 Manslaughter is...

> (c) vehicular...driving a vehicle in the commission of an unlawful act...with gross negligence.

There are, however, some important moral, social and political complexities that this kind of unifying legislation threatens to erase, sometimes at the level of fundamental values.

To begin with a simple example, how convincing is the case for extracting the offence in England and Wales of 'causing death by dangerous driving' from its road traffic context,[58] and placing it in a new Homicide Act? The offence seems at least as at home alongside its road traffic-related siblings, such as the offence of 'dangerous driving', which is the lesser included offence under the Road Traffic Act 1988. That is probably where the lay person in search of guidance on his or her legal obligations—Hart's 'puzzled man'[59]—would expect to find it. More importantly, offences concerned with dangerous driving can be thought of as belonging naturally to the regulatory realm of health and safety. A similar point has been convincingly made, in criticism of the proposal for an offence of so-called 'corporate manslaughter', in supporting the case for an alternative offence of causing death through breach of health and safety laws.[60] The fact that death has been caused need not, in and of itself, inevitably lead us to regard as inappropriate the placing of the relevant prohibition in its regulatory context.[61] Causing death by dangerous driving is one unacceptable face of what is, in general, engagement in an activity—driving—that is regarded as acceptable

---

[55] *R v Poulton* (1832) 5 C & P 329; *R v Enoch* (1850) 5 C & P 539; *R v Malcherek* (1981) 2 All ER 422.

[56] [1993] AC 789.

[57] [2001] Fam 147.

[58] Road Traffic Act 1988, s 1.

[59] HLA Hart, *The Concept of Law* (Oxford, 1961) at 193.

[60] See P Glazebrook, 'A Better Way of Convicting Businesses of Avoidable Deaths and Injuries' [2002] *CLJ* 405.

[61] In saying that I am not, of course, in any sense suggesting that deaths caused on the roads or in the workplace are in some sense less serious than deaths caused in other contexts and treated as

despite the fact that it involves inherent risks of causing death. So the prohibition on causing death by dangerous driving is probably best seen in the context of the attempt, more broadly, to make engagement in the acceptable activity safer.

To provide an extreme contrast: in its worst form as an intended killing, murder is not the unwanted by-product of permitting people to engage in risky activity.[62] Successfully to kill someone and hence commit murder is by definition to engage in a kind of conduct that is wholly unacceptable; and in so far as there are serious doubts about that—as in the case of mercy killing—then the question arises whether such killings should continue to be regarded as murder.[63] By way of contrast, other forms of murder and manslaughter straddle the border between the two kinds of crime, regulatory and non-regulatory. In some instances (say, a gang attack that ends in another's death) the conduct in question that led to the death will—as in cases of intended killing—be wholly unacceptable, period. In other cases—say, deaths caused through medical malpractice or through dangerous (but consensual) sports—murder and manslaughter are being relied on to do much the same job as causing death by reckless driving: policing those who step beyond the boundaries of otherwise tolerated but risky conduct. Perhaps there is a case for a 'culpable homicide' offence based on negligence (below manslaughter) to catch such 'regulatory' cases and protect the offender from the harsher 'murder' or 'manslaughter' label; but consideration of that is beyond the scope of this essay.

Similar issues arise at a more fundamental level. What is commonly considered to be the law of 'homicide' is that part of the law concerned with the prima facie wrong of ending of another's life when that life is already 'in being'.[64] The defences commonly regarded as available wholly to justify or excuse the intentional commission of that prima facie wrong are, correspondingly, focused on the preservation of a life that would otherwise wrongly be ended (self-defence; necessity).[65] Traditionally, this has been more or less the full extent of the criminal law codifier's menu, and it is not hard to see why. A true and full account of justifications for killing would have to address much more controversial instances where the justification is not (or may not be) the preservation of life, as such: examples are abortion, killing in war, taking one's own life, deciding not to resuscitate a dying and untreatable patient, and withdrawing life support from a patient in a persistent vegetative state. Take, by way of example, suicide and

---

murder or manslaughter. Even if the death penalty were to be introduced for causing death by dangerous driving, it would not in any way diminish the case for keeping that offence in a Road Traffic Act.

[62] Subject to what will be said below about death caused in the course of engagements with dangerous people involving armed police officers.

[63] The Law Commission is recommending that the area of mercy killing is the subject of a special review: see Law Commission, *Murder, Manslaughter and Infanticide* (London, 2006).

[64] In other words, when someone has been 'born alive': see n 55 above.

[65] In circumstances where the individual has no choice but to act him- or herself if life is to be saved: see J Horder, 'On the Irrelevance of Motive in Criminal Law' in J Horder (ed), *Oxford Essays in Jurisprudence*, 4th series (Oxford, 2000).

abortion. Without entering into the rights and wrongs of these instances where life is ended unnaturally, they may all stand to be justified or excused, if at all, by values unconnected to the preservation of life. Suicide and abortion are (in some or all circumstances) lawful because to permit these practices—to a greater or to a lesser extent—shows a proper concern for civil liberty and for the right to self-determination. One might question, then, the recent innovative use of Anti-Social Behaviour Orders to prevent people seeking to take their own lives, even when a social cost is imposed when such people must be rescued and treated.[66] A society that can afford to rescue reckless people trying to have fun by crossing the Atlantic on a rubber inflatable hardly needs to trespass on the right to self-determination in the interests of cost-saving.

By way of contrast, the decision not to resuscitate a dying and untreatable patient or to withdraw life support from a patient in a persistent vegetative state may (in many instances) be better justified by considerations of what is in the patient's best interests, rather than by an appeal to the right to self-determination.[67] Something similar might be said about many instances of mercy killing. None the less, these examples share with suicide and abortion the absence of any justification founded in the preservation of life itself. As suggested above, each of these sets of homicide-related concerns (suicide; abortion; withdrawing patient life-support; mercy killing) is best located in its own political or moral—and hence legislative—context, a context partly distinct from that in which the would-be codifier of the law of homicide shapes his or her frame of reference. What lesson, then, should one draw from these examples?

They suggest that the criminal lawyer's ambition to codify the entire law of homicide, if not actually incoherent, rests on the false premise that either the 'preservation of life' or the 'ending of life' itself provides a sufficiently substantial focal point for legislation on all end-of-life issues. In questioning this ambition I should obviously not be taken to be saying that, for example, the question whether life can be ended ceases to be an issue within the domain the law of homicide simply because the killer is a doctor or mother and the victim a patient or foetus. However, the fact that the killing of patients or foetuses can be murder or manslaughter is a conclusion to an argument about the legal status of those killings that is, and should be, in part shaped or determined by moral and political principles outside the life-preservatory domain of homicide. That point, at least, is recognised under Californian penal law relating to abortion, in the legal connection that it establishes between homicide law and abortion law.[68]

Shamefully, England and Wales still lacks proper medical ethics legislation that would relieve the courts of the primary duty to resolve intractable life-or-death

---

[66] In Jan 2006, Amy Dallamura found herself banned under such an order from visiting any beach in Aberystwyth, where she had repeated tried to drown herself; and Kim Sutton from Bath was likewise banned from jumping into rivers, canals or on to railway lines.

[67] Obviously, I am putting aside here the issues raised when someone has made a 'living will' with instructions on how they are (not) to be treated when terminally ill.

[68] See the text following n 57 above.

medical dilemmas using doctrines ill-fitted for the purpose, like necessity, drawn from the domain of life-preservation.[69] The issue has, by and large, simply been ducked by the legislature. In an ideal world, we would not have an all-embracing codified law of homicide so much as separate pieces of legislation divided, according to respect for the plural and conflicting nature of values, very roughly as follows:

(a) Life Preservatory Domain (homicide law):
Issues: eg definition of murder and manslaughter; justifications and complete excuses for murder and manslaughter concerned with life-preservation, such as self-defence and necessity.

(b) Quality of Life Domain (medical ethics law):
Issues: eg Mercy killing; assisted suicide; cessation of life-support for patients.

(c) Domain of Self-determination (law of civil liberties):
Issues: eg abortion; suicide.

(d) Regulatory Domain (law of health and safety):
Issues: eg causing death by dangerous driving; corporate manslaughter (ie causing death through breach of health and safety at work rules).

(e) Domain of National and International Security:
Issues: eg genocide; use of weapons of mass destruction; jurisdiction to try non-nationals for homicide committed overseas.

As indicated above, although each domain is context-sensitive, there can be overlapping and controversy over the territory claimed by each of them. Take the examples where patients die needlessly on the operating table, and where armed police shoot someone wrongly thought to be armed and dangerous. Some might argue that killing in these kinds of cases should be regarded, however serious, first and foremost as a regulatory offence, even if life-preservation was the purported justification for the action that led to the death.[70] They should be regarded as regulatory offences, so the argument runs, because doctors and armed police officers face life-threatening choices as part of their professional, rule-following duties and not—as is the case for ordinary citizens—as unexpected, once-in-a-life-time emergencies for which the doctrines of necessity and self-defence (on which professionals currently have to rely) were designed.[71] Almost needless to say, some would also regard mercy killing as having no claim to special status under any 'quality of life' rubric, because it is a straightforward violation of the right to life protected within the life-preservatory domain. I hope I have done enough, however, to suggest that it is right to regard reform of the law of

---

[69] See *Re A (Conjoined Twins)* [2001] Fam 147.

[70] In that regard, it is perhaps not insignificant that when in 2005 an armed policeman shot an innocent man on the London underground system because he was mistakenly thought to be a terrorist, the only charges brought concerned breach of health and safety laws in connection with the way the operation as a whole was run: www.bbc.co.uk/1/hi/uk/5186050.stm (17 July 2006).

[71] See, further, J Rogers, 'Justifying the Use of Firearms by Policemen and Soldiers: a Response to the Home Office's Review of the Law on the Use of Lethal Force' (1998) 18 *Legal Studies* 486.

homicide within the life-preservatory domain as a modest but coherent and achievable aim, unlike grandiose schemes for the codification of all the law relevant to the commission of homicide.

3

Intentional Killings in French Law

JR SPENCER

I. Introduction: The Legal Background

T HIS CHAPTER DESCRIBES in outline the parts of French criminal law
that cover the ground of murder and voluntary manslaughter in English
law, and the main defences that are potentially applicable. The account it
contains is an elementary one, derived from the relevant statutory provisions and
the discussions of them that are contained in the leading textbooks.[1] In what
follows, the term 'intentional killing' will be used to designate killings done with
intent to kill or to cause grievous bodily harm, and 'intended killing' to refer to
killings done with nothing less than an intent to cause death.

(i) French Legal Sources: the Code Pénal

As is general in continental Europe, the source of French law on the subject is a
Criminal Code. The French Code is called the *Code pénal* (usually abbreviated to
CP). An up-to-date version of the *Code pénal* is published annually by the French
law publishers Dalloz, in a single-volume edition containing brief comments and
references to the most significant case law. An up-to-date version of the text,
without commentary, is also available on *Légifrance*, the French government's
official legal website. On this website the Code also appears in an English
translation. (In this chapter, English versions of the French text have been taken
from this site—though with the substitution in some places of the original
French terms for the English equivalents chosen by the translators.)

---

[1] In particular F Desportes and F Le Gunehec, *Droit pénal général*, 10th edn (Paris, 2003), J Pradel,
Manuel de Droit pénal général, 14th edn (Paris, 2002), and R Merle and A Vitu, *Traité de droit criminel*,
vol. I, *Droit pénal général*, 7th edn (Paris, 1997). A distinguished French colleague (Professor Jean
Pradel) was kind enough to read an earlier draft and offer comments: but for any mistakes in the final
version the responsibility is mine.

39

The current French Criminal Code is modern, dating from 1994—and for this reason it is still widely referred to as the *Nouveau Code pénal* (or NPC). Although this new Code introduced many changes, much of the underlying thought derives from the earlier Code that it replaced—which dated from 1810 and was part of the original Napoleonic codification. A complete picture of French criminal law still frequently requires a backward glance to the earlier Code.

A significant matter that still affects public debate about the law of homicide in France is the fact that it was only in 1981 that the death penalty was abolished. As in England, some of the French rules governing the punishment of homicide still bear the marks of the political compromises needed to bring about the abolition.

(ii) Different Types of Imprisonment; Maximum and Minimum Penalties

There are three types of offence in French law. In ascending order of gravity, these are *contraventions*, *délits* and *crimes*. Each type is handled by a differently constituted court. *Contraventions* are tried by a professional judge who sits alone, or sometimes by the French equivalent of a lay magistrate. *Délits* are tried in a court that in principle consists of three professional judges, but for the less important cases may comprise a single judge who sits alone. *Crimes* are tried by the French version of a jury which, unlike the English version, consists of nine lay people and three professional judges who sit together as a combined panel.

For *crimes* the main punishment prescribed is *réclusion criminelle*. Although this is in theory different from ordinary imprisonment (*emprisonnement*), in practice it amounts to the same thing. When the new Code was being prepared there was a proposal to abolish it, but traditionalists argued that there was value in the stigmatic quality that attached to its name,[2] and the decision was taken to retain it.

The 1810 CP operated with what was known as *la forchette*: the law laid down both a maximum and a minimum penalty, within which the court had a discretion as to sentence; though it could impose a sentence lower than the prescribed minimum if it found the existence of extenuating circumstances (*circonstances atténuantes*). The 1994 CP departs from this by abolishing minimum penalties, so that the penalty prescribed by the relevant article of the CP is (as in English law) the maximum, and the court is usually left free to impose a lesser penalty. However, an exception is made to this in respect of very serious offences. By CP Article 132–18:

> Where an offence is punished[3] by *réclusion criminelle* or criminal detention for life, the court may impose *réclusion criminelle* or detention for a term, or imprisonment for not less than two years.

---

[2] Rather as with penal servitude in England.
[3] Ie, liable to be punished, or punish*able*.

Where an offence is punished by a determinate sentence of *réclusion criminelle* or criminal detention, the court may impose a sentence of *réclusion criminelle* or detention shorter than the maximum, or a sentence of ordinary imprisonment of not less than a year.

However, this is a less serious matter for persons convicted of homicide than at first appears because, when imposing a prison sentence of up to five years, the court is free to make it *sous sursis* (i.e. suspend it).[4] Thus French law, unlike English law, does not subject a defendant who has been convicted of a murder to any mandatory period of imprisonment; and in theory a French court could allow a defendant to 'walk free' after convicting him for murder, even of the most atrocious kind. On this point, French law is obviously very different from English law. That such a possibility exists, and that French public opinion tolerates it, probably relates to the fact that in serious cases the sentence is imposed not by a judge, but by a jury (albeit one composed of nine lay people plus three professional judges). In France, unlike in England, the 'jury' not only decides the formal question of guilt or innocence, but in the case of guilt the jury also determines what the sentence is to be. One of the consequences of this is that the sentences pronounced by the courts in highly emotive cases that attract the attention of the media are felt to have a degree of democratic legitimacy about them which is lacking in England, where in such cases the sentence is decided by a judge alone. Furthermore, where a derisory sentence is imposed in a serious case the prosecutor has a right of appeal.[5]

(iii) The Safety Period

In France, the 'get tough on crime' debate that in England has taken place around the issue of minimum sentences has mainly centred on the related but different question of how much of the sentence imposed by the court the convicted defendant must actually serve. In reaction to an increasing range of possibilities for premature release, the French legislator:

> brought in, by the law of 22 November 1978, a safety period (*période de sûreté*) that prevents, while it runs, the grant of any measure of individualisation [ie premature release]. A very controversial topic, the safety period has been at the centre of political debate, exacerbating the traditional division between those who are said to be soft and those who claim to be tough. The debate intensified after the death penalty was abolished, when the safety period, as applied to life imprisonment, took on the appearance of a substitute for capital punishment.[6]

---

[4] CP Art 132–29. By Art 132–30 it cannot do this if the sentence is imposed for *un crime* and the defendant has received a prison sentence during the previous five years.

[5] But, surprisingly, only since 2000 in a case where the sentence was imposed by a jury.

[6] F Desportes and F Le Gunehec, *Droit pénal général*, 10th edn (Paris, 2003) §1064.

Since the abolition of capital punishment in 1981 the rules governing the safety period have been repeatedly amended, being alternately strengthened and weakened according to the penal tastes of the government of the day, and the resulting law is complicated.

If the discussion here is limited to what is directly relevant to intentional killings, there is no safety period for the offence of ordinary murder (CP Article 222–1); but unless the court decides otherwise, aggravated forms of murder are subject to a safety period of half the sentence where it is a fixed term, or 18 years in the case of a life sentence. The court that imposes the sentence may reduce the safety period—and in certain particularly grave cases (notably sexual murders or the sadistic murder of children) it also has the power to increase it.

The account of the substantive law that follows is limited to the law relating to intentional killings, and does not cover the French equivalents of manslaughter by gross negligence. But it does include a discussion of the general defences that bear on the issues raised in English law by duress, necessity, provocation, diminished responsibility and the use of excessive force in private or public defence.

2. The Substantive Law

(i) The Basic Legislative Scheme

The central element of the French law on intentional killing consists of a basic offence of homicide, called *meurtre*. Despite the similarity of name, this is more narrowly defined than the English crime of murder, because it is limited to homicides carried out with the intention of causing death; and, again unlike murder in England, it does not carry a mandatory life sentence. It is the equivalent of the German offence of *Todschlag*[7] and, as in German law, there are several upgraded versions of the offence, to which a heavier maximum penalty applies. However, unlike in German law there are no downgraded versions, and in particular there is no equivalent of the special German offence of killing on request. Unlike in England, but as in Germany, the defendant who kills by acts that were intended to cause harm short of death does not commit a *meurtre* (or, a fortiori, any of the aggravated versions of this offence); instead, he commits an aggravated version of one of the lesser offences against the person.

The conduct covered by the offence of *meurtre* (in both its simple and its aggravated forms) obviously depends on how French law interprets the meaning of 'intention'. Neither statute nor French case law provides any general definition of intention, and for a discussion of its meaning it is necessary to look at French

---

[7] See Antje du Bois-Pedain, ch 4 below.

legal writing (*la doctrine*). Here, intention is usually described by the synonym *dol* (from the Latin *dolus*). Of *dol* there are two accepted forms, either of which will satisfy the requirement of the Code for intention: *dol direct*, where the forbidden action or the prohibited consequence is desired, and *dol indirect*, where:

> the agent knows that his voluntary act will cause (certainly or almost certainly) a consequence that is not truly desired. Our case law, without saying so expressly, accepts this notion and assimilates *dol indirect* and *dol direct*; so a murder may exist by reason of the knowledge that the blows can result in death (*peuvent donner la mort*) as well as in the desire to produce the precise result, which is the extinction of a life.[8]

Thus in broad terms, intention in French law bears much the same meaning as intention in the current English case law on murder.

French writers also describe a related concept called *dol éventuel* (from the Latin *dolus eventualis*), which is where the agent merely foresees the possibility of the result—the state of mind which English lawyers would call subjective recklessness. In French law this is not treated as a form of intention. There is no suggestion in French law of the German theory of *bedingter Vorsatz*, under which a person is considered to intend the consequence where he not only foresees the risk, but also willingly embraces it.[9] In principle, *dol éventuel* is not a mental state that will support a conviction for *meurtre*, whether in its simple or in one of its aggravated forms.

(ii) The Basic Offence of Homicide (*Meurtre*)

By Article 221–1 CP:

> The wilful causing of the death of another person is murder (*meurtre*). It is punished with thirty years' *réclusion criminelle*.

(iii) Aggravated Forms of Homicide

By Article 221–2:

> A murder which precedes, accompanies or follows another *crime* is punished by *réclusion criminelle* for life.

> A murder which is intended either to prepare or to facilitate a *délit*, or to assist an escape or to ensure the impunity of the author or accomplice, is punished by *réclusion criminelle* for life.

Article 221–3 creates an aggravated version of the offence where there was premeditation.

---

[8] J Pradel, *Manuel de Droit pénal général*, 14th edn (Paris, 2002) §502.
[9] Explained by A Pedain, 'Intention and the Terrorist Example' [2003] *Crim LR* 579 at 591.

Murder committed with premeditation is assassination (*un assassinat*). Assassination is punished by *réclusion criminelle* for life.

Article 221–4 creates a further aggravated form of *meurtre*, also punishable with life imprisonment, where it was committed against one of a range of specified victims. The list was extended in 2003 as part of the French government's 'get tough on crime' policy. The current list consists of nine different categories of victim, ranging from minors aged less than 15, through a group of close relatives, to a spectrum of public officials—from judges to bus-conductors and firemen—to conclude with homosexuals and members of ethnic minorities where the motive was homophobia or racism. (To stress once again the basic point that may appear almost unbelievable to many English readers, the sentence of life imprisonment in these cases is the *maximum*: it is not, as in English law, mandatory.)

(iv) Less Serious Cases of Voluntary Homicide: Death as an Aggravating Factor in Other Offences against the Person

CP Article 222–1 creates an offence of 'torture or acts of barbarity'. This carries 15 years' *réclusion criminelle*. The penalty is higher if any of a list of aggravating factors is present. By Article 222–6, one of these is the unintended death of the victim, in which case the maximum penalty is imprisonment for life.

By Article 222–7 acts of violence causing an unintended death are punished by 15 years' *réclusion criminelle*. In practice, this is probably the offence of which the defendant would have been convicted in a case like *Woolin*,[10] where, as English readers will recall, the defendant lost his temper with his three-month-old son and threw him down on a hard surface, inflicting a fatal fracture of his skull in the process.

By Article 222–23, rape is widely defined as '[a]ny act of sexual penetration, whatever its nature, committed against another person by violence, constraint, threat or surprise'. It is normally punishable with up to 15 years' *réclusion criminelle*; but by Article 222–25 it is punishable by 30 years' *réclusion criminelle* where it resulted in the death of the victim.

---

[10] [1999] 1 AC 82.

(v) Duress, Necessity, Provocation, Excessive Force in Self-defence, Mercy Killing and Diminished Responsibility

(a) General Introduction

According to French legal theory, the matters that are usually lumped together as 'general defences' in English law are divided into three categories: faits justificatifs, causes d'irresponsabilité (or de non-culpabalité) and exemptions de peine.[11] In the first type of case, the 'defence' is seen as making the defendant's conduct positively legal, whereas in the second type of case the defendant's conduct is still regarded as illegal, although he cannot be convicted for it. In the third type of case, by contrast, the defendant's conduct is considered to be illegal and, if prosecuted, he is liable to conviction: but should this happen, then no penalty may be imposed. Whatever the theoretical differences, the practical result in each type of case is identical in one obvious respect, namely that the defendant cannot be punished for conduct for which he would otherwise be punished by the criminal courts; and for present purposes I shall adopt the usual English practice and refer to all three groups collectively as 'defences'.

As to whether the burden of proving general defences falls on the prosecution or the defence, the position in French law is obscure. The older and more traditional writers say that, on principle, the burden of proving any general defence must fall on the defendant, and the case law seems to bear this out.[12] But some modern writers question this and argue that, on the contrary, basic legal principles should require the defendant who raises the defence to have the benefit of the doubt.[13] As in English law 50 years ago, the position in French law is not entirely clear—and discussions of the topic fail to draw the distinction between the 'legal' and the 'evidential' burdens.

To English readers, the relative underdevelopment of this important part of French law may seem surprising; but the situation is understandable in the light of the way that criminal cases in France are tried. In France a serious case is decided by a jury, which (like an English jury) gives no reasons for its decision, but which (unlike an English jury) produces its verdict without any public direction from the judge. A French jury consists of a combined panel of three professional judges sitting with nine laymen to whom the judges give their views on points of law, not by way of a public direction, but privately in the secrecy of the retiring room. In consequence, many points of principle that end up before the Court of Appeal in England never 'show their heads above the parapet' in

---

[11] J Pradel, *Manuel de Droit pénal général*, 14th edn (Paris, 2002) §307, §651 ff; R Merle and A Vitu, *Traité de droit criminel*, vol. I, *Droit pénal général*, 7th edn (Paris, 1997) §§438–442.

[12] J Pradel, *Manuel de procédure pénale*, 10th edn (Paris, 2000) §380.

[13] For a discussion see G. Stefani, G. Levasseur and B. Bouloc, *Procédure pénale*, 17th edn (Paris, 2000) §§126 and 127, and also R Merle and A Vitu, *Traité de droit criminel*, vol. II, *Procédure pénale*, 4th edn (Paris, 1989) §127.

France. The less serious cases, on the other hand, are decided by courts composed of one or more professional judges. These, unlike juries, give reasons for their decisions: but they are usually laconic. In the course of giving them, the judges will usually just list the evidence they have heard and facts that they find proved, without explaining the reasoning that led from one to the other.

(b) Duress and Necessity

French law recognises duress as a defence. This is to be found in Article 122–2 of the *Code pénal*, which says:

> A person is not criminally liable who acted under the influence of a force or constraint which he could not resist.[14]

The defence created by this laconic provision covers the same ground as the two distinct English-law defences of 'duress of threats' and 'duress of circumstances'. The French term for this composite defence is *contrainte*.

Under French law, a general provision of this sort contained in the *Code pénal* applies to any criminal offence in the absence of any statutory provision that explicitly disapplies it, and no such provision exists to take homicide (or any other offence) outside the scope of *contrainte* (or indeed any other general defence). Thus the French equivalent of duress does potentially apply, inter alia, to the French equivalent of murder. In the famous case of Maurice Papon, the *Cour de cassation* ruled that a French official under the Vichy government who was accused of 'crimes against humanity' by collaborating with the German occupiers to help round up Jews and send them to their deaths was not entitled to rely on a defence of *contrainte*, based on his fear of reprisals from the Germans: but this was because the threats of reprisals were insufficiently specific, and not because *contrainte* is in principle inapplicable to crimes against humanity.[15]

In addition to *contrainte*, French criminal law provides a general defence of necessity, which Article 122–7 defines as follows:

> A person is not criminally liable if confronted with a present or imminent danger to himself, another person or property, he performs an act necessary to ensure the safety of the person or property, except where the means used are disproportionate to the seriousness of the threat.

As with *contrainte*, this defence is in principle available to a person charged with any crime, however grave, including murder. But in practice, obviously, the intentional killing of another human being is likely to be treated as 'disproportionate to the seriousness of the threat'.

---

[14] *N'est pas pénalement responsable la personne qui a agi sous l'empire d'une force ou d'une contrainte à laquelle elle n'a pu résister.*

[15] Cour de Cassation (Cass), 23 Jan 1997; *Bulletin des arrêts de la Cour de cassation Chambre criminelle* ('Bull Crim'), 1997 No 32.

(c) Provocation

Under the old CP, French law had a general concept of 'provocation'. This operated as a partial defence, reducing the penalty otherwise applicable. Articles 321, 322 and 323 of the old Code set out the circumstances that could give rise to the defence—which by 1994 looked strangely archaic. Provocation could arise from 'blows or serious violence', burglary committed during daylight hours or a husband discovering his wife in the act of adultery within the matrimonial home. Provocation so defined reduced the penalties otherwise applicable to offences of murder and wounding. The old Code contained a specific offence of castration(!)—and, for good measure, Article 325 provided a defence of provocation where the defendant castrated his victim as 'an immediate reaction to an indecent assault committed with violence'. The partial defence of provocation disappeared with the new Criminal Code, the view prevailing that there was no need for it after minimum penalties were abolished. However, some French writers regret its passing and think that a modernised version of the partial defence of provocation should have been incorporated in the new Code.[16]

(d) Self-defence and Excessive Force in Self-defence

The rules on 'legitimate defence' are contained in Article 122–5:

> A person is not criminally liable if, confronted with an unjustified attack upon himself or upon another, he performs at that moment an action compelled by the necessity of self-defence or the defence of another person, except where the means of defence used are not proportionate to the seriousness of the attack.

> A person is not criminally liable if, to interrupt the commission of a *crime* or a *délit* against property, he performs an act of defence other than wilful murder, where the act is strictly necessary for the intended objective and the means used are proportionate to the gravity of the offence.

French case law provides that the defendant who misunderstood the situation is in principle to be judged on the facts as he believed them to be. So, as in English law, the defendant who uses force that is excessive only because he misread the situation is not guilty if the force he used would have been appropriate had the facts been as imagined. Unlike English law, however, French law does not give the defendant the benefit of a mistake if it was wholly unreasonable.[17] And there is no direct French equivalent of the German defence of *Überschreitung der*

---

[16] F Desportes and F Le Gunehec, *Droit pénal général*, 10th edn (Paris, 2003) §741.
[17] *Ibid*, §730.

Notwehr, which provides a defence for the person who overreacts in panic and uses an unreasonable degree of force in a situation that he has understood correctly.[18]

In England, much of the popular debate about the use of lethal force in defence of person and or property has centred around the case of Tony Martin, the Norfolk farmer who shot an escaping burglar in the back and killed him, who was originally convicted of murder and whose conviction was eventually reduced to manslaughter, not on the ground that on these facts he should have had the benefit of any kind of 'legitimate defence', but because his mental state seemed to give rise a defence of diminished responsibility.[19] Tony Martin's French equivalent is sometimes helped by Article 122–6:

> A person is presumed to have acted in a state of self-defence if he performs an action
>
> 1. to repulse at night an entry to an inhabited place committed by breaking in, violence or deception;
>
> 2. to defend himself against the perpetrators of theft or pillage carried out with violence.

This provision was carried over from the Napoleonic Code of 1810, and in the nineteenth century it was originally interpreted as creating a presumption that was irrebuttable. Thus at one time, for example, it even applied to protect a husband who shot his wife's lover as he climbed into the house, the husband knowing full well who he was and the purpose of his visit.[20] Nowadays, however, the courts treat it as creating a rebuttable presumption only—which means in practice that the householder who shoots an intruder, though normally taken to have acted in self-defence, is convicted if the prosecution can persuade the court that when he shot he was no longer in fear for the safety of himself or of his family. Thus in one case, the householder was convicted where he saw an intruder in the garden and fired a warning shot, at which the intruder ran away: whereupon the householder fired again directly at him, and hit him.[21]

So, as French law currently stands, Tony Martin would probably stand a better chance of acquittal than he would in England; but, depending on the precise facts, he might still fail in his defence. However, if convicted he would still be better off than under English law, for two reasons. First, if he were convicted it would probably not be for *meurtre* because, as we have seen, in French law this requires an intention to kill, and an intention to cause grievous bodily harm is not sufficient. Secondly, even if he was convicted for an offence of *meurtre*, this does not carry a mandatory life sentence. The minimum sentence for a *meurtre* is only a year's imprisonment, and even this can be suspended. So, if convicted, a

---

[18]   See Antje du Bois-Pedain, ch 4 below.
[19]   *Martin* [2001] EWCA Crim 2245, [2003] QB 1.
[20]   Desportes and Le Gunehec, above n 16, §740, quoting Cass, Chambre criminelle, 22 July 1844 [1844] I *Receuil Sirey* 777.
[21]   Cass, Chambre criminelle, 8 July 1942, Bull Crim No 88; Dalloz, *Code pénal* (Paris, 2005) at 128.

French equivalent of Tony Martin might not even go to jail at all, if the court decided to give him a suspended sentence.

(e) Mercy Killing

Like English law, but unlike German law, French law makes no special provision for intended killings carried out at the request of the victim. So in France, voluntary euthanasia—and involuntary euthanasia a fortiori—amounts to *meurtre*. However, as already mentioned, the court has a wide discretion as to sentence. In France a life sentence for a genuine mercy killer would be virtually inconceivable.

Despite this, the issue of euthanasia has recently provoked a great deal of discussion in France.[22] In April 2005, after a lengthy enquiry, the French legislature enacted a new law on the subject,[23] but the scope of it is limited. Whilst it makes it legal for doctors in certain circumstances to withdraw life-supporting treatment, it stops short of legalising the deliberate ending of life by taking positive steps (eg the administration of a fatal dose of medicine in order to put the patient to sleep permanently).

(f) Diminished Responsibility

Although French law no longer provides for a partial defence of provocation, it does have something that closely resembles a partial defence of diminished responsibility, which is contained in CP Article 122–1. The first paragraph of this Article deals with what in English law would be mainly covered by the defence of insanity:

> A person is not criminally liable who, when the act was committed, was suffering from a psychological or neuropsychological disorder which destroyed his discernment or his ability to control his actions.

This Article obviously provides the French defendant with a complete defence where under English law he would fall under the *M'Naghten Rules*.[24] But it goes wider than this, because it potentially covers the case of the mentally disordered defendant who knew what he was doing, but was unable to control himself. Unlike the defence of insanity in English law, it is probably also wide enough to cover the case of the defendant whose self-control was undermined by drink or drugs: at any rate, those which, as in *Kingston*,[25] he had consumed involuntarily.[26]

The second paragraph of Article 122–1 deals with what English law would view as diminished responsibility.

---

[22] See J Pradel, *Manuel de Droit pénal général*, 14th edn (Paris, 2002) §540.
[23] *Loi No 2005–370 du 22 avril 2005 relative aux droits des malades et à la fin de vie.*
[24] *Daniel M'Naghten's case*, 10 Cl & F 200, 8 ER 718.
[25] *Kingston* [1995] 2 AC 355.

A person who, at the time he acted, was suffering from a psychological or neuropsychological disorder which reduced his discernment or impeded his ability to control his actions, remains punishable; however, the court shall take this into account when it decides the penalty and determines its regime.

Unlike section 2 of the Homicide Act 1957, this provision is general and operates in favour of defendants no matter what offence they have been charged with. To that extent, it is like the partial defence in German law of *verminderte Schuld-fähigkeit* (StGB §21).[27] However, unlike the German provision, and unlike section 2 of the Homicide Act, Article 122–1(2) CP fails to lay down any precise legal consequence. All it does is to remind the French court to take account of the defendant's mental state when sentencing him. As one writer puts it:

> So the last line of Article 122–1(2) goes against the traditional tendency of the judges (and the lawyers) to consider at the trial only matters relating to culpability and the types of penalty, without any great reflection on how they are to be carried out, something which is truly essential.[28]

3. Conclusion

From this brief survey, it is clear that the French law of murder differs from our own in a number of strikingly important ways.

In the first place the French, unlike the British, have managed to abolish capital punishment for murder without in the process replacing it with a mandatory life sentence (or indeed with any other form of heavy mandatory penalty). As we have seen, in France the penalty for murder is effectively in the discretion of the court of trial. Secondly, in French law, the equivalent of murder has always been defined in such a way as to limit it to killings that are intended. And thirdly, the crime of murder in French law is in principle subject to the normal range of general defences, including the French equivalents of necessity and duress.

In all of these respects, the French law of murder conforms to the shape that liberal reformers in this country have usually advocated for the law of murder here. That all this can be so in a country which faces similar social problems to our own, and where the media and the general public are at least as prone as they are here to criticise politicians, judges and the courts for being 'soft on crime', seems to me to give our liberal reformers a simple message: *bon courage*.

---

[26] French writers shrink from the conclusion that this Art provides a potential defence for those who are intoxicated voluntarily: F Desportes and F Le Gunehec, *Droit pénal général*, 10th edn (Paris, 2003) §649.

[27] See Antje du Bois Pedain, below, ch 4.

[28] J Pradel, *Manuel de Droit pénal général*, 14th edn (Paris, 2002) at 421.

4. Provisions of the French Criminal Code Relevant to Intentional Homicide

ARTICLE 132–23

In the case of an immediate custodial sentence for a term of ten years or more imposed for offences specifically set out by statute, the convicted person is not entitled to benefit from provisions governing the suspension or division of the penalty, posting to a non-custodial assignment, temporary leave, semi-detention or parole, during the safety period.

The safety period is half that of the custodial sentence or, in case of criminal imprisonment for life, eighteen years. The *Cour d'assises* or trial court may nevertheless by a special decision either extend this period up to two-thirds of the prison sentence or up to twenty-two years in the case of imprisonment for life, or may decide to reduce these periods.

In all the other cases, where it imposes a non-suspended custodial sentence exceeding five years, the court may determine a safety-period during which the convicted person may not be granted the benefit of any one of the modes of execution of penalties referred to under the first paragraph. The length of this safety period may not exceed two-thirds of the penalty imposed, or twenty-two years in the event of life imprisonment. Reductions of sentences granted during the safety period will be deducted only from the portion of the penalty exceeding this period.

ARTICLE 221–1

The wilful causing of the death of another person is murder. It is punished with thirty years' *réclusion criminelle.*

ARTICLE 221–2

A murder which precedes, accompanies or follows another *crime* is punished by *réclusion criminelle* for life.

A murder which is intended either to prepare or to facilitate a *délit*, or to assist an escape or to ensure the impunity of the author or accomplice, is punished by *réclusion criminelle* for life.

The first two paragraphs of article 132–23 governing the safety period are applicable to the offences under the present article.

ARTICLE 221–3

Murder committed with premeditation is assassination. Assassination is punished by a *réclusion criminelle* for life.

The first two paragraphs of article 132–23 governing the safety period apply to the offence under the present article. Nevertheless, where the victim is a minor who is under fifteen years of age and the assassination is preceded by or accompanied by rape, torture or acts of barbarity, the Cour d'assises may by a special decision either increase the safety period to thirty years, or, where it imposes *réclusion criminelle* for life, decide that none of the measures enumerated under Article 132–23 shall be granted to the convicted person. Where the sentence is commuted, and unless the decree of pardon otherwise provides, the safety period is equal to the length of the sentence resulting from the pardon.

ARTICLE 221–4

Murder is punished by *réclusion criminelle* for life where it is committed:

1. against a minor under fifteen years of age;

2. against a natural or legitimate ascendant or the adoptive father or mother;

3. against a person whose particular vulnerability, due to age, sickness or disability, or to any psychic or psychical deficiency or to a state of pregnancy, is apparent or known to the perpetrator;

4. against a judge or prosecutor, a juror, an advocate, a legal professional officer or a public officer, a member of the Gendarmerie, a civil servant belonging to the national police, the customs, the penitentiary administration or on any other person holding public authority, a fireman (whether professional or volunteer), the accredited warden of a building or group of buildings or an agent carrying out on behalf of the tenant the duty of caring for or watching an inhabited building in pursuance of article L. 127.1 of the Code of Construction and Habitation, in the exercise or at the occasion of the exercise of his functions or mission, when the capacity of the victim is known or apparent to the perpetrator;

4*bis* Against the partner, direct ascendants or descendants of the persons mentioned in paragraph 4 above, or on any other person habitually living with them, by reason of the duties that they carry out;

4*ter* Against the agent of a public transport organisation or any other person entrusted with a public service mission, such as a health professional, in the exercise of his functions, when the capacity of the victim is known to the perpetrator;

5. Against a witness, a victim or civil party, either to prevent him from denouncing the action, filing a complaint or making a statement before a court, or because of his denunciation, complaint or statement.

6. By reason of the victim's belonging, or not belonging (real or supposed) to a particular ethnic group, nation, race or religion.

7. By reason of the victim's sexual orientation.

The first two paragraphs of Article 132–23 governing the safety period are applicable to the offences set out under the present article. Nevertheless, where the victim is a minor under of fifteen years of age and the murder is preceded by or accompanied by rape, torture or acts of barbarity, the Cour d'assises may by a special decision either increase the safety period to thirty years, or, where it orders life imprisonment, decide that none of the measures enumerated under article 132–23 shall be granted to the convicted person; where the penalty is commuted, and unless the decree of pardon otherwise provides, the safety period is then equal to the length of the sentence resulting from the pardon.

ARTICLE 222–1

The subjection of a person to torture or to acts of barbarity is punished by fifteen years' *réclusion criminelle.*

The first two paragraphs of Article 132–23 governing the safety period are applicable to the offence set out under the present article.

ARTICLE 222–6

The offence defined under Article 222–1 is punished by *réclusion criminelle* for life where it brought about the death of the victim without intent to cause it.

The first two paragraphs of Article 132–23 governing the safety period are applicable to the offence set out under the present article.

ARTICLE 222–7

Acts of violence causing an unintended death are punished by fifteen years' *réclusion criminelle.*

ARTICLE 222–23

Any act of sexual penetration, whatever its nature, committed against another person by violence, constraint, threat or surprise, is rape.

Rape is punished by fifteen years' *réclusion criminelle.*

ARTICLE 222–25

Rape is punished by thirty years' *réclusion criminelle* where it caused the death of the victim.

The first two paragraphs of Article 132–23 governing the safety period are applicable to the offence set out under the present article.

4

Intentional Killings: The German Law

ANTJE DU BOIS-PEDAIN

1. Introduction

THIS EXPOSITION COVERS the German law relating to conduct which under English law would be classified as murder or voluntary manslaughter, and includes a discussion of the general defences that bear on the issues raised in English law by duress, necessity, provocation, diminished responsibility and the use of excessive force in public or private defence. The term 'intentional killings' is used throughout to designate killings performed with an intention to cause death or grievous bodily harm (GBH). The term 'intended killings' is reserved for killings executed with an intention to kill, the latter being used synonymously with an intention to cause death. Unless this is clearly indicated in either text or footnotes, what is presented is the standard position taken by the courts and shared by almost all writers on the subject.[1]

The German Penal Code (*Strafgesetzbuch*, StGB) contains two homicide offences which are the terminological equivalents of the English offences of murder and voluntary manslaughter: § 211[2] (*Mord*; meaning 'murder') and § 212

---

[1] The main commentaries which have been drawn on are: K Lackner and K Kühl, *Strafgesetzbuch mit Erläuterungen*, 25th edn (Munich, 2004); subsequently cited as Lackner/Kühl *StGB*, para and annotation; H Tröndle and T Fischer, *Strafgesetzbuch und Nebengesetze: Kommentar*, 53rd edn (Munich, 2006); subsequently cited as Tröndle/Fischer *StGB*, para and annotation; W Joecks and K Miebach, *Münchener Kommentar zum Strafgesetzbuch, Band 3 (§§ 185–262 StGB)* (Munich, 2003), subsequently cited as (name of commentator) in *MüKo-StGB* para and annotation; B Jähnke, HW Laufhütte and W Odersky (eds), *Strafgesetzbuch: Leipziger Kommentar: Großkommentar*, multi vols, update no 44, §§ 211–217 (Berlin, 2002), subsequently cited as *LK-StGB* para and annotation; A Schönke and H Schröder (with T Lenckner, P Cramer *et al*), *Strafgesetzbuch: Kommentar*, 27th edn (Munich, 2006); subsequently cited as Schönke/Schröder *StGB* para and annotation; U Kindhäuser, U Neumann and HU Paeffgen (eds), *Nomos-Kommentar zum Strafgesetzbuch*, 2nd edn (Baden-Baden, 2005) 2 vols, subsequently cited as (name of commentator) in *Nomos-StGB* para and annotation.

[2] If not otherwise marked, all provisions cited in this chapter are provisions of the *Strafgesetzbuch* (German Penal Code: 'StGB'). I follow German convention by citing these provisions as 'paras' (§),

(*Totschlag*, meaning 'voluntary manslaughter' or 'voluntary homicide'). German law also recognises two other voluntary homicide offences of lesser severity. These are § 213 (*Minder schwerer Fall des Totschlags* or 'less severe case of voluntary homicide') and § 216 (*Tötung auf Verlangen* or 'killing on request').[3] The German texts and an unofficial translation of the main provisions of German law discussed in this chapter are set out in section 5 below.

The structure of this chapter is as follows: Section 2 introduces the legal and doctrinal context in which the German homicide offences operate. This discussion covers in particular the concept of intention, the existence in German law of constructive crimes for intended wrongdoing short of homicide which 'results in death', and the main available defences. Section 3 then presents the specific homicide offences of the StGB[4] and their penalties. This section also explains the composition of the trial courts and the appeals process in cases concerning intentional killings. The conclusion (Section 4) addresses the main academic criticisms of the German murder offence and highlights the merits of the German scheme from a comparative perspective.

2. The Legal and Doctrinal Context

The aim of this section is to enable a preliminary comparison of the potential reach of voluntary homicide offences in German and English law.

(i) The *Mens Rea* Requirement for Voluntary Homicide and the Role of Result-Qualified Offences

German law insists on an intention to kill as the necessary *mens rea* for any voluntary homicide offence. At first blush, this might suggest that German law would refuse to treat as *Mord* or *Totschlag* any set of facts which English law classifies as murder on the basis that death was caused with an intention to cause GBH. But this is in fact not the case. The German definition of 'intention' is wider than the reading which the English courts have given to this term. German law

---

and by indicating sub-sections with italic Roman numerals. Thus, the citation '§ 1 *I* StGB' indicates section 1, sub-section 1 of the German Penal Code.

[3] I do not discuss the specific murder offences contained in the German 'Code of Crimes Against International Law' (*Völkerstrafgesetzbuch*, VStGB), where the intended killing of a person who belongs to a protected group can be one of the modes of commission of the crime of genocide (see § 6 *I* No 1 VStGB), of a crime against humanity (see § 7 *I* No 1 VStGB) and of a war crime (see § 8 *I* No 1 VStGB). I also do not cover offences against the foetus (§§ 218 ff StGB) and involuntary manslaughter (§ 222 StGB).

[4] These are: §§ 211, 212, 213 and 216. §§ 214, 215 and 217 have been abolished through legislative reform at different points in time.

recognises *dolus eventualis* as a form of intention.[5] An intention to kill in the form of *dolus eventualis* is made out when the defendant realises that his conduct creates a risk of death for another human being and takes a 'so be it' attitude towards the possibility that death will result.[6] The potentially wide reach of *dolus eventualis* in homicide law is somewhat contained by the Federal Court of Justice (*Bundesgerichtshof*, BGH) through its 'threshold theory' (*Hemmschwellentheorie*).[7] Briefly, the idea is that since there is such a strong taboo against killing, forming an intention to kill requires the defendant to cross an internal psychological threshold that is not necessarily crossed when a defendant forms an intention to use violence. This means that even if the defendant's violent conduct endangered the victim's life or caused serious injuries, the trial court should not be too quick to conclude that intent to kill in the form of *dolus eventualis* was present, but rather ask itself whether the evidence proves that the defendant in his mind crossed that threshold.[8]

The recognition of *dolus eventualis* in the German system means that in practice there is a large overlap between what English law regards as murder under the constructive variant of this offence and what German law classifies as *Mord* or *Totschlag* because of the presence of an intention to kill in the form of *dolus eventualis*.[9] In some respects German law may even be more strict than English law (notably in cases of uncompleted killings, in which German courts can, with the help of the notion of *dolus eventualis*, arrive at a conviction for attempted murder in many situations where English courts have to make do with a conviction for wounding or causing grievous bodily harm with intent under section 18 of the Offences Against the Person Act 1861).

However, there remains an important group of cases where English law would convict someone of a homicide offence but German law would not. These are

---

[5] For an explanation of *dolus eventualis* see, *inter alia*, HH Jescheck and T Weigend, *Lehrbuch des Strafrechts Allgemeiner Teil*, 5th edn (Berlin, 1996) (hereafter Jescheck/Weigend *AT*) 299–303; and C Roxin, *Strafrecht Allgemeiner Teil I Grundlagen. Der Aufbau der Verbrechenslehre*, 4th edn (Munich, 2006) (hereafter: Roxin *AT-1*) 445–78.

[6] For details see A Pedain, 'Intention and the Terrorist Example' [2003] *Crim LR* 579 at 591 and Roxin, above n 5.

[7] See BGHSt 36, 1 at 15. German cases are not referred to by the name(s) of the defendant(s), since the names of all parties are anonymised before the case is reported. They are identified instead by file number and/or reference to the published case report. As an aid to memory, writers and commentators sometimes make up their own descriptive labels for important cases, and in the academic literature the case is then referred to by that name. The BGH itself does not refer to its previous decisions by these informal names.

[8] On the difficulties created by the 'threshold theory' for prosecutors and trial courts see T Trück, 'Die Problematik der Rechtsprechung des BGH zum bedingten Tötungsvorsatz' [2005] *Neue Zeitschrift für Strafrecht (NStZ)* 233.

[9] For recent cases of violent conduct by defendants where the BGH overturned the trial court's finding that an intention to kill was not proven and sent the cases back for re-trial see BGH 1 StR 410/05—judgment of 13 Dec 2005 (3-year-old hit violently on the head in a context of prolonged physical mistreatment) and BGH 5 StR 290/04—judgment of 26 Jan 2005 (argument between drunken acquaintances spirals out of control; a witness not participating in the argument is kicked in the head in a spontaneous act of aggression against her).

cases where, broadly speaking, the defendant intends to cause some physical harm but is merely reckless or negligent with respect to the death which in fact results. In English law these cases are treated as murder provided that grievous bodily harm was intended. In German law, by contrast, these situations are covered by special, so-called 'result-qualified' offences against the person.[10] Conviction of these offences requires that the specific risk of death inherent in the commission of the basic offence must have materialised (*Zurechnung*) and that it was foreseeable for the agent that death might result (*Fahrlässigkeit*), provided no higher degree of recklessness is stipulated. Hence, in a case like *Hayward*[11] German law would convict the defendant merely of an offence of intentionally causing physical injury if it could not be established that he was at least reckless as to whether his actions would also cause death.

The most important of these result-qualified offences is § 227 (*Körperverletzung mit Todesfolge* or 'bodily injury resulting in death').[12] § 227 was, for instance, applied in a case where the defendant had attacked the victim with a plastic hammer, knocked him unconscious and, erroneously believing that he had died, strung him up to create the impression that he had committed suicide. The victim died by suffocation.[13] Similar aggravated versions of basic offences by reason of the fact that death ensued from the commission of the basic offence exist in respect of almost all other offences against the person. The stipulated penalty range for many of these offences, including § 227, is 'imprisonment for no less than 3 years'[14] (which for less serious cases is reduced to imprisonment of between one and 10 years).[15] Certain sexual offences, kidnapping, robbery and arson are punishable with 'imprisonment for life or for no less than 10 years' when the death of the victim is caused through 'gross recklessness' (*Leichtfertigkeit*) of the defendant.[16] Some of these provisions may well be applicable to fact

---

[10] On result-qualified offences generally see JR Spencer and A Pedain, 'Approaches to Strict and Constructive Liability in Continental Criminal Law' in AP Simester (ed), *Appraising Strict Liability* (Oxford and New York, 2005) 237 at 242.

[11] (1908) 21 Cox 692.

[12] Note that for the application of § 227 an intention to cause any, even minor, bodily injury suffices, provided that the defendant was at least reckless as to whether his actions would cause death.

[13] See BGH NStZ 1992, 333 ('faked suicide case').

[14] 'No less than three years' means, in practice, anywhere between 3 and 15 years, since § 38 *I* stipulates that imprisonment cannot be 'for life' unless the law explicitly says so, and § 38 *II* stipulates that the maximum length of a sentence which is not 'for life' is 15 years.

[15] See § 221 (*Aussetzung*, exposure to the elements): qualification in sub-sections *III* and *IV*; § 235 (*Entziehung Minderjähriger*: removal of a minor from parental care and control): qualification in sub-sections *V* and *VI*; § 239 (*Freiheitsberaubung*: false imprisonment): qualification in sub-sections *IV* and *V*.

[16] See § 176b (*Sexueller Mißbrauch von Kindern mit Todesfolge*: sexual abuse of a child resulting in death); § 178 (*Vergewaltigung oder sexuelle Nötigung mit Todesfolge*: rape or sexual assault resulting in death); § 239a (*Erpresserischer Menschenraub*: kidnapping for ransom) and § 239b (*Geiselnahme*: hostage taking): qualifications in sub-sections *III* and *IV*; § 251 (*Raub mit Todesfolge*: robbery resulting in death); § 306c (*Brandstiftung mit Todesfolge*: arson resulting in death).

situations where English law would find that an intention to cause GBH was present, and hence arrive at a murder conviction.[17]

(ii) Generally Available Defences

(a) Self-defence and Justifying Necessity

German law recognises the classic justificatory defences of self-defence (*Notwehr*, § 32) and justifying necessity (*Rechtfertigender Notstand*, § 34). Self-defence, as in English law, requires that the defendant act in order to ward off a present attack on himself or on another person, and entitles him to use as much force as is necessary to bring the attack to an end.[18] Justifying necessity applies in cases where the defendant acts in order to protect his own or another person's life, limb, liberty, honour, property or other legally protected interest, provided that the harm he is likely to cause is not disproportionate to the harm he is trying to avert.[19] Both defences can, in principle, apply to voluntary homicide offences, though in practice it is unlikely that either of them will be made out in a case of murder because of the special motivational or circumstantial elements which must be present under German law to turn an intended killing into murder.[20] Moreover, the proportionality requirement which is part of the defence of justifying necessity leaves little room for the application of this defence even in cases of intended killings which are not murder; most German writers consider that it is *never* proportionate to sacrifice one innocent life in order to save one or more others.[21]

(b) Excessive Self-defence and Exculpatory Necessity

The German Penal Code also contains two general 'excusatory' defences of excessive self-defence (§ 33, *Überschreitung der Notwehr*) and of exculpatory

---

[17] A defendant like *Woollin* [1999] 1 AC 82 who, in a moment of exasperation, threw his baby son across the room towards his pram and missed, with the result that the baby fell onto a hard surface and died, would have looked at a conviction under § 227 StGB.

[18] For details see Roxin *AT-1* 654–719; Jescheck/Weigend *AT* 334–48.

[19] For details see Roxin *AT-1* 720–74; Jescheck/Weigend *AT* 359–65.

[20] See the exposition and discussion of § 211 in section 3(ii)(a) below.

[21] For the impermissibility of balancing (innocent) life against life see Lenckner/Perron in Schönke/Schröder *StGB* § 34 marg no 31, Roxin *AT-1* 738–9. These writers often argue that § 35 (exculpatory necessity) should apply instead. This solution is confirmed in BGHSt 48, 255 (BGH 1 StR 489/02—judgment of 25 Mar 2003: 'family tyrant'), where the Federal Court of Justice denied a frightened and subjectively helpless woman who killed her husband in his sleep after she had endured years of physical abuse the justificatory defence of § 34, but quashed her conviction for voluntary manslaughter on the basis that § 35 might apply if she subjectively believed that there was no other way for her to escape from her husband's violence, and this assessment of her situation was either correct or reasonable in the circumstances. (§ 32 could not apply in the defendant's favour because she killed her husband outside the context of a present or immediately anticipated unlawful attack on her).

necessity (§ 35, *Entschuldigender Notstand*), both of which lead to a full acquittal. The rationale behind these exculpatory defences is that a criminal conviction would be inappropriate in view of the pressure with which the agent was confronted (§ 33) or the serious conflict of interest in which he was caught up (§ 35).

The application of § 33 (excessive self-defence) requires that the defendant exceed the degree of force he is entitled to use in self-defence due to confusion, fear or shock. This provision protects defendants whose response is objectively excessive, provided that this is due to any of the three listed mental reactions to the situations in which they find themselves.[22] The rule covers excessive use of force arising from misjudgements concerning the appropriateness of the response as well as genuine overreactions.[23] By contrast, general 'mistake of fact' rules (§ 16) apply to defendants who mistakenly believe facts to exist which, had they been present, would have entitled them to respond to the situation in self-defence in the way in which they in fact do.[24] This means that defendants do not just have a defence if they acted adequately 'on the facts as they honestly believed them to be',[25] but can also avail themselves of a full defence in cases where their excessive use of force in response to an unlawful attack results from confusion, fear or shock (§ 33).[26]

§ 35 (exculpatory necessity) kicks in when the defendant commits an unlawful act in order to protect himself or a person close to him against a serious danger to life, limb or liberty which could not otherwise have been averted. In the context of this provision, for a full acquittal any mistake of fact must be reasonable (§ 35

---

[22] See generally Roxin *AT-1* 991–1002; Jescheck/Weigend *AT* 490–3. Thus, § 33 is not available to defendants who exceed the bounds of self-defence because of anger or hatred against the attacker. If defendants overreact from a mixture of causes, the courts have usually demanded that confusion, fear or shock dominate (BGHSt 3, 194 at 198; BGH GA 1969, 23 at 24), but have recently been more generous to defendants, suggesting that the relevant consideration is whether the defendant's conduct is significantly affected by confusion, fear or shock, whatever other reactions may be present (BGH StV 1999, 148). A defendant like the one in *Martin* [2001] EWCA Crim 2245; [2003] QB 1 would be likely to be acquitted under § 33.

[23] Thus, § 33 can benefit a perpetrator who hits an attacker with a blunt instrument 'as hard as he can' on the head, realising that this is clearly more force than is necessary to knock the attacker unconscious, but doing so out of fear that he may not succeed in knocking the attacker out if he tries to use only as much force as he thinks is needed. See further Roxin *AT-1* 997–8 and Jescheck/Weigend *AT* 492.

[24] This rule covers both factual errors concerning whether the victim is engaged in an unlawful attack on the defendant or another person, and any factual errors which lead to a belief that the attack is more forceful or dangerous than it in fact is and thereby affect the degree of force that it would be legitimate to use in reply (for example, an erroneous belief that the attacker has a loaded gun, failure to realise that the attacker is a young child, physically handicapped or mentally confused, etc). See Jescheck/Weigend *AT* 350 and 462–7.

[25] See *ibid.*

[26] Note that *excessive* responses by perpetrators who *mistakenly believe that they are being attacked* are not covered by § 33. In order to bring § 33 into play, the attack must be real. See Roxin *AT-1* 1003–4.

II).[27] The catalogue of protected rights in § 35 is much narrower than it is in the justificatory version of the necessity defence. Essentially, for § 35 there must be a *serious threat* to the *physical safety* of the defendant or another person close to the defendant. The threat can arise from human behaviour or from natural causes. The preconditions for the application of the defence are very similar to those for duress by threats and duress of circumstances in English law.

(c) Lack of Capacity Arising from Mental Causes, Insanity and Unfitness to Plead

The provision which comes closest to an insanity defence in German criminal law is § 20 (*Schuldunfähigkeit wegen seelischer Störungen* or 'lack of capacity arising from mental causes'). This is a provision of substantive criminal law. It excludes criminal responsibility for persons who at the time of the deed were affected by a mental condition which made it *impossible* for them to realise that their conduct was wrong or to act in accordance with this insight. The triggering conditions are set out as: pathological emotional disorder (*krankhafte seelische Störung*), severe mental disturbance (*tiefgreifende Bewusstseinsstörung*), severe mental retardation (*Schwachsinn*) and any other severe mental abnormality (*schwere andere seelische Abartigkeit*). Some of these states are permanent and outside the defendant's control (for instance, mental retardation or schizophrenia). Others can be transient and/or arise from external causes.[28] In particular, high levels of intoxication can lead to the application of § 20, as they can put defendants into an abnormal state of mind in which they are no longer able to judge their conduct as wrong or to control their actions. Case law requires that this possibility be considered and, if necessary, investigated further by the trial court if the defendant's blood alcohol level at the time of the deed may have exceeded 0.3 %.[29] When it comes to the application of § 20, no distinction can be drawn between defendants who can, and defendants who cannot, be blamed for their lack of capacity at the time of the deed.[30] Both voluntary and involuntary intoxication can lead to the application of § 20,[31] which results in a full acquittal (not an

---

[27] See generally Roxin *AT-1* 962–91; Jescheck/Weigend *AT* 479–88. If the mistake is unreasonable, the reduced penalty scales set out in § 49 apply.

[28] See Roxin *AT-1* 886–902; Jescheck/Weigend *AT* 437–43.

[29] See BGH StV 1990, 107 (blood alcohol level higher than 0.3 % is an 'important indication' of lack of capacity). But see also BGH NStZ 1987, 545 (no error in law if the trial court concludes on an evaluation of all the evidence that the defendant did not lack capacity despite a blood alcohol concentration of 0.394 %).

[30] For details see Roxin *AT-1* 894, W Theune, 'Auswirkungen des normalpsychologischen (psychogenen) Affekts auf die Schuldfähigkeit sowie den Schuld- und Rechtsfolgenausspruch' [1999] *NStZ* 273 at 280. Jescheck/Weigend (*AT* 439) fail to distinguish clearly between a voluntarily caused lack of capacity (blameworthiness is irrelevant) and a voluntarily caused state which merely 'reduces' capacity (mitigation of sentence may be denied: see below).

[31] Note that defendants can sometimes be convicted of a fall-back offence of 'dangerous intoxication' (*Vollrausch*, § 323a), and those who formed an intention to commit the deed before they became

acquittal 'by reason of insanity', as in English law). However, the trial court orders the defendant to be remitted to a psychiatric hospital for treatment if it expects the defendant to engage in serious unlawful conduct in the future, and for this reason considers him a grave danger to the public (§§ 63, 67).[32]

Some defendants who are not liable for their deeds under § 20 suffer from conditions which also make them unfit to plead (*Verhandlungsunfähigkeit*).[33] Persons who are unfit to plead cannot stand trial.[34] Whether they in fact do is largely a function of how obvious the defendant's defective state is to outsiders, and when the prosecution and/or court become aware of it. If the prosecution realises during its investigations that the suspect 'lacked capacity' in the sense defined by § 20 at the time of the act, and is unfit to plead now, it can place the case immediately on a track directed at the defendant's confinement for the protection of the public (*Sicherungsverfahren*, § 71 StGB read in conjunction with §§ 413 ff StPO[35]). If the trial has already begun when it becomes evident to the prosecution that the defendant is unfit to plead, the prosecution can withdraw the charge from the trial court with a view to using the confinement procedure instead.[36] In cases where it appears to the court when the charge is brought that the defendant is unfit to plead, the court will refuse to 'open the trial'.[37] After the trial has begun proceedings will be halted permanently when enduring unfitness to plead becomes apparent.[38] It will then be incumbent upon the prosecution to begin the confinement procedure. As for the evidential standard, the court cannot hold a trial if it has serious concerns that the defendant may be unfit to

---

intoxicated may be held criminally liable for their conduct in application of the principle of *actio libera in causa*. On the offence of 'dangerous intoxication' see JR Spencer and A Pedain, 'Approaches to Strict and Constructive Liability in Continental Criminal Law' in AP Simester (ed), *Appraising Strict Liability* (Oxford and New York, 2005) at 244–5. On the reach of the principle of *actio libera in causa* see Roxin *AT-1* 895 and 914–24; Jescheck/Weigend *AT* 439 and 445–8.

[32] It is important to note that the fact that the defendant committed an unlawful act for which he cannot be held responsible due to a lack of capacity (§ 20) is only *one* of the preconditions for the application of § 63 (remittance to a psychiatric hospital). The application of § 63 further requires that the pathological condition which caused the lack of capacity persists, and that the court considers it highly likely that because of it the defendant will in the future commit other serious deeds, for which he cannot be held responsible due to lack of capacity. If these preconditions obtain, the court *must* find the defendant liable to be detained in a psychiatric hospital until such time as he no longer poses a risk to the public (see BGH NStZ-RR 2005, 370). If alcohol addiction caused the deed, the court can order compulsory treatment in a rehabilitation clinic (§ 64).

[33] There is no necessary link between lack of capacity and unfitness to plead. Unfitness to plead can arise from different causes and after the crime has been committed with capacity; a perfectly responsible agent can later become unfit to plead. Conversely, many persons who suffer from conditions that make them pathologically incapable of realising that their actions at the time of the deed were wrong, or to act in accordance with this insight, do possess the grasp on reality necessary to understand the charge before the court and to instruct counsel.

[34] See L Meyer-Goßner, *Strafprozessordnung. Mit GVG und Nebengesetzen,* 49th edn (Munich, 2006; subsequently cited as Meyer-Goßner *StPO*, para and annotation) introduction, marg no 97.

[35] 'StPO' is short for *Strafprozessordnung*, the German Code of Criminal Procedure.

[36] Meyer-Goßner *StPO* § 413 marg no 3.

[37] See § 204 StPO.

[38] Usually in a judgment of 'abandonment of proceedings' (§ 260 *III* StPO); outside the trial, through an order of abandonment of proceedings (§ 206a StPO).

plead.[39] The defence can influence what happens by raising concerns about the defendant's fitness to plead with the court. But there is no formal rule that fitness to plead will only be tested if the defendant queries it or offers evidence to support the contention that he is unfit to plead. It is for the court to assure itself that the defendant is fit to plead. If the appeal court finds that, for whatever reason, the trial court failed to notice that the defendant was unfit to plead, the case will be aborted at this stage.[40]

(d) General Partial Defence of Diminished Responsibility

Unlike English law, which restricts the concept of partial defences to murder, German law contains a general partial defence of diminished responsibility which leads to mitigation of sentence (§ 21, *Verminderte Schuldfähigkeit*).[41] The provision is conceptualised as a logical extension of the recognition of a full defence based on 'lack of capacity due to mental causes' in § 20. It requires that, on account of one of the triggering conditions set out in § 20,[42] the defendant's ability to realise that his conduct is wrong, or to act in accordance with this insight, is *significantly reduced* at the time of the deed. The triggering conditions cover all the mental states which, in English law, can establish a defendant's diminished responsibility under section 2 of the Homicide Act 1957. In addition, they extend to abnormal mental states which would not qualify under section 2 of the Homicide Act 1957 because they are insufficiently severe, transient, self-induced, externally caused and the like. As regards intoxication, the courts will have to investigate the possibility that the defendant qualifies for the application of § 21 if his level of intoxication at the time of the commission of the offence exceeded a blood alcohol level of 0.2 %.[43]

Importantly, though, mitigation of sentence under § 21 is *optional* in the sense that the trial court can refuse to grant it when the mitigating factors are outweighed by aggravating ones.[44] This is not an arbitrary power given to the courts. Rather, it follows naturally from the legislative choice to classify as *mitigating factors* mental states which *reduce* the defendant's ability to realise the wrongness of his conduct or to act in accordance with this realisation. Mitigating factors do not affect liability, but sentence. Their presence means that the court, when passing sentence, has to ask itself whether *in the case before it* these factors are a good reason to impose on the defendant a less severe punishment. The

---

[39] See BGH NStZ 1984, 520, Meyer-Goßner *StPO* § 261 marg no 34.

[40] See BGHSt 24, 208 at 212; BGHSt 32, 275 at 290.

[41] See generally Roxin *AT-1* 902–11; Jescheck/Weigend *AT* 443–4.

[42] For a list of these conditions see the text above at n 28.

[43] See BGH StV 1997, 460 (which clarifies that there is no presumption that responsibility is diminished by reason of this degree of intoxication); Roxin *AT-1* 904; Jescheck/Weigend *AT* 448.

[44] See BGH 3 StR 479/03—decision of 27 Jan 2004 and the summary of recent case law by W Theune, 'Die Beurteilung der Schuldfähigkeit in der Rechtsprechung des Bundesgerichtshofs 2. Teil' [2005] *Neue Zeitschrift für Strafrecht, Rechtsprechungsreport (NStZ-RR)* 329 at 334–5.

answer is 'yes' if the mitigating factors make the defendant's conduct less blameworthy. The answer is 'no' if despite these factors the defendant deserves the full force of blame. Full blame is deserved when he either culpably put himself in a state in which he would be a danger to others, or when some other aggravating factor for which the defendant is responsible makes his crime particularly bad.[45] The BGH has stressed repeatedly that defendants whose appreciation of the wrongness of their actions, or their ability to act according to that appreciation, is impeded by reason of a mental state that results from voluntary consumption of alcohol[46] are unlikely to deserve mitigation under § 21, particularly in cases where defendants know that they tend to act violently when intoxicated.[47]

If mitigation is granted, significantly reduced punishment scales apply. These are set out in § 49 (*Besondere gesetzliche Milderungsgründe*). But (as with § 20) the application of § 21 is not an occasion of unalloyed joy for defendants. Alongside and in addition to imposing the (reduced) criminal penalty, the trial court may order that the defendant be remitted to a psychiatric hospital if on account of his mental condition he continues to pose a grave risk to public safety (§ 63), or order his compulsory treatment in a rehabilitation clinic if alcohol addiction caused the deed (§ 64).

Procedurally, the two capacity-related defences in German law operate differently from their rough parallels in English law. Both lack of capacity (§ 20) and diminished responsibility (§ 21) are defences which are investigated by the court of its own motion when hearing the evidence led by the prosecution on the charge. The defence neither has to raise the point, nor put forward facts (no evidential burden), nor does the defendant carry any legal burden of proof. Because these defences have a bearing on the culpability of the defendant, the standard of proof for any finding against the defendant is 'beyond reasonable doubt' (§ 261 StPO) and must be made by a two-thirds majority of the judges (§ 263 StPO); the court's obligation to hear all available evidence is strict (§ 244 StPO); and the *in dubio pro reo* rule applies.[48]

However, especially in relation to the application of § 21 it is important to bear in mind that there is no procedural separation between conviction and sentence in a German criminal trial. The trial ends with an acquittal or with conviction

---

[45] In German law, aggravating factors can only be held against the defendant if he is responsible for them in the sense that he knew of their existence or realised that they might result from his actions (see § 46 StGB).

[46] Different considerations apply where these states result from the consumption of other drugs. See BGH 5 StR 93/04—judgment of 17 Aug 2004.

[47] See especially BGH 5 StR 428/03—judgment of 30 Mar 2004; BGH 5 StR 93/04—judgment of 17 Aug 2004.

[48] See Meyer-Goßner *StPO* § 261 marg no 26ff. Before any of the restraining measures explained in the text at n 32 above can be imposed on a defendant who successfully relied on either defence, the court must again be *convinced beyond reasonable doubt* that the defendant acted without, or with diminished, capacity. The upshot of this is that if it cannot be decided whether the defendant had, or did nor have, capacity, he can neither be convicted of the offence with which he is charged nor have the restraining measures imposed on him. See Jescheck/Weigend *AT* 809; BGHSt 34, 22 at 26.

and sentence, as the case may be. Facts which matter in regard to mitigation of sentence are investigated along with facts on which conviction for the offence is based. In practice, this may well mean that if the defendant denies the crime altogether, some mitigating aspect which could only have been put before the court by the defendant himself may not be investigated at all, because the court simply never becomes aware of it.

3. Voluntary Homicide in German Law

German homicide law is based on a recognition that even where particularly serious wrongdoing—the intended killing of another human being—is in issue, the culpability of individual killers in the light of all the circumstances of their respective deeds differs so significantly that it would be inappropriate to categorise all of them as perpetrators of the gravest crime of all: murder. Hence it adopts a tripartite model:[49] a 'standard' voluntary homicide offence (§ 212) which provides the baseline for the criminal liability of those who kill with intent to kill, and from where the law reaches out to identify particularly serious cases, classified as murder (§ 211), and (in the opposite direction) less serious cases of voluntary manslaughter (§§ 213, 216).[50]

(i) The Basic Homicide Offence: Voluntary Homicide, § 212 (*Totschlag*)

(a) Definition

The basic homicide offence in German criminal law is *Totschlag* (§ 212), subsequently referred to as 'voluntary homicide' or 'voluntary manslaughter'. This offence is defined in § 212 as 'any killing of a human being carried out with an intention to kill which is not murder'. This somewhat clumsy definition raises

---

[49] See Neumann in *Nomos-StGB* Vor § 211 marg no 136; Lackner/Kühl *StGB* § 211 marg no 22.

[50] By referring to murder as a particularly serious instance of voluntary homicide I do not mean to make a technical point about the relation between the two offences in German law. The German courts are locked in persistent disagreement with academic commentators over whether voluntary homicide and murder are separate offences, or whether murder is an aggravated case of voluntary homicide. In German law, this technical classification has repercussions for the liability of secondary participants. In essence, the dispute centres around whether the secondary party to a killing which is murder by reason of one of the perpetrator-related criteria set out in the first or third group of 'qualifying factors' of § 211 is always a secondary party to murder, or only if the secondary party also exhibits this qualifying factor himself. The position of the courts on the relationship between the offences of voluntary homicide and murder entails the first result, the view preferred by academic commentators the second. See Neumann in *Nomos-StGB* Vor § 211 marg no 141–2.

few difficulties in practice. The courts apply § 212 to intended killings unless the additional preconditions for murder (§ 211) or for a 'less serious case of voluntary homicide' (§ 213) or a 'killing on request' (§ 216) are made out.

(b) Sentence

The sentence for voluntary homicide is 'no less than 5 years' imprisonment' (§ 212 *I*). Read in conjunction with § 38, which stipulates that imprisonment cannot be 'for life' unless the law explicitly says so and lays down 15 years as the maximum length of a sentence which is not 'for life', this means that for a standard intended homicide the court can impose a prison sentence of between five and 15 years. In addition, § 212 *II* entitles the court to impose a life sentence 'in especially serious cases'. According to the case law of the higher courts, the trial court must identify particular aggravating factors which increase the culpability of the defendant. It is not enough for the trial court simply to say that the defendant's conduct came within a hair's breadth of fulfilling one or more of the qualifying criteria which make an intended killing murder.[51]

(c) Voluntary Homicide in Mitigating Circumstances by Reason of Diminished Responsibility (§§ 212, 21, 49 I)

Since the provision concerning diminished responsibility applies to all offences, the basic homicide offence can also be committed in mitigating circumstances by reason of the fact that the defendant suffered from one of the triggering conditions set out in § 20, provided that this substantially reduced his ability to appreciate the wrongfulness of his conduct or his ability to act in accordance with this insight at the time of the commission of the offence (see the discussion of § 21 above). Defendants like *Doughty*[52] or *Smith*[53] would be likely to be slotted in here.

Where §§ 21, 49 *I* apply to a standard homicide case (§ 212 *I*), the sentence will be one of imprisonment of between two years and 11 years and three months (§ 49 *I* No. 2 and 3, read in conjunction with § 38). Where §§ 21, 49 *I* apply to a particularly serious homicide (§ 212 *II*), the sentence will be one of imprisonment for between three and 15 years (§ 49 *I* No. 1, read in conjunction with § 38).

---

[51]   See BGH NJW 1982, 2264 at 2265; BGH NStZ 1993, 342; BGH NStZ-RR 1999, 101 and recently BGH 5 StR 395/03—decision of 20 Jan 2004.

[52]   (1986) 83 CrApp R 319. He would not be able to rely on provocation (§ 213, alternative 1), but his fractured nerves as a result of the baby's persistent crying may well qualify as an abnormal state of mind within the meaning of § 21, or lead to the acceptance of 'another less serious case' within the meaning of § 213, alternative 2.

[53]   [2001] 1 AC 146. On the facts, it is unlikely that Smith would be able to rely on provocation concurrently with diminished responsibility, since the victim's denial that he stole Smith's tools of trade (whether false or true) is unlikely to qualify as 'physical or verbal abuse' within the meaning of § 213, alternative 1.

It is important to note that the same aspect of the defendant's psychological state or make-up at the time of the deed which might convince the court to refrain from finding that the homicide is 'especially serious' (§ 212 *II*) can also suggest that the defendant's responsibility may be diminished (§ 21). In such a situation, § 50 stipulates that the defendant cannot profit from the same mitigating factor more than once.[54] This is particularly relevant in cases where intoxicated or paranoid defendants have killed their victims with great brutality.[55] If in light of their mental state the court decides to treat the case as a standard rather than a particularly serious homicide, it cannot reduce the penalty scale further by reason of diminished responsibility.[56]

(ii) Murder, § 211 (*Mord*)

(a) Definition

An intended killing is murder if one of the qualifying factors listed in § 211 (*Mord*) obtains. § 211 singles out as murderers perpetrators who kill with intent to do so:

(1) out of a lust for killing (*Mordlust*), [or] in order to find sexual gratification (*zur Befriedigung des Geschlechtstriebs*), [or] motivated by greed (*Habgier*) or by other despicable reasons (*sonstige niedrige Beweggründe*); [or]
(2) deviously (*heimtückisch*) or cruelly (*grausam*) or using means capable of causing widespread mayhem (*mit gemeingefährlichen Mitteln*); [or]
(3) in order to enable or to cover up the commission of another crime.

The factors in the first and the third groups are perpetrator-focused. The factors in the second group are deed-focused. In accordance with the principle of culpability, which requires that only matters in respect of which the defendant is subjectively at fault can be held against him, an internal element is read into all the qualifying factors. This means that it is never sufficient for the defendant merely to act in a manner which is 'objectively' despicable, dangerous and the like. He must be aware of the circumstances which lead to this classification of his conduct, and must mean to act in such a manner.[57]

Many of these qualifying factors are fairly straightforward in their application. A lust to kill is present when the perpetrator takes pleasure in the destruction of a

---

[54] Lackner/Kühl *StGB* § 46 marg no 17.
[55] For an intoxicated killer who battered his girlfriend to death see BGH 5 StR 395/03—decision of 24 Jan 2004. For a paranoid killer who stabbed a hunter who blocked his path to mushrooms in the forest see BGH 2 StR 230/03—decision of 11 Sept 2003.
[56] In practice these principles can sometimes be hard to apply (as is illustrated by the decisions cited in the preceding footnote, where the trial courts got it all wrong). The rule has to be that the mitigating factor must be applied where it gives the defendant the largest discount on sentence.
[57] The precise subjective element for each of the qualifying factors differs, as it is formulated so as to match the objective element of the qualifying factor.

human life as such.[58] A killing 'in order to satisfy the perpetrator's sexual desires' is made out when the perpetrator strives to achieve sexual gratification through the actions which lead to the victim's death,[59] or kills the victim because he wants to use the victim's corpse for sexual purposes.[60] Greed covers contract killers, those who kill for an inheritance and killings in the course of uncompleted burglaries and robberies.[61] What motivations should count as 'despicable' has proven more troublesome. The legal definition is vague (perhaps unacceptably so), and the BGH's interpretation along the lines of 'motives which are generally recognised to be of the basest sort' or 'utterly contemptible' is of limited assistance to trial courts.[62] The degree of elasticity which inevitably results from this definition is indeed problematic, and the tensions arising from it have not been satisfactorily resolved.[63] At the same time, these difficulties are perhaps to be preferred to the obverse situation, the risk of over-inclusiveness generated by the inflexible definitions of some of the other qualifying factors, in that the elasticity enables courts to avoid murder convictions under this heading where, with a view to the totality of the circumstances, a mandatory life sentence would be undeserved.[64]

An intended killing is classified as 'devious' (*heimtückisch*) if the perpetrator relies on the fact that the victim is unprepared for any attack on his or her safety to perform the deed.[65] Killings which cause prolonged or gratuitous intense suffering to the victim are cruel.[66] Means used to kill are 'capable of causing mayhem' if the perpetrator has no way of containing their effects on other people

---

[58]   See BGH NJW 1953, 1440; BGHSt 34, 59, 61; BGH NJW 1994, 2629.

[59]   This covers both cases where the act of killing itself gives the perpetrator sexual pleasure (as in BGHSt 7, 353) and cases where a violent sexual act such as forcible rape is performed with *dolus eventualis* in respect of the victim's death (as in BGHSt 9, 101, 105).

[60]   The BGH has recently had occasion to point out that this alternative covers situations where sexual gratification arises from eating human flesh, rather than from more straightforward necrophilic interaction with the corpse. See BGH 2 StR 310/04—judgment of 22 Apr 2005 ('the cannibal from Rothenburg').

[61]   See BGHSt 39, 160; BGHSt 42, 203.

[62]   See BGHSt 3, 132. For a critical review of the case law see Neumann in *Nomos-StGB* § 211 marg no 27–45. Motives that are politically (BGH 5 StR 306/03—judgment of 24 June 2004: terrorist explosion in the discotheque 'La Belle') or culturally grounded (BGH 2 StR 550/99—judgment of 2 Feb 2000 ('honour killing'); see also BGH NJW 2004, 1466) can be base.

[63]   The courts regularly experience difficulties when they try to apply the notion of 'despicable reasons' to perpetrators who act from a bundle of motives, some more despicable than others, or out of jealousy or hatred of their partner in an intimate relationship with a history of prolonged conflict between the partners.

[64]   How the courts deal with the obverse problem is explained in sub-section (b) below.

[65]   For relevant case law see Tröndle/Fischer *StGB* § 211 marg no 16. The definition is unhappy to say the least. A perpetrator can be 'devious' if he attacks a jogger in the forest out of the blue (since the victim, whom he had never met before, did not expect to be attacked: see BGH 2 StR 236/05—judgment of 13 July 2005), but will not be devious if his victim is a baby or a very small child who is in any case too young to recognise an attack on his life for what it is (see BGH 2 StR 561/05—judgment of 10 Mar 2006).

[66]   See BGHSt 3, 180; BGHSt 3, 264. The subjective requirement of this qualifying factor is an unfeeling and cruel attitude on the part of the perpetrator. Hence, a person who does something objectively very cruel (such as overseeing the mass execution of 60 prisoners of war, as a warning and

and unavoidably puts more people than his intended victim at risk.[67] The desire to enable or to prevent the detection of another crime is often seen as a special case of despicable motivation. Interpreted in this way, the ruthless prioritisation of self-interest over innocent life which is typical for killings which fall into this category may not in all cases be sufficient to justify the 'upgrading' of the killing to murder. It would be preferable to abolish this qualification, and instead consider the desire to enable or to prevent the detection of another crime in the context of the evaluation of whether the killing is 'devious'.[68]

In summary, what makes an intended killing murder is a particularly appalling or antisocial motive, a particularly base mode of attack on the victim or an extra, 'gratuitous', danger to the public resulting from the means used. What underlies this catalogue of qualifying aggravating conditions is the idea that a murderer evinces a qualitatively greater anti-social personal disposition than other offenders who kill, and that this disposition is manifested by the motives for which or the way in which he acts.[69] He and/or his actions are simply 'more evil' than those of the 'ordinary killer'.

(b) The Punishment for Murder: Life Imprisonment

Murder carries a mandatory life sentence. Unless the defendant's responsibility was diminished as defined by § 21 (which justifies the application of a reduced sentencing scale), the court has no legal authority to impose a lesser sentence in a case of murder which it views as somewhat less grave. This has led to challenges to the fairness of a life sentence in cases where an 'upgrading element' (which makes the deed murder) is present concurrently with a 'downgrading element' (which would make the deed a less serious case of voluntary homicide if only one were not forced to 'upgrade' it to murder by reason of the presence of a qualifying condition from the catalogue in § 211). For instance, if an abused wife kills her husband in his sleep after drugging him with liquor, this counts as a 'devious' killing. If her mental state was not sufficiently deranged to draw her into the fold of diminished responsibility, she would have to be given a life sentence for murder, despite the fact that she also (as an abused wife) responded to provocation and, were it not for the *manner* (deviously) in which she killed her husband, would have fallen under § 213 and faced a maximum sentence of 10 years' (and a minimum sentence of one year's) imprisonment.

In response to these cases, where a life sentence seems disproportionate because of the presence of an otherwise mitigating factor, academic writers have

---

collective punishment for an offence against occupying troops) may subjectively not be motivated by cruelty if what motivates him is simply a desire to comply with superior orders: see BGH 5 StR 115/03—decision of 17 June 2004 *(Engel's Case)*.

[67] BGHSt 38, 353, 354; Neumann in *Nomos-StGB* § 211 marg no 85–89.

[68] See Neumann in *Nomos-StGB* § 211 marg no 97ff.

[69] See Tröndle/Fischer *StGB* § 211 marg no 2.

suggested that one should read into § 211 an implied restriction that the provision only applies to the most appalling types of killings, which would enable the courts to avoid classifying the deed as murder in cases where a 'downgrading element' is present concurrently with an 'upgrading' one.[70] The courts, however, have gone down a different route. Their response to the situation has been to view themselves as 'constitutionally authorised' to impose a lesser sentence than life, contrary to the letter of the statute, in cases where the imposition of the mandatory life sentence results in disproportionate punishment. This extraordinary 'constitutional competence to disregard the mandatory life sentence' is used very rarely and is seen as troubling, both from the perspective of legal doctrine and from the perspective of legal policy.[71]

This might be taken to show that even in a legal system where an effort has been made to define murder narrowly so as to bring within its scope only the most serious cases of voluntary homicide, a mandatory life sentence is still capable of causing grave injustice in untypical cases. Judicial responses aimed at avoiding injustice in particular cases come at the expense of wreaking havoc in legal doctrine, and of claiming an authority for disregarding the law on an *ad hoc* basis for which there is no support whatsoever in constitutional law or doctrine.[72] Arguably the cure is no worse than the ill it is meant to address, but it does come at considerable expense.

(c) Punishment for Murder Committed in a State of Diminished Responsibility

Where § 21 applies to a person who has committed murder, the sentence will be one of imprisonment for between three and 15 years (§ 49 *I* No. 1, read in conjunction with § 38).[73]

---

[70] Corrective readings ('*positive*' or '*negative Typenkorrektur*') are supported by many academic writers. As an open attempt to read into § 211 an evaluative discretion which is manifestly not there, these suggestions are rejected by the courts as an indefensible interpretation of the provision as it stands. See Tröndle/Fischer *StGB* § 211 marg no 3.

[71] BGHSt 30, 105 (Großer Senat); see also BVerfGE 45, 187, 259 ff. See also Neumann in *Nomos-StGB* Vor § 211 marg no 144–150.

[72] Only the constitutional court has the power to 'disapply' and declare invalid legislation the application of which leads to an unconstitutional result. Other courts are called upon to interpret laws in ways that avoid violations of the constitution; but where the language of the statute does not allow for the constitutionally required reading as one possible reading of it, the only route left open to the ordinary court is to draw the Constitutional Court's attention to the situation and ask it to declare that the offending law is invalid (*Richtervorlage; Grundgesetz*, Art. 100).

[73] For a recent application see BGH 5 StR 351/03—decision of 31 Mar 2004. This case concerned a socially dysfunctional 21-year-old mother of a 2-year-old child who eventually simply walked out on the child and did not return to her flat. The child died from dehydration after 3 days. The BGH upheld the mother's conviction for murder (based on the cruelty of leaving the child to die of thirst, alone and in agony) but quashed the life sentence, pointing out that the evidence indicated an increasing inability to cope with the simple daily tasks of life typical of serious depression which qualified for § 21.

(iii) Provoked Killings and Other Less Serious Cases of Voluntary Homicide, § 213

(a) Definition

§ 213 applies to provoked killings and to other 'less serious cases' of voluntary homicide which are not murder. The definition of provocation is strict. The victim must have directed physical or verbal abuse against the perpetrator or against one of his close relatives. The perpetrator must have lost his temper and must have been carried away thereby to commit the deed. There must be no grounds for blaming the perpetrator for his loss of temper. Such grounds excluding the application of § 213 exist where the perpetrator gave the victim reason to act as provocatively as he or she did, for instance by insulting or abusing the victim first, before the victim responded in kind. This requires a moral evaluation of the interaction between victim and perpetrator immediately prior to the deed. Only if the perpetrator was—morally speaking—the 'wronged party' in the circumstances leading up to the deed will he be able to rely on provocation.[74]

Other cases of less serious killing do not (like provocation) require a defendant to have acted for an understandable reason. Rather, they are characterised by features which mean that the defendant acted in distress, or in a state of mind that significantly affected his ability to master his violent impulses and to maintain control over his reactions. The following have been recognised as less serious: Intended killings motivated by fear or extreme distress:[75] intended killings motivated by compassion for a suffering victim,[76] and intended killings 'on the borderline of self-defence'.[77] The courts have also been prepared to accept that intended killings performed by defendants who were uninhibited and prone to use violence as a result of the prior consumption of drink or drugs *can* be less serious, but whether they are depends on an evaluation of their conduct as a whole. There is no fixed rule either way.

---

[74] For details see Neumann in *Nomos-StGB* § 213 marg no 6–18. § 213; alternative 1 was applied in a case where a husband killed his wife in response to an unprovoked physical attack by her with a knife, during which she also tried to kick him in the groin: BGH 4 StR 37/95—decision of 9 Feb 1995.

[75] In BGH NStZ-RR 2006, 270, the defendant killed his 2-month-old severely disabled son partly out of pity for his suffering and partly because of the strain on his wife and marriage arising from this extremely difficult situation, for which he did not want to 'abdicate responsibility'. In BGH NStZ-RR 2005, 168, the defendant killed her newborn baby, her fourth child, after hiding her pregnancy from the rest of her family out of fear that her partner would make good his threat to leave her if she got pregnant again.

[76] See BGHSt 27, 209.

[77] For more examples see Tröndle/Fischer *StGB* § 213 marg no 13; Schneider in *Müko-StGB* § 213 marg no 46ff.

(b) Sentence

If a killing is accepted as 'less serious' under § 213, the punishment is imprisonment of between one and 10 years.[78]

(c) Double Mitigation of Sentence in Less Serious Cases of Voluntary Manslaughter

Where § 213 and §§ 21, 49 *I* apply concurrently (this is possible wherever § 213 applies for a reason other than the abnormal mental state which founds the application of § 21), the defendant ultimately can expect a sentence of between three months and seven and a half years' imprisonment (§ 49 *I* No. 2 and 3).

(iv) Killing on Request, § 216 (*Tötung auf Verlangen*)

§ 216 is a special case of a mitigated homicide, where the killing is performed at the express and earnest request of the victim. The punishment is low (six months' to five years' imprisonment), and if the defendant acted in an abnormal state of mind which diminished his responsibility, as well as at the express and earnest request of the person killed, 'double mitigation' results in a reduced punishment scale of one month's to three years and nine months' imprisonment. This would be the punishment a defendant like *Cocker*[79] would be looking at under German law.

(v) The Composition of the Trial Court and the Appeals Process

For charges under §§ 211, 212, 213 and for any of the death-result-qualified offences discussed in this Chapter, the first instance tribunal of fact is the District Court (*Landgericht*), which sits as a collegiate court (*Schwurgericht*)[80] composed of three professional judges and two lay judges (so-called *Schöffen*).[81] Since a killing on request (§ 216) is not a serious crime, the prosecution can in theory bring the case before a Magistrate's Court (*Amtsgericht*),[82] but in practice it is likely to bring the charge before the District Court so as not to pre-empt the

---

[78] In the cases cited in n 75 above, the BGH quashed sentences of 6 and 4 years' imprisonment respectively as too high in view of the mitigating factors.

[79] *The Times*, 27 May 1989.

[80] See § 74 *II* GVG (*Gerichtsverfassungsgesetz*, Act on the Composition and Jurisdiction of the Courts).

[81] See § 76 GVG.

[82] Cases in which the prosecution does not expect the imposition of a sentence of more than 2 years' imprisonment can be brought before a single judge (§ 25 *II* GVG); cases in which the prosecution does not expect the imposition of a sentence of more than 4 years' imprisonment can be brought before a magistrate sitting with two lay judges (*Schöffengericht*, §§ 28, 29 *I* GVG).

possibility of a conviction for a more serious homicide offence[83] or the imposition of a longer sentence than four years. Professional and lay judges sit and deliberate together.

Judgments of the District Court in criminal cases can be appealed to the Federal Court of Justice (BGH).[84] Both the prosecution and the defence have the right to appeal.[85] This type of appeal is called '*Revision*'. It can only be based on a legal error, and in order for the appeal to succeed this must be an error on which the decision rests.[86] If the BGH quashes the trial court's judgment or sentence, it also declares to what extent the facts are to be re-heard.[87] Factual findings which are not affected by the error in law which the trial court made are preserved. If the findings are unchallenged but the court convicted for the wrong offence, the BGH can correct the sentence but otherwise preserve the trial court's judgment. If it is clear that the defendant committed no offence, the BGH can acquit directly.[88] The BGH can dispose of the appeal by 'decision' (*Beschluss*) if all the judges on the panel consider that the appeal is 'obviously ill-founded'[89] or that the defendant's appeal is well-founded.[90] In all other cases it holds a hearing and decides by judgment (*Urteil*).[91]

4. The German Scheme: A Critical Assessment

Academic criticism of the German law of murder centres around three main issues: (1) the alleged unworkability of a scheme that aims to provide a typology of most heinous killings; (2) the claim that the perpetrator-focused qualifying factors are wedded to an unsavoury theory of character-based criminal liability (*Täterstrafrecht*) which punishes people for who they are rather than for what they have done'[92] and (3) the alleged inability of the courts to apply the qualifying factors in a coherent and predictable manner. Often, the favoured

---

[83]   This would be possible provided that the defendant were duly warned by the trial court that he may face conviction for a more serious crime.

[84]   See § 333 StPO.

[85]   See § 296 StPO.

[86]   See §§ 337, 338 StPO.

[87]   See § 353 StPO.

[88]   See § 354 *I* StPO.

[89]   See § 349 *II* StPO.

[90]   See § 349 *IV* StPO.

[91]   See § 353 StPO.

[92]   This claim is often linked to the admittedly dubious pedigree of the provision (it was redrafted in 1941). See further S Thomas, *Die Geschichte des Mordparagraphen. Eine normgenetische Untersuchung bis in die Gegenwart* (Bochum, 1985).

alternative is a return to the earlier definition of murder as 'a premeditated killing' which the current provision replaced.[93]

In my view, none of these criticisms are particularly convincing. There is nothing intrinsically problematic about a catalogue of qualifying factors which identify killings which are typically more repulsive and serious than other intended killings, and the reason they are more serious. While some of the qualifying factors in § 211 should indeed be removed or re-drafted so as to avoid the risk of over-inclusiveness (this applies, in particular, to 'deviousness' and to 'the aim of enabling the commission or avoiding the detection of another offence'),[94] it appears to me that the principle behind the provision is sound. Some of the qualifying factors are also quite appropriately perpetrator-focused. These factors try to identify particularly callous motivations behind the deed. They are, in essence, not about a particular character trait as such, but about a particular attitude that was evinced by the deed. Read in this way, they are perfectly compatible with the culpability principle. The generality of the notion of 'despicable motives' and the resulting elasticity of its application is indeed a problem for legal certainty: but the risks are contained by the fact that the courts apply this qualifying factor with restraint. In practice, it serves as a 'threshold criterion' rather than as an open door. The very rarity of occasions on which courts have to resort to their 'exceptional competence to disapply the mandatory life sentence' in murder cases is indirect testimony to the fact that the present law for the most part succeeds in identifying those killings which are indeed more severe than other killings.[95]

The present catalogue of qualifying factors is certainly preferable to a definition of murder through the concept of premeditation. Some of the most heinous killings are not premeditated, but spontaneous, and could be captured by the notion of premeditation only if the delay between intention and execution were reduced almost to vanishing point (think only of the brutal rapist or robber who, suddenly realising that his victim has recognised him, without thinking bashes his victim to death). Conversely, some of the least serious killings *are* premeditated, and their perpetrators have spent a long time deliberating over the perceived need to kill (for instance killings motivated by compassion for suffering, or killings by individuals victimised through years of domestic abuse). A move away from the current, differentiated set of qualifying factors would not be a move in the right direction.

One of the strongest critics of the German law of murder, Professor Gerhard Wolf, recently remarked that the impetus for reform is weakened by the fact that,

---

[93] See G Wolf, 'Mörder oder Totschläger? Zum 60jährigen Bestehen des § 211 StGB' in K Amelung *et al, Strafrecht, Biorecht, Rechtsphilosophie: Festschrift für Hans-Ludwig Schreiber zum 70. Geburtstag* (Heidelberg, 2003) 519 at 531.

[94] Similarly Lackner/Kühl *StGB* Vor § 211 marg no 20.

[95] This is not an argument in support of retaining the mandatory life sentence for murder. After all, there are still cases where the courts have to disapply this penalty in order to avoid the imposition of a disproportionate punishment.

flawed as the definition of murder is, it 'usually does not lead to convictions of the wrong people'.[96] This, for a German academic, is little reason to stick with the current law if improvement seems possible. A view from across the channel suggests a more charitable perspective. In England, where reform is driven by a realisation that the law of murder is too broad and frequently leads to unjust convictions and disproportionate punishments,[97] a legislative scheme that (whether by design or by default) leads to just results would be cause for celebration.

5. The Main Provisions of the Penal Code

(i) 'Special Part' (*Besonderer Teil*) Provisions Concerned with Intentional Killings[98]

(a) § 211 Mord

(i) *Der Mörder wird mit lebenslanger Freiheitsstrafe bestraft.*

(ii) *Mörder ist, wer*

aus Mordlust, zur Befriedigung des Geschlechtstriebs, aus Habgier oder sonst aus niedrigen Beweggründen,

heimtückisch oder grausam oder mit gemeingefährlichen Mitteln oder um eine andere Straftat zu ermöglichen oder zu verdecken,

einen Menschen tötet.

(b) § 211 Murder (translation)

(i) A person who commits murder shall be punished with imprisonment for life.

(ii) A person commits murder when he kills another human being

out of a lust for killing, [or] in order to satisfy his sexual desires, [or] motivated by greed or by other despicable reasons,

[or] deviously or cruelly or with means capable of causing widespread mayhem, or in order to enable or to cover up the commission of another crime.

---

[96] Wolf, n 93 above, at 519.

[97] For the driving concerns behind the reform in England see Law Commission for England and Wales, *A New Homicide Act for England and Wales?*, Consultation Paper No 177 (London, 2005), especially at paras 1.4–1.29 and 1.49–1.91.

[98] From the 'special part' of the German Penal Code: §§ 211, 212, 213, 216 and 227.

(c) § 212 Totschlag

(i) *Wer einen Menschen tötet, ohne Mörder zu sein, wird als Totschläger mit Freiheitsstrafe nicht unter fünf Jahren bestraft.*

(ii) *In besonders schweren Fällen ist auf lebenslange Freiheitsstrafe zu erkennen.*

(d) § 212 (Voluntary) Manslaughter (translation)

(i) A person who kills another human being without being a murderer shall be punished for manslaughter with imprisonment for no less than five years.

(ii) In especially serious cases a sentence of imprisonment for life shall be imposed.

(e) § 213 Minder schwerer Fall des Totschlags

War der Totschläger ohne eigene Schuld durch eine ihm oder einem Angehörigen zugefügte Misshandlung oder schwere Beleidigung von dem getöteten Menschen zum Zorn gereizt und hierdurch auf der Stelle zur Tat hingerissen worden oder liegt sonst ein minder schwerer Fall vor, so ist die Strafe Freiheitsstrafe von einem Jahr bis zu 10 Jahren.

(f) § 213 Less Serious Case of (Voluntary) Manslaughter (translation)

If the person committing manslaughter was through no fault of his own provoked to lose his temper by physical or verbal abuse from the person killed directed at himself or at a close relative and was thereby immediately carried away to commit the act, or in the event of an otherwise less serious case, the punishment shall be imprisonment between one year and ten years.

(g) § 216 Tötung auf Verlangen

(i) *Ist jemand durch das ausdrückliche und ernstliche Verlangen des Getöteten zur Tötung bestimmt worden, so ist auf Freiheitsstrafe von sechs Monaten bis zu fünf Jahren zu erkennen.*

(ii) *Der Versuch ist strafbar.*

(h) § 216 Killing on Request (translation)

(i) Where the person who killed another was induced to kill by an express and earnest request of the person killed, the punishment shall be imprisonment between six months and five years.

(ii) An attempt is punishable.

(i) § 227 Körperverletzung mit Todesfolge

(i) *Verursacht der Täter durch die Körperverletzung (§§ 223 bis 226) den Tod der verletzten Person, so ist die Strafe Freiheitsstrafe nicht unter drei Jahren* [Körperverletzung, § 223, is the intended causation of bodily injury].

(ii) In minder schweren Fällen ist auf Freiheitsstrafe von einem Jahr bis zu zehn Jahren zu erkennen.

(j) § 227 Bodily Injury Resulting in Death (translation)

(i) If the perpetrator causes the death of the injured person through the infliction of bodily injury, the punishment shall be imprisonment for no less than three years.

(ii) In less serious cases a custodial sentence of between one year's and ten years' imprisonment shall be imposed.

(ii) 'General Part' Provisions (*Allgemeiner Teil*) Discussed in this Chapter[99]

(a) § 20 Schuldunfähigkeit wegen seelischer Störungen

Ohne Schuld handelt, wer bei Begehung der Tat wegen einer krankhaften seelischen Störung, wegen einer tiefgreifenden Bewußtseinsstörung oder wegen Schwachsinns oder einer schweren anderen seelischen Abartigkeit unfähig ist, das Unrecht der Tat einzusehen oder nach dieser Einsicht zu handeln.

(b) § 20 Lack of Capacity Arising from Mental Causes (translation)

A person who, at the time of the commission of the offence, is by reason of a pathological emotional disorder, a severe mental disturbance, severe mental retardation or some other severe mental abnormality unable to appreciate the wrongfulness of his conduct, or to act in accordance with this insight, cannot be held criminally liable [literally: acts without guilt].

(c) § 21 Verminderte Schuldfähigkeit

Ist die Fähigkeit des Täters, das Unrecht der Tat einzusehen oder nach dieser Einsicht zu handeln, aus einem der in § 20 bezeichneten Gründe bei Begehung der Tat erheblich vermindert, so kann die Strafe nach § 49 Abs. 1 gemildert werden.

(d) § 21 Diminished Responsibility (translation)

If, at the time of the commission of the offence, the perpetrator's ability to appreciate the wrongfulness of his conduct, or his ability to act in accordance with this insight, is substantially reduced because of one of the reasons indicated in § 20, the punishment may be mitigated pursuant to § 49 (i).

(e) § 32 Notwehr

(i) Wer eine Tat begeht, die durch Notwehr geboten ist, handelt nicht rechtswidrig.

---

[99] §§ 20, 21, 32, 33, 34, 35, 38, 49 and 50.

(ii) Notwehr ist die Verteidigung, die erforderlich ist, um einen gegenwärtigen rechtswidrigen Angriff von sich oder einem anderen abzuwenden.

(f) § 32 Self-defence (translation)

(i) A person who does an act which is necessitated by self-defence acts lawfully.

(ii) Self-defence is the degree of force necessary to repel a present unlawful attack directed against oneself or another person.

(g) § 33 Überschreitung der Notwehr

Überschreitet der Täter die Grenzen der Notwehr aus Verwirrung, Furcht oder Schrecken, so wird er nicht bestraft.

(h) § 33 Excessive Self-defence (translation)

A person who exceeds the boundaries of self-defence due to confusion, fear or shock shall not be punished.

(i) § 34 Rechtfertigender Notstand

Wer in einer gegenwärtigen, nicht anders abwendbaren Gefahr für Leben, Leib, Freiheit, Ehre, Eigentum oder ein anderes Rechtsgut eine Tat begeht, um die Gefahr von sich oder einem anderen abzuwenden, handelt nicht rechtswidrig, wenn bei Abwägung der widerstreitenden Interessen, namentlich der betroffenen Rechtsgüter und des Grades der ihnen drohenden Gefahren, das geschützte Interesse das beeinträchtigte wesentlich überwiegt. Dies gilt jedoch nur, soweit die Tat ein angemessenes Mittel ist, die Gefahr abzuwenden.

(j) § 34 Justifying Necessity (translation)

A person who, when faced with an imminent danger which cannot otherwise be averted to life, limb, liberty, honour, property or another legally protected interest, acts in order to avert the danger from himself or another, does not act unlawfully, if, upon weighing the conflicting interests, in particular the affected legal interests and the degree of danger threatening them, the protected interest substantially outweighs the one interfered with; provided that the act is a proportionate means of averting the danger.

(k) § 35 Entschuldigender Notstand

(i) Wer in einer gegenwärtigen, nicht anders abwendbaren Gefahr für Leben, Leib oder Freiheit eine rechtswidrige Tat begeht, um die Gefahr von sich, einem Angehörigen oder einer anderen ihm nahestehenden Person abzuwenden, handelt ohne Schuld. Dies gilt nicht, soweit dem Täter nach den Umständen, namentlich weil er die Gefahr selbst verursacht hat oder weil er in einem besonderen Rechtsverhältnis stand, zugemutet werden

konnte, die Gefahr hinzunehmen; jedoch kann die Strafe nach § 49 Abs. 1 gemildert werden, wenn der Täter nicht mit Rücksicht auf ein besonderes Rechtsverhältnis die Gefahr hinzunehmen hatte.

(ii) Nimmt der Täter bei Begehung der Tat irrig Umstände an, welche ihn nach Absatz 1 entschuldigen würden, so wird er nur dann bestraft, wenn er den Irrtum vermeiden konnte. Die Strafe ist nach § 49 Abs. 1 zu mildern.

(l) § 35 Exculpatory Necessity (translation)

(i) A person who, when faced with an imminent danger to life, limb or liberty which cannot otherwise be averted, commits an unlawful act in order to avert the danger from himself, a relative or a person close to him, shall not be held criminally liable for his act [literally: acts without guilt]. This shall not apply in circumstances where the perpetrator could have been expected to put up with the risk, for instance because he caused the danger or because of a special legal relationship; in these cases the court can mitigate punishment in application of § 49 (i) unless the perpetrator was under a specific legal duty to assume the risk.

(ii) If the perpetrator at the time of the commission of the offence mistakenly believes that circumstances exist which, if true, would excuse him under subsection (i), he is only liable to punishment if he could have avoided the mistake. The punishment shall be mitigated pursuant to § 49(i).

(m) § 38 Dauer der Freiheitsstrafe

(i)Die Freiheitsstrafe ist zeitig, wenn das Gesetz nicht lebenslange Freiheitsstrafe androht.

(ii) Das Höchstmaß der zeitigen Freiheitsstrafe ist fünfzehn Jahre, ihr Mindestmaß ein Monat.

(n) § 38 Length of imprisonment (translation)

(i) Imprisonment is for a fixed term unless the law expressly stipulates imprisonment for life.

(ii) The maximum length of a fixed term of imprisonment is 15 years; the minimum length is one month.

(o) § 49 Besondere gesetzliche Milderungsgründe

(i) Ist eine Milderung nach dieser Vorschrift vorgeschrieben oder zugelassen, so gilt für die Milderung folgendes:

1. An die Stelle von lebenslanger Freiheitsstrafe tritt Freiheitsstrafe nicht unter drei Jahren.

2. Bei zeitiger Freiheitsstrafe darf höchstens auf drei Viertel des angedrohten Höchstmaßes erkannt werden. Bei Geldstrafe gilt dasselbe für die Höchstzahl der Tagessätze.

3. Das erhöhte Mindestmaß einer Freiheitsstrafe ermäßigt sich im Falle eines Mindestmaßes von zehn oder fünf Jahren auf zwei Jahre,

im Falle eines Mindestmaßes von drei oder zwei Jahren auf sechs Monate,

im Falle eines Mindestmaßes von einem Jahr auf drei Monate,

im übrigen auf das gesetzliche Mindestmaß.

(ii) [omitted]

(p) § 49 Special Statutory Mitigating Circumstances (translation)

(i) If mitigation of sentence is prescribed or permitted according to this provision, the following shall apply for such mitigation:

1. Imprisonment for no less than three years takes the place of imprisonment for life.

2. In cases of imprisonment for a fixed term, at most three quarters of the maximum term provided for may be imposed. In the case of a fine the same shall apply to the maximum number of daily rates.

3. An increased minimum term of imprisonment shall be reduced:

in the case of a minimum term of 10 or five years, to three years,

in the case of a minimum term of three or two years, to six months,

in the case of a minimum term of one year, to three months,

in other cases to the statutory minimum.

(ii) [omitted]

(q) § 50 Zusammentreffen von Milderungsgründen

Ein Umstand, der allein oder mit anderen Umständen die Annahme eines minder schweren Falles begründet und der zugleich ein besonderer gesetzlicher Milderungsgrund nach § 49 ist, darf nur einmal berücksichtigt werden.

(r) § 50 More Than One Occasion for Mitigation (translation)

A factor which, alone or in combination with other factors, justifies the assumption that the case is less serious and is simultaneously a special statutory mitigating circumstance under § 49, may only be considered once.

(iii) Further Explanatory Notes

A. Whenever a provision in the German Penal Code does not specify a lesser state of *mens rea* than intention, intention is required with regard to all the elements of the *actus reus*. This follows from § 15.

B. Unless an explicit exception applies, defendants are always judged on the facts as they believed them to be (see § 16).

C. Whenever a provision sets out a heavier penalty for an offence by virtue of it having led to a particularly serious result (as § 227 does), the defendant has to have been at least reckless as to whether his act would cause the serious result (§ 18).

D. Whenever a provision sets out a minimum penalty of at least one year's imprisonment (*Verbrechen*), an attempt is punishable (§§ 12, 23). Whenever a provision sets out a lesser minimum penalty (*Vergehen*), attempts are only punishable if the provision in question explicitly provides for it. Hence, in § 216, there was a need to state that the attempt was punishable, whereas in §§ 211, 212 and 213 an attempt is punishable under the general rule.

5

Two Models of Murder: Patterns of Criminalisation in the United States

CLAIRE FINKELSTEIN

1. Introduction

U NITED STATES MURDER law displays a high degree of consistency in its core doctrines from one jurisdiction to another. Nearly every state allows conviction for murder based on a defendant's participation in certain 'predicate' felonies at the time the killing took place (the so-called 'felony murder' doctrine).[1] Nearly every state distinguishes different 'degrees' of murder, and most states treat premeditation as the basis for charging a defendant with the higher grade of murder.[2] Nearly every state allows a partial defence of provocation or 'extreme emotional disturbance' which reduces a charge of murder to manslaughter. All states that impose the death penalty require a jury or judge to do so on the basis of formally identified aggravating and mitigating factors.[3] And all states routinely allow a certain set of defences to murder, such as self-defence, necessity, defence of others, defence of habitation and law-enforcement. Very few states allow duress as a defence to murder.[4]

Despite these commonalities, there are significant differences in the formal structure of murder law from state to state. For example, nearly all American jurisdictions have a 'felony-murder' doctrine, but in some there is a list of predicate felonies in the murder statute itself, while in others the entire doctrine

---

[1] See 40 American Jurisprudence 2D Homicide § 64 (2006).
[2] As we shall see, however, there are important differences among jurisdictions regarding the meaning of premeditation.
[3] This is constitutionally mandated. See *Furman v Georgia* 408 US 238 (1972), *Gregg v Georgia* 428 US 153 (1976), *Woodson v North Carolina* 428 US 280 (1976).
[4] A small handful of jurisdictions allow the duress defence to murder under certain limited circumstances. See *Spunaugle v State* 946 P2d 246 (Okla Crim App 1997).

stems from judicial decision-making.[5] Some jurisdictions, using an older template, treat provocation as a kind of partial justification, allowing, for example, a reduction in the grade and degree of the offence if the defendant killed in response to certain conventional triggers. Other jurisdictions, following the Model Penal Code, treat provocation under the rubric of 'extreme emotional disturbance', and in these jurisdictions provocation is more akin to an excuse based on impaired mental state.[6]

In many cases, however, these formal differences do not represent an actual difference in practice. For example, despite the fact that felony murder is codified in some jurisdictions and not in others, the judicially-defined list of predicate felonies is nearly the same in all jurisdictions. The same may be true of the provocation defence and its modern MPC-inspired variant, extreme emotional disturbance. The wide divergence in the formal structure of these defences may not translate into as wide a divergence in practice as one might expect on the basis of the official doctrine.

This Chapter will mainly deal with the formal aspects of murder law in the United States, but it will also examine significant patterns of criminalisation effected through judicial decision-making. As suggested above, the question we shall address is whether the divergences among formal approaches to murder in the United States represent a significant variation in actual practice or whether formal differences are less important than we might suppose for the uniformity of practice. It will also address what is perhaps the most significant difference among US jurisdictions in drawing the line between first and second degree murder, namely the meaning accorded to the term 'premeditation'.

The Chapter will focus on two jurisdictions: California and New York. The patterns of criminalisation in these two jurisdictions typify the two predominant approaches to homicide law in the US. We shall call California a Type I statute and New York a Type II statute.[7] Type I statutes reflect the traditional pattern inherited from the common law. They are identified by a normative approach to the mens rea for murder 'malice aforethought' and the inclusion of other normative concepts 'unlawfully', by identifying the forbidden conduct in act rather than result terms 'killing' rather than 'causing death', and by an absence of statutory direction on matters like felony murder and its associated doctrines. Type II statutes reflect an effort at reform initiated by the drafters of the Model Penal Code. They are most significantly distinguished from Type I statutes by their approach to mental state terms. Type II statutes replace the normative language of the traditional approach to mens rea with a more fine-grained series of mental state categories, and the distinctions in homicide law usually track

---

[5] New York is an example of the former and California of the latter.
[6] Model Penal Code § 210.3(b) (Proposed Official Draft 1982) (hereinafter MPC). 14 states, of which the best example is New York, have adopted the latter approach. See NY Pen.Law § 125.25.
[7] While other jurisdictions will not be discussed, the Appendix to this ch provides a list of states according to whether they are Type I, Type II, a mix of elements from both models, or 'other'.

these more psychologically nuanced categories of mental state. They also tend to favour result over conduct elements to define the actus reus of murder, to offer more precise legislative direction in the areas of felony murder and in defences, and more generally to eschew the inclusion of any normative elements in the formulation of the conduct requirement.

The Chapter will suggest that along several dimensions the difference between Type I and Type II murder statutes is important in practice, but perhaps not in the way that the drafters of the new wave of murder statutes had intended. It will suggest in particular that although many of the formal differences in the different patterns of criminalisation do not reflect differences in actual practice, the increased clarity of the reformed murder statutes has helped to improve the consistency and predictability of judicial decision-making under them. Ironically, the new wave of MPC-type statutes has also influenced jurisdictions that have not revised their criminal codes, since traditional jurisdictions have begun re-interpreting their own statutes in light of MPC-inspired principles.

Finally, we shall turn to a discussion of different approaches to degrees of murder. This Chapter identifies two such approaches. As this distinction does not appear to correspond to the basic distinction between Type I and Type II jurisdictions, we shall discuss this question under separate heading. A basic question that arises in this area is whether the usual criterion for distinguishing first from second degree murder—premeditation—captures the distinction between those murders we consider the worst, and so most deserving of punishment, and those we consider of somewhat lesser gravity. As we shall see, there is reason to question this use of the notion of premeditation.

2. Type I Statutes—California

(i) Basic Definition

California retains the old common law definition of murder. Section 187 of the California Penal Code defines murder as 'the unlawful killing of a human being, or a foetus, with malice aforethought'.[8] California takes the traditional approach to mens rea, as do a majority of US jurisdictions.[9] And while a number of states have rejected the traditional approach in favour of some variant of the Model

---

[8] 1970 Cal Laws ch 1311, § 1. The words 'or a fetus' were added after the case of *Keeler v Superior Court* 470 P2d 617 (1970) (setting aside murder charges for a defendant who attacked his pregnant ex-wife, killing her foetus).

[9] See *American Jurisprudence* 2d, *Homicide*, § 37, citing in addition Arizona, Idaho, Indiana, New Hampshire, Rhode Island, Tennessee, Texas and Virginia as among the jurisdictions taking this traditional approach to the mental element in murder.

Penal Code approach, federal law still retains the Type I model.[10] It is unfortunate that more jurisdictions have not followed the MPC example, as the mental state element in the traditional murder statute creates great unclarity. Type II statutes (such as New York's, discussed below) significantly enhance the precision of the mental state element in murder.

(ii) Mens Rea

While the expression 'malice aforethought' is not defined under California law, the Penal Code does make some attempt to clarify the term 'malice' (§ 188). Malice is divided into two categories: 'express' and 'implied'. The Code defines 'express malice' as 'when there is manifested a deliberate intention unlawfully to take away the life of a fellow creature', ie when the defendant had a purpose to kill. The definition of malice leaves at least two questions unanswered. First, what does § 188 do with cases in which the defendant *knows* he will bring about the victim's death, but has no *intent* to do so? Secondly, what about cases in which the defendant intends to bring about grievous bodily injury but death results instead?

While these questions are not addressed in the murder laws themselves, California Jury Instructions shed some light on them. Section 8.11 limits express malice to cases in which 'there is manifested an intention unlawfully to kill a human being'. What counts as a 'manifested intention' in this context? Most jurisdictions with the express/implied malice formulation treat express malice as requiring 'deliberation' or a design to take life. The 'malice' in this context thus appears to mean the same thing as 'aforethought', and the latter term does not convey any additional information.[11] The import of the distinction between express and implied malice is mainly that express malice is intentional killing, while implied malice refers to highly reckless killing (sometimes called 'depraved heart murder') or killing that takes place in the course of a dangerous felony.

Thus far we have been discussing whether intent to kill supplies a *necessary* condition for malice aforethought in California, and the answer is clear that it does not. By contrast, matters are less settled on the question of whether an intent to kill provides a *sufficient* condition for express malice. One argument advanced in support of the position that more should be required is that if intent is sufficient for express malice, there will be no room left over for the category of voluntary manslaughter. As one justice of the California Supreme Court explained:

---

[10] 18 USCS § 1111(a) (defining murder as 'the unlawful killing of a human being with malice aforethought').

[11] See *Littleton v State* 88 Tex Crim 614 (1921).

a defendant who announced his intent to kill, and then took methodical steps to do so, could not pursue the compromise verdict of voluntary manslaughter on the theory that intoxication or other mental condition had clouded his awareness of his duty to act within the law.[12]

This is arguably problematic, because where the defendant's intent to kill is itself the product of an impaired mental state, the defendant should be found guilty of voluntary manslaughter instead of murder. But if intent is sufficient to establish malice, that possibility would be foreclosed. So it remains unclear whether express malice is synonymous with intent or whether it requires an additional normative element that goes beyond intent. As we shall see when we consider the line between first and second degree murder, the same debate will be revisited in that context from the opposite side: if more than mere intention is necessary for express malice, how will we distinguish ordinary malice from premeditation? The concept of premeditation is easier to define if express malice is limited to ordinary intent, and premeditation would then require further reflection, over and above intent. The problem, however, then becomes that it is not at all clear that the distinction between brief and extended reflection captures the distinction between ordinary murders and the murders that we wish to punish at the very highest level. Are murders committed with longer lead times really worse, morally speaking? The Type II approach to mental states somewhat alleviates these difficulties, as we shall see below.

In California, as in many other jurisdictions, 'implied malice' is when 'the circumstances attending the killing show an abandoned and malignant heart' (§ 188). California jury instructions further define implied malice as when:

1. The killing resulted from an intentional act;
2. The natural consequences of the act are dangerous to human life; and
3. The act was deliberately performed with knowledge of the danger to, and with conscious disregard for, human life.[13]

Thus a defendant who blows up an aeroplane to collect the insurance money on the cargo is guilty of the murder of the pilot, despite the fact that he does not intend to kill him. His culpability is 'implied' on the basis of his knowledge that he would kill him when he acted.[14] Similarly, a defendant who intends to inflict grievous bodily injury (but not death) would also be covered by the implied malice provision and would satisfy the definition of murder if the victim died as

---

[12] *People v Wright* 28 Cal Rptr 3d 708 (2005), Brown J concurring.
[13] California Jury Instructions Code (CALJIC) § 8.11 'Malice Aforethought Defined'.
[14] The defendant in this kind of case would sometimes be said 'obliquely' to intend to kill the pilot. This locution, however, is misleading, as the defendant does not, strictly speaking, have any kind of intention at all with respect to the pilot. 'Intent' or 'intention' is usually defined as a 'conscious purpose' to bring something about, where purpose implies desiring or aiming at the object in question. Thus if the defendant is aware that the pilot's death will result, but does not aim at or desire it, he does not intend it.

a result of the act. The same would be true of the defendant who was aware that he was inflicting a serious risk of bodily injury, even if he did not intend to impose such injuries.

In addition to covering knowing and extremely reckless (depraved heart) killings, this section is the statutory basis for the felony murder rule in California. While most states that allow felony murder convictions contain explicit statutory provisions authorising such convictions and providing a list of 'predicate' felonies, California's felony murder rule is entirely case-based. In California, there are three judicially imposed restrictions on the felonies that can count as predicates for purposes of felony murder: (1) the requirement that the predicate felony be 'inherently dangerous', (2) the requirement that the felony not 'merge' with the homicide, and (3) the requirement that the killing take place 'in furtherance' of the felony. Articulating these limitations has occupied an inordinate amount of judicial attention, and to the extent that none can be eliminated by more precise codification, the greater legislative involvement in shaping doctrine we find in Type I statutes is preferable.

The 'inherently dangerous' requirement restricts predicate felonies to those that are particularly likely to cause death or serious bodily injury. This is a nearly universal limitation in jurisdictions whose felony murder rule is judge-made.[15] In California, whether a felony is inherently dangerous is to be determined 'in the abstract', meaning that a judge should ask whether the type of felony in question is of an inherently dangerous nature, putting aside the facts of the particular case.[16] Such an approach would rule out felonies like fraud, embezzlement, medical malpractice, and sometimes even crimes like burglary or kidnapping. The alternative to this approach in some jurisdictions is to say that the dangerousness of the felony should be assessed 'in the particular circumstances of the case'. Under this test courts are more likely to find the predicate felony to be inherently dangerous.[17]

The second judicial restriction on the felony murder rule in California, as well as in most jurisdictions, is the requirement that the felony that causes the victim's death not be too close in nature to the killing itself. The obvious example illustrating such concerns is the assault that results in a death. Imagine a murder case in which the prosecution cannot prove the required mens rea for that crime. Without the merger restriction, the prosecution could charge the defendant with assault and then use the assault as the predicate to secure the defendant's murder conviction without having to prove mens rea. The restriction on the prosecution's ability to behave in this way is thus a logical as well as policy-based one: it makes little sense to think of one felony as the basis of a conviction for a different

---

[15] An exception appears in jurisdictions that modify their felony murder rules to require that the defendant also had a conscious disregard of the risk to human life: *Com v Wojcik* 686 NE2d 452 (1997).

[16] See *People v Williams* 63 Cal 2d 452, 458 (1965).

[17] See eg *Chapman v State* 467 SE 2d 497 (Ga 1997).

felony if the two felonies are so close in nature that they should really be considered one.[18] As the famous case of *People v Ireland* held, a felony that forms an 'integral part of the homicide' should be thought to 'merge' with the homicide, and thus fail to supply an independent basis for a felony-murder conviction.[19]

The third requirement is that the killing take place in the course of the commission of, or 'in furtherance' of, the felony. That is, it must not be the case that the killing is entirely incidental and unconnected to the underlying felony. But exactly what that means is unclear. The more common approach is dubbed the 'agency' approach, meaning that the killing must result from the defendant's own agency or from one of his confederates (partners-in-crime).[20] Other jurisdictions have followed the less stringent 'proximate cause' approach, according to which the killing must merely have been proximately caused by the commission of the felony.[21] In the former sort of jurisdiction, it has been held that the killing of a felon by the victim of a convenience store robbery did not satisfy the 'in furtherance' of requirement, and the defendant could not be convicted under the felony-murder doctrine.[22] On the other hand, a defendant who murdered a victim he had raped was found to have killed 'in furtherance' of the predicate felony, despite the fact that the rape was long over by the time the killing occurred.[23] It is thus not necessary that the killing and the predicate felony take place in quick succession, although the lapse of time is a factor to be considered in determining whether this requirement is satisfied. Jurisdictions with this restriction are agreed that mere coincidence in time of homicide and predicate felony is insufficient.[24]

Nothing in the formal structure of the implied malice provision mandates any of the aforementioned restrictions, but nevertheless they are applied as consistently as if they were an official part of the legislative scheme. One might question the legitimacy of having extensive judicially created rules establishing the structure of crimes based on minimal legislative guidance. Among other concerns one might have is whether potential defendants receive adequate notice of the potential illegality of their conduct when the details of the elements of the offence are all established by judicial decision. Despite the nearly uniform rejection of common law crimes in the present day, as well as the rejection of novel interpretations of statutory offences, courts have mostly ignored this problem.[25]

---

[18] For further discussion of the merger doctrine see C Finkelstein, 'Merger and Felony Murder' in A Duff and SP Green (eds), *Defining Crimes: Essays on the Criominal Law's Special Part* (Oxford, 2005).

[19] 70 Cal 2d 522 (1969).

[20] *State v Canola* 374 A2d 20 (1977).

[21] *Commonwealth v Redline 137 A2d 472 (1958)*

[22] *State v Canola* 374 A 2d 20 (NJ 1977).

[23] *People v Castro* 27 Cal App 4th 578 (1994).

[24] See *People v Alvarez* 14 Cal 4th 155 (1996).

[25] Paul Robinson has argued that even criminal codes often fail to place people on notice of their obligations to the extent drafters expect: 'Code drafters fool themselves when they formulate such

One can argue in defence of the California scheme that all three of the above restrictions place limitations on when a conviction can be based on implied malice above and beyond those stated in the statute. Thus arguably a defendant is not disadvantaged by the statutory notice he receives, given that the judiciary has merely afforded him protections in excess of those accorded by the legislature. But this argument suffers from the defect that the California implied malice provision does not place a defendant on notice that he could be convicted on the basis of mere participation in a felony in which death results. The defendant must read prior cases to determine that fact. The entire felony murder rule, in other words, is not at all apparent from the face of the implied malice provision, so the limitations on such convictions are not the only judicial contribution to this doctrine. In general, the concerns with notice and our system's wariness of common law crimes should supply a reason to favour a more statutorily precise scheme, such as that adopted in New York. The latter approach is discussed below.

Finally, § 189 of the California Penal Code establishes the different degrees of murder by defining first degree murder as follows:

> All murder which is perpetrated by means of a destructive device or explosive, a weapon of mass destruction, knowing use of ammunition designed primarily to penetrate metal or armor, poison, lying in wait, torture, or by any other kind of willful, deliberate, and premeditated killing, or which is committed in the perpetration of, or attempt to perpetrate, arson, rape, carjacking, robbery, burglary, mayhem, kidnapping, train wrecking . . . or any murder which is perpetrated by means of discharging a firearm from a motor vehicle, intentionally at another person outside of the vehicle with the intent to inflict death, is murder of the first degree.

The statute then holds that 'all other kinds of murders are of the second degree'. This kind of provision is modelled on the original 1794 Pennsylvania statute, which defined first degree murder as 'intentional killing', and defined the latter phrase as '[k]illing by means of poison, or by lying in wait, or by any other kind of willful, deliberate and premeditated killing' (18 Pa.C.S.A. § 2502). This continues to be the most common formulation of first degree murder, although, as discussed below, there is wide variation in the approach to the line between first and second degree murder, due to divergence of opinion as to the meaning of 'willful, deliberate and premeditated'.

It is important to be clear that this kind of degree-raising provision does not substitute for mens rea. Instead, it has the effect of elevating a killing that has already met the requirements for murder (by satisfying the condition of either express or implied malice in § 188) to first degree murder if the killing was done

provisions on the assumption that they will in fact govern people's behavior': PH Robinson, 'Are Criminal Codes Irrelevant?' (1994) 68 *Southern California Law Review* 159 at 166. Juries apparently have serious difficulty comprehending and following jury instructions as well. One would expect the problem of comprehension and receipt of the law to be far more extensive when the legal sources potential defendants must interpret are judicial opinions.

in any of the specified ways. For example, let us suppose a defendant accidentally kills his victim in the course of committing armed robbery. Such a defendant would satisfy the requirement of 'implied malice' under § 188 by virtue of the fact that the killing took place in the course, and in furtherance, of an inherently dangerous felony. He would thus be guilty of murder. Under the above provision, he would be guilty of first degree murder by virtue of the fact that 'robbery' is one of the degree-raising factors in § 189. Finally, that the killing took place in the course of a robbery would count again as an aggravating factor for purpose of the death penalty (Cal Pen Code § 190.2). The most difficult and important question about this section arises in interpreting the concept of premeditation. We turn to that question in the final section.

(iii) Actus Reus

One of the interesting formal distinctions among homicide laws is whether the actus reus is described as a conduct or as a result element. Thus various statutes, like California's, define the actus reus as 'killing', while others contain the term 'causing death'. The question is whether this difference is purely stylistic, or whether it has significance for defendants who fall under the statute. While courts have not focused on the distinction, there are several reasons to favour the MPC 'causing death' formulation over the more traditional 'killing' version of the actus reus.

First, as other commentators have noted, the expression 'killing' is in fact a compound concept, combining conduct and result elements. Robinson and Grall argue that 'such combinations create ambiguities and undermine consistency in the operation of the Code, given that mens rea can vary depending on the sort of element to which it applies'.[26]

Secondly, the choice of actus reus in the case in which an involuntariness defence is asserted has potentially significant implications. In general, if a defendant suffers from an involuntary condition such as epilepsy, sleep walking, hypnosis or the like, he can claim the defence as long as he did not contrive or anticipate the onset of the involuntary condition. But what about a defendant who was aware that the involuntary condition was likely to occur? Consider a defendant who gets into his car and drives, knowing he is subject to frequent epileptic seizures. Courts have held that such defendants are not entitled to claim an involuntariness defence to a resulting homicide.[27] Yet it is hard to justify this result, given that at the time the defendant kills he is not engaging in any voluntary act.

---

[26] PH Robinson and JA Grall, 'Element Analysis in Defining Criminal Liability: The Model Penal Code and Beyond' (1983) 35 *Stanford Law Review* 681 at 709.

[27] For a further discussion of this point see C Finkelstein, 'Involuntary Crimes, Voluntarily Committed' in S Shute and AP Simester (eds), *Criminal Law Theory: Doctrines of the General Part* (Oxford, 2002).

One answer to this dilemma is to say that if the defendant voluntarily chooses to drive, knowing that he is subject to epileptic seizures, he voluntarily causes death, because his risky behaviour is the proximate cause of the victim's death. (Of course whether he has the mens rea for the relevant homicide offence is another question—in all likelihood he will have the mens rea for manslaughter but not for murder in such cases.) Notice, however, that there is some difficulty with this solution in the case of conduct crimes. Does a defendant who voluntarily takes a drug that will make him unconscious at the time he later enters a store to rob it 'enter a building unlawfully with intent to commit a crime therein' *voluntarily*? It is difficult to see how a defendant can be understood as entering a building voluntarily at the moment that he swallows a pill, sees a hypnotist or goes to sleep (and later sleepwalks). And arguably when murder is defined as 'killing' rather than 'causing the death of', we would encounter the same difficulty. Does a defendant who gets into his car knowing he is subject to epileptic seizures then and there 'kill' his victim? The term 'killing' may be less elastic with respect to time frame than the expression 'causing death of'. This may give us one reason to favour the latter approach to the actus reus requirement.

There are several other variations in the formulation of the actus reus worth noting. The first concerns the time period for bringing about the victim's death. Traditionally criminal codes did not specify the period of time within which the victim must die for the actus reus of homicide to be satisfied. Any time limitations therefore stemmed from interpretation of the basic actus reus— 'causing death' or 'killing'. The question then becomes whether those concepts contain an implicit limitation on the permissible gap between the defendant's action and the victim's death. At common law, the rule was assumed to be that the victim must die within 'a year and a day' of the defendant's infliction of the victim's injury.[28] In California, however, § 194 now explicitly provides that if death occurs beyond three years and a day after the act of the defendant's that caused it, 'there shall be a rebuttable presumption that the killing was not criminal'. The prosecution may be able to overcome this presumption, but the Code does not say how.

A second source of variation in actus reus concerns the identification of special classes of victims and particular circumstances. For example, as mentioned above, the California legislature amended its homicide provision after the *Keeler* case to include foetuses among the class of protected persons. And nearly all jurisdictions impose enhanced penalties for certain classes of victims, usually police officers and other law enforcement officers at a minimum. In California, § 190 sets forth enhanced penalties for the killing of various kinds of 'peace officers'. Subsection (b) authorises a sentence of 25 years to life if the victim was a peace officer killed while engaged in the performance of his or her duties, as long as the defendant knew or should have known that this was the case. Subsection

---

[28]   40 American Jurisprudence 2d, Homicide, § 13.

(c) establishes a sentence of life without the possibility of parole under the conditions listed in (b) when the defendant intended to kill or intended to inflict great bodily injury on a peace officer, when the defendant personally used a dangerous weapon, or when the defendant used a firearm in the commission of the offence. In addition, California Penal Code § 190.25 sets forth a mandatory term of life without the possibility of parole for the murder of 'the operator of a bus, taxicab, streetcar, cable car, trackless trolley, or other motor vehicle operated on land'. Section 190.2 also contains special provisions relating to the murder of a federal law enforcement officer, a firefighter, a witness to a crime, a prosecutor, judge or elected official.

There are also provisions for 'special circumstances' which would establish a mandatory sentence of either life without the possibility of parole or death. The list includes conditions such as that the murder was intentional and carried out for financial gain; the defendant was previously convicted of murder; the murder was committed by mean of an explosive device; the murder was committed for the purpose of avoiding lawful arrest or escaping from custody or the murder was especially heinous, atrocious or cruel; the defendant intentionally killed the victim by means of lying in wait; the victim was intentionally killed because of race, colour, religion, etc, or; the murder was committed in the course of committing another specific felony. Finally, § 190.03 establishes a minimum penalty of life in prison without the possibility of parole for any 'hate crime murder', meaning a killing motivated by animus on the basis of race or religion.

(iv) Defences to Murder

The next category to consider is the structure of affirmative defences to murder under California law. The defendant has the burden in this state of establishing any affirmative defences he may wish to assert to a charge of homicide (§ 189.5). The following are defences specific to homicide.

Excusable Homicide (§ 195) is an act 'committed by accident and misfortune . . . with usual and ordinary caution, and without any unlawful intent'. It also includes acts performed 'in the heat of passion, upon any sudden and sufficient provocation or combat', provided that no 'undue advantage' is taken, no dangerous weapon is used, and the killing is not performed 'in a cruel or unusual manner'. In the case of heat of passion killing, however, the defendant may be convicted of voluntary manslaughter under § 192 (see below).

Justifiable Homicide (§ 197) includes acts to defend oneself or another person against murder, great bodily injury or certain other felonies. It also contains a broad privilege allowing deadly force committed 'in defence of habitation, property, or person, against one who manifestly intends or endeavors, by violence or surprise, to commit a felony, or against one who manifestly intends and endeavors, in a violent, riotous or tumultuous manner, to enter the habitation of another for the purpose of offering violence to any person therein'. Thus the thief who intends to use force to steal someone's wallet subjects himself to the permissible use of lethal force by the victim. In addition, under this provision, a bare fear that another is about to commit a felony against one is insufficient to justify the use of lethal force. Instead, California law suggests that the fear must be reasonable (§ 198).

(v) Lesser Offences

Finally, manslaughter in California tracks the definition of murder (§ 192), but it lacks the element of malice aforethought. There are three types of manslaughter: voluntary, involuntary and vehicular. Voluntary manslaughter is defined as killing 'upon a sudden quarrel or heat of passion'. That is, voluntary manslaughter identifies cases either in which a defendant's murder charge is reduced to manslaughter on account of provocation, or in which a defendant forms an intention to harm the victim, and hence is probably reckless with respect to his death, but acts out of emotion and so does not form a fully fledged, reflective intention to kill. A defendant in this category, however, who displays depraved indifference to the value of human life will probably be guilty of second degree murder. Involuntary manslaughter is defined as killing 'in the commission of an unlawful act, not amounting to felony; or in the commission of a lawful act which might produce death, in an unlawful manner, or without due caution and circumspection'. This provision contains a lesser analogue to the felony murder doctrine: the misdemeanour-manslaughter rule. In cases to which this doctrine applies, a defendant will be guilty of manslaughter if he killed in the course of committing a misdemeanour.

Vehicular manslaughter is itself divided into two types: (1) gross vehicular manslaughter while intoxicated, defined as 'the unlawful killing of a human being without malice aforethought, in the driving of a vehicle . . . and the killing was either the proximate result of the commission of an unlawful act, not amounting to a felony, and with gross negligence, or the proximate result of the commission of a lawful act which might produce death, in an unlawful manner, and with gross negligence' (§ 191.5); and (2) vehicular manslaughter, defined as 'operating a vehicle in the commission of an unlawful act, not amounting to felony, and with gross negligence; or operating a vehicle in the commission of a lawful act which might produce death, in an unlawful manner, and with gross negligence' (§192.5). A lesser offence of this same provision punishes the same conduct without gross negligence.

3. Type II Statutes—New York

The New York Penal Code was entirely revised in the 1960s, and the new statute patterned largely after the American Law Institute's Model Penal Code (MPC).

Since that time, many other murder statutes in the United States have also been revised to follow this model. One of the central innovations of the MPC, as well as the revised New York Penal Code is the more precise approach to mens rea. The advance in thinking about mens rea is what best characterises Type II statutes. As already suggested, it gives ample reason to favour the Type II model.

(i) Basic Definition

Like the MPC, New York offers a basic definition of homicide first (§ 125.00) and then distinguishes murder and manslaughter from homicide largely in terms of the different mental state requirements for those crimes. Homicide is defined as:

> conduct which causes the death of a person or an unborn child with which a female has been pregnant for more than twenty-four weeks under circumstances constituting murder, manslaughter in the first degree, manslaughter in the second degree, criminally negligent homicide, abortion in the first degree or self-abortion in the first degree (§ 125.00).

This is also the structure of the MPC, which identifies a basic definition of homicide (MPC § 210.0) and then distinguishes different types of homicide based on the mental state that applies to it. In this respect, the MPC and New York can be usefully compared to other jurisdictions on this point, such as those listed in Part 6(D) of this Article, which tend not to identify homicide in a separate provision, but skip directly to specific homicide offences instead.

(ii) Mens Rea

Like the MPC, New York officially articulates four different mental states (§ 15.00(6)). Section 15.05 defines these mental states as follows:

> 1.Intentionally: A person acts intentionally with respect to a result or to conduct . . . when his conscious objective is to cause such result or to engage in such conduct.

> 2.Knowingly: A person acts knowingly with respect to conduct or to a circumstance described by a statute defining an offence when he is aware that his conduct is of such nature or that such circumstance exists.

> 3.Recklessly: A person acts recklessly with respect to a result or to a circumstance described by a statute defining an offence when he is aware of and consciously disregards a substantial and unjustifiable risk that such result will occur or that such circumstance exists.

> 4.Criminal Negligence: A person acts with criminal negligence with respect to a result or to a circumstance described by a statute defining an offence when he fails to perceive a substantial and unjustifiable risk that such result will occur or that such circumstance exists.

The definition of murder in the second degree (§ 125.25) then adds various mental states or circumstances to the homicide to make the killing murder. A homicide will constitute second degree murder if the defendant caused the death with (1) intent, (2) depraved indifference, or (3) the killing took place during the commission of one of a list of enumerated felonies. Second degree murder in New York is thus that jurisdiction's basic murder provision. In many other jurisdictions it would be classified as first degree murder.

Curiously, New York's second degree murder provision does not exactly track these fine-grained mental state distinctions set out in § 15.00(6). The first category of second degree murder is when 'with intent to cause the death of another person, [the defendant] causes the death of such person or of a third person...' (§125.25(1)).[29] The next category is depraved indifference killing, the nearly universal form of murder based on killing in a heightened state of recklessness (§ 125.25(2)). Conspicuously missing from this definition are killings that are knowing but not intentional. This was in all likelihood an oversight, in view of the fact that the comparable provision in the MPC, after which the New York Code is modelled, defines murder as criminal homicide committed 'purposely or knowingly' (MPC § 210.2). The omission of 'knowingly' is probably harmless error, since knowing killings, killings in which a defendant knew that death would result from his conduct, even if it was not his 'conscious object' to produce that death, would probably be covered by the second kind of second degree murder, as set out in §125.25(2). That is, arguably §125.25's depraved indifference provision would provision would be satisfied by a defendant who knew that death would result from his conduct, even if it was not his 'conscious object' to produce that death. But the omission of the 'knowing' mental state represents at the least a loss in clarity. And it is just barely possible that a defendant could kill knowingly and without justification but attempt to deny liability on the ground that the killing was not done with 'depraved indifference'. The theoretical possibility of such a defence is clear under the New York statute, even if such cases have not arisen in practice.

Finally, § 125.25(3) sets out the felony murder provision, with a list of predicate felonies. That list includes robbery, burglary, kidnapping, arson and rape in the first degree, among others. This provision also departs from the comparable MPC provision, which technically eliminates felony murder. What MPC § 210.2(1)(b) puts in its place is a rebuttable presumption of the required 'extreme indifference' if the defendant is engaged in the commission of any of the listed felonies (robbery, rape, deviate sexual intercourse by force or threat of force, arson, burglary, kidnapping or felonious escape). Thus, under the MPC, if the defendant can demonstrate that he did not act recklessly when he committed one of the aforementioned felonies, he will not be guilty of murder for the

---

[29] Notice that this provision allows for what is sometimes called 'transferred intent', where the victim is a person other than the one whose death was intended. This would apply whether or not the defendant was aware of the risk to the third party.

resulting death. This seems preferable to the New York approach, as it firmly makes the enhanced culpability for killing during a felony a matter of mens rea.

New York courts have interpreted this provision to set out an exhaustive list of acceptable predicate felonies for felony murder purposes. Thus the problems arising from the three restrictions on felony murder we saw in California—the inherently dangerous requirement, absence of merger, and the 'in furtherance of' requirement—is thought to be obviated in this jurisdiction.[30] New York courts *could* have viewed this matter differently, however. They might have concluded that the statutory list of felonies supplied *potential* predicate felonies, conditioned on whether, under the circumstances, the felony satisfied these three conditions.

For example, consider a burglary where the defendant breaks in to steal a television and ends up killing the owner. California courts have struggled with burglary as a predicate felony, and opinion is divided on whether, for example, a burglary merges with the homicide. In New York, courts have held that because burglary is on the list of predicate felonies, there is no need to question whether it additionally satisfies the traditional common law requirements. But another approach would ask whether, under the circumstances of this specific crime, it makes sense to treat burglary as a predicate felony for felony murder purposes. The point is especially clear with respect to merger. It seems likely that the applicability of this doctrine should depend on the circumstances, unlike what New York courts have supposed. If the defendant is charged with burglary because he broke into a dwelling for the purpose of killing the inhabitants, then arguably the burglary does merge with the homicide. But if he broke in to steal the television, arguably there should be no merger.[31] The same might be said of the inherent dangerousness doctrine, although an impediment to the particular-istic approach in this case would be the fact that courts in jurisdictions taking a common law approach to felony murder have long favoured the abstract approach, and not entirely without reason. The particularistic approach threatens to make all felonies inherently dangerous since in the particular circumstances of the case, the felonious activity will always turn out to have been dangerous, given that it caused a death. Finally, with regard to the 'in furtherance of' requirement, it is hard to see how a court's approach could be anything other than particular-istic. Thus if this requirement makes sense, it makes sense to apply it to both statutory and non-statutory predicate felonies.

---

[30] See *People v Miller* 297 NE 2d 85 (1973) (rejecting the suggestion that the burglary merges with the homicide).

[31] Of course this approach produces the paradoxical result that the former can be proven a murderer without demonstrating his intent to kill, whereas the latter must be shown to have such intent, and thus arguably the defendant who commits the lesser offence is treated more harshly than the defendant who commits the greater. But there will also be significant discontinuities if we take the statutorily enumerated approach as well. These problems seem to be simply part and parcel of the felony murder doctrine. They are among the many reasons that the doctrine is often reviled in academic writing on the subject. For a discussion of the issues connected with merger see C Finkelstein, 'Merger and Felony Murder' in A Duff and SP Green (eds), *Defining Crimes: Essays on the Criminal Law's Special Part* (Oxford, 2005).

If Type II jurisdictions see the turn to codification as eliminating all judicial discretion in areas of this sort, the divergence between Type I and Type II statutes will be greater than we would otherwise expect, since much of the consistency in doctrine depends on the fact that judges have common reactions to certain consistent patterns of fact. The consistency of judicial intuitions arguably creates de facto doctrinal consistency even in the face of broad de jure variation. Thus while greater codification is in general laudable, it should be tempered by more liberal principles of judicial interpretation than the those New York courts have adopted.

(iii) Actus Reus

The New York Code defines the actus reus of murder as 'causing death', rather than 'killing' as in California. As discussed above, the former seems a preferable formulation, as it disentangles conduct from result more clearly and avoids some of the causation problems associated with conduct crimes, particularly when an involuntariness defence is asserted.

Section 125.27 sets out the definition of first degree murder. It is the same as the first type of second degree murder (intentionally causing death), with the addition of a special victims and circumstances provision. It identifies the following factors, among others, as a basis for upgrading the degree of murder: the victim was a police officer performing his official duties and the defendant knew or should have known that this was the case; the defendant was confined in a state correctional facility; the victim was a witness to a crime; and the crime was intended to prevent the victim's testimony in criminal proceedings; the killing was performed for money; the killing was performed in the course of the defendant's committing or attempting to commit a felony from a statutory list of felonies;[32] the defendant caused the death of an additional person or persons; the defendant had already been convicted of murder; the defendant tortured the victim; or the victim was killed in furtherance of an act of terrorism.[33] A conviction of murder in the first degree makes a defendant eligible for the death penalty.

New York does not follow the Model Penal Code entirely, insofar as the latter recommends the elimination of the distinction between degrees of murder. But New York distinguishes itself from the traditional treatment of first degree murder in rejecting the concept of premeditation. When we consider the issue of degrees of murder below, we will see that it is highly questionable whether premeditation captures common intuitions about which are the worst killings. A

---

[32] The list here is substantially the same as the list presented in part (3) of § 125.25 (murder in the second degree).

[33] Several conditions omitted.

special victims provision, such as New York has incorporated, seems the preferable course if a jurisdiction is to retain a distinction between degrees of murder.

(iv) Defences to Murder

Section 125.25(1) presents two defences to intentional murder (in the second degree): the defendant acted 'under the influence of extreme emotional disturbance for which there was a reasonable explanation or excuse', or the defendant merely assisted another to commit suicide. The first defence—extreme emotional disturbance—is a revised version of the provocation defence, once again taken from the MPC formulation of that defence. Unlike provocation, the extreme emotional disturbance defence in the New York statute is intended to focus primarily on the defendant's psychological state, rather than on the 'provoking' element. The defendant can be convicted of manslaughter in the first degree under § 125.20, when he intentionally causes the death of another person,

> under circumstances which do not constitute murder because he acts under the influence of extreme emotional disturbance…The fact that homicide was committed under the influence of extreme emotional disturbance constitutes a mitigating circumstance reducing murder to manslaughter in the first degree and need not be proved in any prosecution initiated under this subdivision.

Section 125.25 then sets out the conditions under which acting under the influence of 'extreme emotional disturbance' constitutes an affirmative defence to murder:

> The defendant acted under the influence of extreme emotional disturbance for which there was a reasonable explanation or excuse, the reasonableness of which is to be determined from the viewpoint of a person in the defendant's situation under the circumstances as the defendant believed them to be.

This provision represents a significant formal change from the traditional approach to provocation, such as we saw in California. It typifies MPC-inspired reform in focusing more on actual culpability and states of mind in lieu of objective criteria in assessing a defendant's culpability. There is some reason to believe, however, that despite the quite significant difference between extreme emotional disturbance formulations and the traditional provocation formulation, the actual practices in the two types of jurisdictions may not differ as much as might be supposed. For example, traditional jurisdictions tend to consider whether defendants are actually provoked at the time they kill, even if they squarely satisfy the statutory criteria for a provocation defence on the basis of external factors.[34] Conversely, defendants who kill in a state of extreme emotional disturbance will not have a defence if there was no reasonable explanation or

---

[34] See W. Lafave, *Criminal Law*, 3rd edn (2000), § 7.10(e).

excuse for their emotional state. What counts as a reasonable explanation or excuse is of course subject to judicial elaboration, but the cases in which judges are apt to find the condition satisfied are likely to resemble those in which the old provocation defence would have held.

The foregoing discussion has examined the central elements that distinguish Type I from Type II murder statutes. We turn now to another crucial distinction among American jurisdictions in their approach to murder, namely that between two different treatments of the line between first and second degree murder. As this distinction does not particularly correlate with the features of our two types of murder statutes we will treat this feature separately.

4. Degrees of Murder

While all American jurisdictions distinguish different degrees of murder, the basis for the distinction varies from state to state. Among states that have retained the traditional 'malice aforethought' definition of the mental state requirement for murder, some states treat *express* malice as itself adequate for first degree murder.[35] Other states have a degree-raising provision that requires the killing to be committed in a particular way or be 'willful, deliberate, and premeditated'.[36] Despite the Model Penal Code's rejection of degrees of murder and New York's idiosyncratic special victims approach to first degree murder, most Type II states still define first degree murder in a separate provision as requiring 'premeditation' or a 'deliberate design' to take the life of another. The usual question that arises in any jurisdiction containing a premeditation provision is whether a defendant who kills intentionally satisfies this element merely by virtue of his intent to kill, or whether a more elaborate plan and advance reflection or deliberation is required for premeditation. The issue is important in cases in which a defendant forms an immediate intention to kill without having deliberated on that intention for a lengthy period of time. A number of jurisdictions do indeed regard intention as sufficient for premeditation, despite the fact that the

---

[35] See *American Jurisprudence* 2d, *Homicide*, § 39 (citing Delaware as one such example). A small number of other states even appear to authorise first degree murder convictions in the absence of premeditation (even interpreted as mere intention) and hold that a killing that is committed by an act 'imminently dangerous to others and evincing a depraved mind . . . without a premeditated design to effect the death of any individual' can still count as first degree murder (see 40 *American Jurisprudence* 2d § 41, citing New Mexico and the state of Washington.

[36] Examples are California, Michigan, Nebraska, Florida and Wyoming. Some states even take the position that first and second degree murder are identical, except that second degree murder signifies the presence of a mitigating factor such as an unreasonable belief in the availability of a justification. See *People v Porter* 168 Ill 2d 201 (1995).

mens rea for murder can be satisfied by intention, and premeditation is a further concept elevating a 'murder' to first degree murder.[37]

In *State v Guthrie*,[38] for example, the defendant was a dishwasher who attacked a teasing co-worker with a knife. Jury instruction number eight said that '[t]o constitute a willful, deliberate and premeditated killing, it is not necessary that the intention to kill should exist for any particular length of time prior to the actual killing; it is only necessary that such intention should have come into existence for the first time at the time of such killing, or at any time previously'. Jury instruction number 10 said that 'in order to constitute a "premeditated" murder an intent to kill need exist only for an instant'. The Supreme Court of West Virginia rejected these instructions, saying that 'there must be some period between the formation of the intent to kill and the actual killing, which indicates the killing is by prior calculation and design'.[39] It went on to explain that there must be 'an opportunity for some reflection on the intention to kill after it is formed'.[40] Other jurisdictions appear to agree.[41]

Despite the rejection of instantaneous premeditation by a number of states, the view of premeditation reflected in the *Guthrie* jury instructions is all too common. California, for example, has consistently endorsed it,[42] and Pennsylvania also appears to accept it,[43] along with other states such as Alaska,[44] Idaho,[45] Iowa, Kansas, Massachusetts, North Carolina, Virginia, Wisconsin and others. There is no particular connection between a jurisdiction's approach to premeditation and its formal criminalisation scheme for murder (ie whether it is Type I or Type II). It bears noting, however, that the chief benefit of a Type II criminalisation scheme, namely the greater precision in mens rea, is at least partially lost if that scheme is combined with a view of premeditation that equates that concept with mere intent. The reason for this should be clear. The Model Penal Code type of scheme distinguishes intent or purpose from knowledge, allowing us to say both that a defendant who intends to kill, but is aware there is a low probability she will succeed in doing so, satisfies the mens rea for murder, and that a defendant who is aware he will kill, without any intention to kill, satisfies that mens rea as well. Defendants who impose a grave risk of death on others satisfy the mens rea for murder only if their killing shows particular indifference to those persons' welfare. If premeditation is satisfied by intent alone, second degree murder will consist only of the smaller category of those who kill knowingly but not intentionally (ie as the by-product of some other

---

[37] See, eg, *Commonwealth v Carrol*, 194 A2d 911 (1963).
[38] *State v Guthrie* 461 SE 2d 163 (1995).
[39] 461 SE 2d 163, 181 (1995).
[40] *Ibid.*
[41] Rhode Island, Massachusetts, Minnesota, Ohio, Florida and Nevada, to name a few.
[42] *People v Anderson* 447 P 2d 942 (1968).
[43] *Commonwealth v Carroll* 194 A 2d 911 (1963).
[44] *Young v State* 428 So. 2d 155 (Ala Crim App 1982).
[45] *State v Phinney* 13 Idaho 307, 89 P 634 (1907).

activity) or those who kill with reckless indifference. But it is far from apparent that all intentional murders are worse than all knowing or reckless indifference murders. This is a point that has been made often enough, but it bears repeating, because many legal actors continue to assume that intentional murder is more morally culpable than any of the other categories.

Consider the defendant who sets out to kill his enemy by throwing a baseball at his head. He realises this method has a low chance of success, but he adopts it anyway, because his enemy lives next to a ball field and the defendant supposes he is more likely to avoid detection if a stray baseball caused the victim's death. Now compare this defendant to one who decides to blow up a bus in order to gain attention for his political causes. He is not guilty of intentional murder, because he really does not care whether anyone is killed. Indeed, he is not guilty of knowing killing, because he does not know whether anyone is on the bus when he blows it up. But he nevertheless satisfies the mens rea for murder, because he behaves with reckless indifference towards the value of human life.[46] As we compare these two defendants, there is little reason to think the former more morally blameworthy than the latter. If anything, the latter defendant seems more blameworthy in his very degree of indifference to whether and how many victims of his attack there may be. Yet the view that equates intention and premeditation would grade the former defendant's offence higher than the latter's, and for no reason other than that he satisfies the mens rea for murder by way of intention rather than knowledge or reckless indifference. Worse, this approach runs the risk of making all murder fall into the category of first degree murder, since arguably even defendants who act with knowledge or reckless indifference acts 'intention- ally' in a broader sense, and only defendants guilty of involuntary manslaughter do not. But since involuntary manslaughter would not satisfy the requirements for murder anyway, all, or nearly all, murders would be first degree, and there would be few to no second degree murders, with the possible exception of felony murder convictions.

On the face of it, the better approach to premeditation is the one that treats that concept as requiring additional planning and reflection over and above the intent to kill or awareness of killing. This additional factor can be spelled out in any number of ways. The most common version of this approach treats premedi- tation as requiring an opportunity for deliberation, where the defendant has a chance to reflect on his plan and either proceed or turn back.

Despite the fact that the advance reflection and deliberation approach makes the concept of premeditation more coherent, there is ample reason to question whether states should not follow the Model Penal Code's lead and eliminate degrees of murder entirely. Most notably, the advance deliberation view of premeditation encounters the difficulty that the worst murders are very often *not*

---

[46] These two examples are discussed in M Keiter, 'With Malice Toward All: The Increased Lethality of Violence Reshapes Transferred Intent and Attempted Murder Law (2003–4) 38 University of Southern Florida Law Rev 261 at 265.

the ones committed with premeditation, under any interpretation of that concept. The grisly California case of *People v Anderson* is a case in point.[47] In *Anderson*, the defendant sexually assaulted the victim, a 10-year-old girl, and then killed her by inflicting over 60 stab wounds on her nude body. On appeal the court found that the defendant's behaviour constituted an 'explosion of violence' rather than a 'preconceived design' and found the evidence accordingly insufficient to support a finding of premeditation. By contrast, a mercy killing in which the defendant killed his terminally ill father with a single gunshot wound to the head was found, in another jurisdiction applying the same criteria, to satisfy the requirements for premeditation and hence for first degree murder.[48] Surely, however, the defendant in Anderson more aptly captures common intuitions of which killers are most deserving of severe punishment, and mercy killers and other intentional killers do not seem to compare in wickedness.

Notice that the foregoing problem is at least somewhat alleviated on the view of premeditation that treats that concept as synonymous with intention, since Anderson might have been found to have acted intentionally but not with advance reflection. But, first, we have seen that this approach has other serious difficulties, such as the fact that it leaves the line between first and second degree murder mysterious. In particular, to make sense of the line between first and second degree murder on this approach we would need to identify a class of murders that are less than fully intentional, and hence qualify for second rather than first degree murder, but that nevertheless satisfy the mental state for murder. We would also need to be convinced that murders of this type were deserving of less punishment than intentional killings, and this might reintroduce the problems we saw with the more standard approach to premeditation. And, secondly, it is not clear that all killers of Anderson's ilk will always be shown to have killed intentionally, so they may not meet the requirements for premeditation even under this second approach.

An entirely different approach would reject premeditation as a basis for distinguishing first from second degree murder, and treat objective factors as establishing the category of first degree murder instead. Thus, as we have seen, New York homicide law defines murder in the first degree as intentional killing where the victim is a police officer or an employee of a state or local correctional facility, or where the crime is committed while the defendant is in custody or serving a life sentence.[49] Ordinary premeditated murder remains murder in the second degree. Once again, however, it is unclear whether this approach captures common intuitions about what constitutes the worst murders. Is the murder of a police officer *always* worse, and deserving of more punishment, than any murder of any ordinary citizen, no matter how wanton or cruel the latter might be? While

---

[47]   447 P2d 942 (1968).
[48]   *State v Forrest*, 362 SE 2d 252 (NC 1987).
[49]   NY Pen Law § 125.27 Murder in the First Degree.

presumably it makes sense from a deterrence standpoint to offer special protection to police officers and other legal officials, it is not clear that such treatment can be justified on retributive grounds.

5. Conclusion

The greatest reason to favour statutes in the Model Penal Code mode, which this Chapter has dubbed 'Type II statutes', is their improvement in clarity in mental states and the corresponding improvement in defining types of homicide corresponding to those mental states. As we saw in considering New York's penal law, not all states that adopt the MPC's basic approach to mental states have consistently applied those fine-grained distinctions in revising their homicide provisions. The improvement in precision gained by adopting the MPC gradations in mental state is obviously limited by whether these gradations are consistently applied in structuring particular offences. Once the MPC approach to mental states is accepted, however, the related concepts in homicide law tend to follow naturally. As we have also seen, once a jurisdiction adopts the MPC formulations of mental state and the corresponding categories in homicide law, there is a strong pull towards distinguishing premeditation sharply from intent. For it muddies the waters considerably, once a jurisdiction has adopted the fine-grained approach to mental states, to treat premeditation as coextensive with intention. But the traditional view of premeditation as requiring advance deliberation often fails to comport with our intuitions about moral culpability. Aligning the category of first degree murder with the killings that reflect greatest moral turpitude is a significant challenge for any jurisdiction that identifies degrees of murder.

6. The Classification of State Jurisdictions

What follows is an attempt broadly to classify jurisdictions into the two categories discussed above, which this Chapter has called 'Type I' and 'Type II'. This list is a rough and ready classification, and some might disagree with the classifications suggested here. Please note that this list includes only the 50 American states, and omits American territories or other American jurisdictions.

(A) The following is a list of jurisdictions that can be classified as 'Type I' statutes, meaning that they have retained the common law definition in broad outlines: California, District of Columbia, Florida, Illinois, Idaho, Iowa, Kansas, Mississippi, Montana, Nevada, New Mexico, Oklahoma, Rhode Island, South Carolina.

(B) The following is a list of jurisdictions that can be classified as 'Type II' statutes, meaning that they broadly follow the New York or MPC model: Alabama, Arizona, Arkansas, Colorado, Connecticut, Hawaii, Indiana, Kentucky, Maine, New Hampshire, New Jersey, New York, North Dakota, Oregon, Pennsylvania, Texas, Utah.

(C) Jurisdictions containing a mix of elements from the above categories are: Alaska, Delaware, Georgia, Louisiana, Maryland, Massachusetts, Michigan, Minnesota, Nebraska, Ohio,
South Dakota, Tennessee.

(D) Jurisdictions with no discernible pattern are: North Carolina, Missouri, Vermont, Washington, West Virginia, Wisconsin, Wyoming.

6

Murder and Related Issues: An Analysis of the Law in Canada

WINIFRED H HOLLAND

1. Murder[1]

(i) An Overview[2]

UNDER THE CANADIAN Constitution[3] criminal law is a matter within federal legislative competence, and so, unlike the US or Australia, Canada has one uniform system of criminal law that applies across the country.[4]

The homicide provisions are found within Part VIII of the *Criminal Code*[5] and section 229, which defines murder, provides:

Culpable homicide is murder

---

[1] Manslaughter and other related offences, including causing death by criminal negligence, dangerous driving causing death and impaired driving causing death are outside the scope of this Chapter.

[2] www.canlii.org is a very useful website which permits free access to Canadian legislation (federal and provincial) and decisions from all provinces.

[3] Constitution Act, 1867 (UK), 30 & 21 Vict, c 3, reprinted in RSC 1985, App II, No 5, s 91(27), (formerly The British North America Act).

[4] The provinces can create *regulatory* offences and can impose penal consequences (*ibid* s 92), but cannot create 'criminal' offences.

[5] Part VIII of the *Criminal Code*, RSC 1985 C C-46, as amended. All references to s numbers are to ss of the *Criminal Code* (unless otherwise indicated). Part VIII 'Offences Against the Person and Reputation' includes the s on 'Homicide'. That s includes a definition of 'culpable homicide'; the poorly drafted causation provisions; the ss dealing with murder; manslaughter (all culpable homicide that is not murder or infanticide) and infanticide and a s defining first degree murder. It also includes the offence of killing an unborn child in the act of birth (s 238), and separate provisions dealing with attempts to commit murder (s 239) and accessory after the fact to murder (s 240), both necessitated because of the increased punishment for such offences (maximum of life imprisonment). Other provisions dealing with the parole eligibility for first and second degree murder are found in Part XXII of the *Code* on 'Sentencing'.

(a) where the person who causes the death of a human being

(i) means to cause his death, or

(ii) means to cause him bodily harm that he knows is likely to cause his death and is reckless whether death ensues or not;

(b) where a person meaning to cause death to a human being or meaning to cause him bodily harm that he knows is likely to cause his death, and being reckless whether death ensues or not, by accident or mistake causes death to another human being, notwithstanding that he does not mean to cause death or bodily harm to that human being; or

(c) where a person, for an unlawful object, does anything that he knows or ought to know is likely to cause death, and thereby causes death to a human being, notwithstanding that he desires to effect his object without causing death or bodily harm to any human being.

A conviction for murder under section 229 carries a mandatory sentence of life imprisonment (section 235(1)). In the case of first degree murder there is no parole eligibility for 25 years[6] (subject to section 745.6(1) which permits the possibility of judicial review of the parole ineligibility period after 15 years).[7] In the case of second degree murders (all murders which are not first degree) the period of parole ineligibility is anywhere from 10 to 25 years.[8]

(ii) Proof of Culpable Homicide

Section 229 is rather tortuous in that it requires proof of culpable homicide as a necessary first step in establishing murder ('culpable homicide is murder where . . .').[9] If culpable homicide has been established, but the Crown cannot prove that the accused had the requisite intent for murder, then the accused will be convicted of manslaughter.[10]

Culpable homicide is dealt with in the *Code* in sections 222 to 228. A person commits culpable homicide when he causes the death of a human being in one of the ways specified in section 225(5). In the vast majority of cases the subsections relied on are 222(5)(a) 'by means of an unlawful act' or (b) 'by criminal negligence'.[11] While those sections are of key significance in manslaughter cases, they do not play a major role in the vast majority of murder cases, since there is

---

[6] S 745(a).

[7] That possibility does not apply in the case of multiple murders where the period of parole ineligibility cannot be reviewed (s 745.6(2)).

[8] *Code*, ss 235 and 745. The period is determined by the judge (s 745.4) but he or she must give the jury the option of recommending the requisite period. The jury is not obliged to make a recommendation, and if it does make one, the judge is not obliged to follow it.

[9] It follows the English Draft Code of 1879.

[10] S 234. The third, and rarely encountered form of culpable homicide, infanticide, is defined in s 233. It is discussed in more detail below.

[11] S 222(5)(c) and (d) are seldom used ((c) causing death by threats, fear of violence or deception and (d) wilfully frightening children or sick persons).

usually no problem in establishing that death was caused by an unlawful act[12] and the most contentious issue is whether the accused possessed the requisite mens rea.

The issue of causation, however, does deserve brief mention. The culpable homicide provisions speak of 'causing the death[13] of a human being'[14] and the *Code*, without attempting to define causation, contains a number of poorly drafted examples of causation in action (sections 224–228). Because these provisions are poorly drafted, and even tautologous, courts have tended to ignore them and have developed their own rules on causation.[15] The general rule, which applies to all homicide cases, is that a person causes a death when his conduct can be described as 'outside the *de minimis* range' in relation to the death of the victim. That rule, described in one case as a 'sweeping rule of accountability',[16] has been challenged as contrary to section 7 of the *Charter*. However, in a recent decision, *Nette*, the Supreme Court by a five to four majority affirmed the rule but indicated that it was preferable that the rule be reworded so as to require that the act be a 'significant contributing cause' in relation to the death. The majority specifically disavowed any intention to alter the law, and indicated it was simply making the rule easier for jurors to understand by avoiding Latin expressions, and by expressing the rule positively rather than negatively. A minority of the court was of the view that the redrafting meant a change in substance and that the rewording would be interpreted as creating a more stringent rule on causation. It seems clear, especially following the clarification of the rules in *Nette*, that the causation rules in England and Canada are relatively similar in their application.[17]

There is, however, a more stringent causation rule (the '*Harbottle* rule') which applies *only* to parties to first degree murder within section 231(5).[18] It is first degree murder under section 231(5) where the murder is 'caused by that person'

---

[17] Theoretically culpable homicide caused by criminal negligence could be used as a foundation for murder, but in practice is extremely unlikely to do so. One example might be that of a parent who withholds necessaries of life in order to kill a dependent child. Incidentally this would also involve an unlawful act (failure to provide necessaries under s 215).

[13] S 222(1): A person commits homicide when, directly or indirectly, by any means, he causes the death of a human being.

[14] 'Human being' is defined in s 223—the child must have proceeded in a living state from its mother but it is immaterial whether it has breathed, has an independent circulation or the navel string has been severed. The archaic language used indicates the vintage of this provision. It is homicide when a person causes injury to a child before or during its birth if the child dies of the injury after becoming a human being: s 223(2).

[15] See *Smithers v R* [1978] 1 SCR 506, but note that more recently in *Nette* [2001] 3 SCR 488 the Supreme Court emphasised that courts should be applying both statutory and common law rules.

[16] *R. v F(DL)* (1989), 73 CR (3d) 391 (Alta CA).

[17] The 'thin-skull' rule is alive and well in Canada: see *Smithers*, n 15 above, and it was approved more recently in *Creighton* [1993] 3 SCR 3 (SCC) and survived a *Charter* challenge in *Cribbin* (1994) 89 CCC (3d) 67 (Ont CA). While there are no cases similar to the English decision in *Blaue* [1975] 1 WLR 1411 (Eng CA) on the refusal by a Jehovah's Witness to have a blood transfusion, it is assumed that the finding would be similar.

[18] *Harbottle* [1993] 3 SCR 306. It will also apply under s 231(6) which is worded similarly.

while committing or attempting to commit one of a list of enumerated offences (including kidnapping and sexual assault), and the Supreme Court held that the Crown must establish that the actions of the accused were a 'substantial and integral cause of death'. To be liable for first degree murder (with ensuing ineligibility for parole for 25 years) the accused will usually have had actual physical contact with the victim. In *Harbottle*, for example, the accused held the legs of the victim while his co-accused strangled her. It was held that his participation was sufficient to render the party liable for first degree murder (section 214(5), now section 231(5)). On the other hand if he had simply kept watch at the door or sat in a getaway car he would have been guilty only of second degree murder.[19]

(iii) The Impact of the *Charter*[20] on Murder: The Supreme Court strikes down 'Felony Murder'

Prior to the Supreme Court of Canada's decisions in *Vallaincourt*[21] and *Martineau*[22] there were two separate *Code* provisions dealing with murder: the present section 229 (formerly section 212) and another section dealing with 'felony murder'[23] (section 230, formerly section 213), but those decisions resulted in the striking down of the 'felony murder' provisions of the *Code*, leaving only what is now section 229.

In *Vaillancourt* the Court considered the constitutionality of section 213(d) which provided that it was murder where the accused caused the death during the course of one of the listed triggering offences (or subsequent flight after commission), the *accused used a weapon or had it upon his person, and death ensued as a consequence*. The Court found that section 213(d) infringed section 7 of the *Charter*[24] and the government was unsuccessful in its attempt to have the section upheld under section 1.[25] Under the impugned subsection, an accused

---

[19] There are dicta suggesting that both could have been convicted of first degree murder under s 231(2) (planned and deliberate murder) even though the decision to kill the victim was formed quite shortly before her death.

[20] *Canadian Charter of Rights and Freedoms*, Part I of the *Constitution Act*, 1982, being Sched B to the Canada Act 1982 (UK), c 11.

[21] [1987] 2 SCR 636, 39 CCC (3d) 118.

[22] [1990] 2 SCR 633, 58 CCC (3d) 353.

[23] This is a nickname because Canada has never used the felony/misdemeanour distinction.

[24] S 7 provides: '[e]veryone has the right to life, liberty and security of the person and the right not to be deprived thereof except in accordance with the principles of fundamental justice'. In the *BC Motor Vehicle Reference case (Reference re s 94(2) of the Motor Vehicle Act (BC)* [1985] 2 SCR 486, one of the most important decisions ever delivered by the Court, the Supreme Court had decided that s 7 permitted substantive review of legislation and it was not confined to a review of procedural issues. In *Vallaincourt* the Court also found a violation of s 11(d) of the *Charter* (the presumption of innocence).

[25] S 1 provides: 'The Canadian Charter of Rights and Freedoms guarantees the rights and freedoms set out in it subject only to such reasonable limits prescribed by law as can be demonstrably justified in a free and democratic society'. The onus is on the government to justify infringement of

could be convicted of murder in the absence of objective foresight of death, a principle that the Court considered to be a fundamental principle of criminal liability. Following that decision there was a cosmetic repeal of the subsection in 1991, and it no longer appears in the *Code*.

In its subsequent decision in *Martineau* the Supreme Court considered another of the 'felony murder' subsections, now still printed in the *Code* as section 230(a) (formerly section 213(a)). Under that provision it was murder where the accused 'means to cause bodily harm for the purpose of facilitating the commission' of one of the triggering offences (or flight afterwards). That, too, was found to be contrary to the *Charter*. A majority of the Court went even further than it was prepared to go in *Vaillancourt,* and held that *subjective* foresight of death is a constitutional requirement for murder, and a provision defining murder as requiring anything less than that level of mens rea was unconstitutional, and could not be saved under section 1.[26] Since those Supreme Court decisions the felony murder sections of the *Code* have been a dead letter but, because they have never been repealed by Parliament, they are still printed in the *Code*, which must create confusion for anyone who happens to read it.

The *Charter* has also had an impact on other murder provisions. For example what is now section 229(c) (formerly section 212(c)) (discussed in more detail below) was used quite frequently during the 1980s prior to the decisions in *Vaillancourt* and *Martineau.* However, since the Supreme Court had held in *Martineau* that murder requires proof of subjective foresight of death then section 229(c), which contains the words 'ought to know', was clearly problematic and in *Martineau* the Court had indicated that its reasoning cast serious, if not fatal, doubt on the objective portion of section 229(c). It was unclear whether that rendered the whole section suspect, but in *Meiler*[27] the Ontario Court of Appeal held that the objective portion of the section ('ought to know') was unconstitutional, but otherwise upheld the section. Thus section 229(c) now requires proof of an unlawful object, and that the accused did something that *he knew* was likely to cause death and thereby caused death, notwithstanding that he did not desire that death.

The *Charter* has also played a significant role in interpreting the first degree murder provisions (section 231).[28]

Charter rights. The key decision on the point is *Oakes* [1986] 1 SCR 103. There have been innumerable appeals to the Supreme Court on the interpretation of this ruling. A detailed consideration of the ruling is outside the scope of this Ch.

  [26] See also *Sit* [1991] 3 SCR 124, 66 CCC (3d) 449.

  [27] (1999), 136 CCC (3d) 11 (Ont CA).

  [28] Discussed in more detail below.

(iv) The Mens Rea of Murder under Section 229

(a) Section 229(a)(i): Means to Cause Death

This subsection covers the paradigm case of murder where the accused's purpose was to cause the death of the victim. Since the accused's motive for killing the victim is irrelevant, 'mercy killing'[29] is included in this section, along with the most vicious and depraved murders. The section speaks of meaning to cause 'his death' which seems to assume the existence of a particular victim (transferred intent is addressed in section 229(b)). However this section must surely also cover the case of the terrorist who plants a bomb hoping to cause the death of anyone caught in the ensuing explosion.

English courts have been grappling over the past 40 to 50 years with the requisite intent for murder, stretching from the notorious decision in *DPP v Smith*[30] to the more recent decisions in *Moloney, Hancock, Nedrick* and *Woollin*.[31] Canadian courts, on the other hand, seem to have given the matter much less consideration (perhaps not surprisingly, given that there is an extended definition of murder under section 229(a)(ii) (discussed below)) and as a consequence the mental element under section 229(a)(i) has not been the subject of extensive discussion.

Does this subsection include other mental states, for example 'oblique intent', where consequences are foreseen as virtually certain but were not desired by the accused? In other contexts Canadian courts have approved of the use of 'oblique intent', for example under the section dealing with promotion of racial hatred,[32] but the issue does not appear to have arisen in the context of murder. However, it seems generally assumed that the classic bomb in the aeroplane, where the accused wanted to collect insurance proceeds but hoped not to kill the crew when the bomb exploded in flight, would be found to have the requisite intent for

---

[29] *Latimer* [2001] 1 SCR 3 (discussed in more detail below, in sect 4(ii)(b)). There has been much criticism of the failure to acknowledge the acceptability of some forms of euthanasia (see eg the Special Senate Committee on Euthanasia and Assisted Suicide, *Of Life and Death* (Ottawa, 1995) advocating a new offence of compassionate homicide.

[30] [1961] AC 290.

[31] *Moloney* [1985] AC 905, [1985] 1 All ER 1025 (HL); *Hancock* [1986] AC 455, [1986] 2 WLR 357 (HL); *Nedrick* [1986] 1 WLR 1025, (1986) 83 Cr App R 267 (CA); *Woollin* [1999] 1 AC 82, [1998] 3 WLR 382 (HL).

[32] *Buzzanga and Durocher* (1979) 49 CCC (2d) 369 (Ont CA). Wilfully promoting hatred included the situation where accused foresaw that the promotion of hatred was certain or morally certain to result from distribution of a pamphlet. It was applied in *Chartrand* (1994) 31 CR (4th) 1 (SCC). Although Canadian courts have acknowledged the legitimacy of 'oblique intent', there are no Canadian authorities exploring whether the accused himself must be aware of the inevitability of the consequences.

murder.[33] It can certainly be argued that a doctor who administers large quantities of medication for the immediate purpose of relieving the patient's suffering and who knows that the drugs will certainly hasten death, should be held to have intended the death, though one would anticipate that prosecutorial discretion would play a significant role in such cases.

Under Canadian law, one issue that deserves mention in the context of proof of intent is that of the so-called 'rolled-up charge' where multiple defences have been raised by the accused, most commonly self-defence, intoxication and provocation. The jury may reject each individual defence but should it still consider the *cumulative* effect of all of them on the issue of whether the accused had the requisite intent for murder?[34] This argument has an impact on both section 229 (a)(i) and section 229(a)(ii) but is best considered after a discussion of defences to murder. That issue is clearly related to the issue of proof of intent but is better dealt with after consideration of the defences to murder.

(b) Section 229(a)(ii): Means to Cause him Bodily bodily harm that he knows is likely to cause his death, and is reckless whether death ensues or not

This subsection has proved more problematic than that discussed above. It is awkwardly expressed and its meaning is not clear. Cory J in *Nygaard*[35] states that the culpability scale between what are now section 229(a)(i) and (ii) 'varies so little as to be indistinguishable'. In both *Nygaard* and *Cooper* (below) Cory J opined that the part of the section that refers to recklessness is redundant, because once it is established that the accused intentionally caused bodily harm, knowing that death was likely, then almost inevitably it will be found that the accused was reckless about the ensuing death.

In *Cooper*[36] the accused became angry with the deceased, grabbed her by the throat with both hands and shook her. He said he could recall nothing after that until he awoke in his car and found her body beside him (he had consumed a considerable quantity of alcohol). The Supreme Court held that the requisite mens rea for murder under section 212(a)(ii) (now section 229(a)(ii)) represents only a slight relaxation of the mens rea for intentional killing. There must be subjective intent to cause bodily harm, and subjective knowledge that the bodily harm is of such a nature that it is *likely* to result in death. While the mens rea

---

[33] See, eg, D Stuart, *Canadian Criminal Law*, 4th edn (Toronto, 2001) at 219 who, while accepting that this would constitute intention, doubts the value of a concept such as 'foresight of certainty' which in his opinion is an unnecessarily complicated and esoteric adjunct to the comprehensible concept of intention.

[34] See, eg, *Nealy* (1986) 30 CCC (3d) 460 (Ont CA), approved obiter in *Robinson* [1996] 1 SCR 683 (SCC). This is discussed more fully at the conclusion of sect 4(iii).

[35] [1989] 2 SCR 1074.

[36] [1993] 1 SCR 146, 78 CCC (3d) 289.

must be concurrent with the impugned act, it is not always necessary for the act and the intent to be completely concurrent. Where there is a series of wrongful acts resulting in death, it is sufficient that the mens rea at some point coincides with the acts. Nor was it necessary for the Crown to establish that the intent persisted throughout the entire act of strangulation. (Lamer J, dissenting, was of the view that intentionally choking someone for a few seconds might not fall within the section since there was no intention to cause death, or to cause harm that he knew was likely to cause death, particularly in a case where alcohol played a role).

Situations of pure recklessness, for example driving at 100 kph along a busy street knowing that pedestrians are exposed to serous risk, fall outside the murder provisions because there is no intent to cause harm (as required by this subsection), and even if oblique intent can be utilised, the consequence is not practically certain to result. But what of the terrorist who places a bomb and gives notice of it, intending to cause panic, alarm and confusion but with the expectation that it will be disarmed before it explodes? What if the bomb explodes unexpectedly thereby killing bystanders—is he guilty of murder? He certainly falls outside section 229(a)(i), but what of (ii)? There may well be a problem in convicting him under section 229(a)(ii) because he did not have the intent to cause bodily harm, and even if oblique intent were argued, it may be doubtful whether bodily harm was certain or virtually certain to result. In any event it might be simpler to use section 229(c) (below) in such a situation.

Is murder ever appropriate in cases involving transmission of HIV? What about the accused who is HIV positive and has been warned not to have sex without informing his partners of his status and that he must never have unprotected sex? What if he goes ahead anyway, and infects the victim who subsequently dies? These cases are certainly problematic and there is no easy solution. Prosecutions have been brought under a number of provisions including criminal negligence causing bodily harm, sexual assault, aggravated assault and so on,[37] with the courts being forced to shoe-horn a new problem into existing offences. Because of the difficulties in establishing mens rea, it has generally been the view that murder or attempted murder charges would not be successful in this situation. However, just recently, and somewhat surprisingly, the accused, Azega, who knowingly infected two women who subsequently died of AIDS, has been charged with first degree murder. Since it is unlikely that the

---

[37] In *Cuerrier* [1998] 2 SCR 371, the Supreme Court approved of the use of aggravated assault (assault that inter alia endangers life) reasoning that the complainant's consent had been vitiated by the non-disclosure of the accused's status, which was found to constitute fraud. The later Supreme Court decision in *Williams* (2003) 176 CCC (3d) 449 (SCC) illustrates some of the difficulties in this area. The accused was charged with aggravated assault (assault endangering life). The Crown could not establish that the transmission occurred after the accused was aware of his status (the relationship existed both before and after he was tested and, if transmission occurred before he was aware of being HIV positive, then the Crown could not establish the concurrence of actus reus and mens rea) and the solution was to enter a conviction for *attempted* aggravated assault.

accused intended to kill the women, it is assumed that the Crown will be relying on section 229(a)(ii)—but even that seems problematic. It seems doubtful whether he intended to cause bodily harm—and even the use of oblique intent in this situation also presents problems, given that the consequence (the bodily harm by transmission of the virus) was not virtually certain to occur, nor is it likely that the Crown will be able to establish that the accused had foresight of *death*. On numerous occasions, and for a number of reasons, the trial in this case has been delayed. As of June 2007, the prediction is that it will commence in the autumn of this year.

The subsection requires proof that the accused knew that the bodily harm was 'likely' to cause death, and such terms are likely to tempt judges to go into a detailed explanation of degrees of probability. As far as directions to the jury are concerned, the best advice seems to be to stick as closely as possible to the actual words used in the subsection. Efforts to explain what is meant by 'likely' may well provide a ground of appeal and are best avoided.[38]

In *Nygaard and Schimmens*,[39] the Supreme Court held that what is now section 229(a)(ii) can be used in conjunction with section 231(2) so that this second type of murder can constitute first degree murder that is 'planned and deliberate'. The two accused had planned and executed a vicious attack on the victim with a baseball bat, knowing full well it could result in his death, and it was held that intention to carry out such an assault leading to the victim's death could constitute a planned and deliberate first degree murder.

(c) Section 229(b): Transferred Intent

Culpable homicide is murder:

> (b) where a person meaning to cause death to a human being or meaning to cause him bodily harm that he knows is likely to cause his death, and being reckless whether death ensues or not, by accident or mistake causes death to another human being, notwithstanding that he does not mean to cause death or bodily harm to that human being.

This is one of the few *Code* provisions that expressly recognise transferred intent, although the courts have also recognised the common law doctrine of 'transferred malice'.[40]

The section covers both accidental and mistaken deaths. A shoots at B but hits C instead and also A shoots at B thinking he is C. In *Droste*[41] the accused, intending to kill his wife, soaked the inside of the car with gasoline. A fire started

---

[38] See, eg, *Edelenbos* (2004) 187 CCC (3d) 465 (Ont CA)(although no prejudice was shown in the particular facts of the case); *Dove* (2004) 187 CCC (3d) 506 (BC CA).

[39] Above n 35.

[40] *Deakin* (1974) 16 CCC (2d) 1 (Man CA) and approved obiter in *Droste* (No 2) (1984) 10 CCC (3d) 404 (SCC).

[41] *Ibid.*

and their two children were killed but he and the wife survived. He was convicted of the first degree murder of the children. This situation is clearly within section 229(b) and so D was certainly guilty of murder, but was it first degree murder on the basis that it was 'planned and deliberate'? The Supreme Court agreed that it was. Dickson J for the majority relied on the Court's earlier decision in *Farrant*[42] that section 231 (the first degree murder section) is only a sentence-classifying provision and that the distinction between first and second degree murder is not based on intent. It did not matter that he had planned the death of the wife, not the children—it was simply a matter of statutory construction and there was no need to apply the common law doctrine of transferred intent (though, obiter, the court approved of its use had it been necessary to resort to it).

Is section 229(b) applicable where A intending to kill *himself*, by accident or mistake kills another? In *Fontaine*[43] the accused, intending to commit suicide, deliberately drove his car with three passengers into a parked trailer, killing one and injuring the other passengers. On appeal it was held that the section does not apply in this situation because the intention to commit suicide carries a lesser moral blameworthiness than the intention to kill another (attempted suicide is not even an offence) and the two situations are so different that this should not be encompassed within section 229(b).

(d) Section 229(c): Unlawful Object Murder

Culpable homicide is murder:

> (c) where a person, for an unlawful object, does anything that he knows or ought to know is likely to cause death, and thereby causes death to a human being, notwith-standing that he desires to effect his object without causing death or bodily harm to any human being.

This section, formerly used with some regularity, has for the time being fallen out of favour. It is based on the English Draft Code of 1878 and has been in *Code* since 1892, with only some cosmetic changes.

The leading decision on this subsection is *Vasil*.[44] In that case the accused, a chronic alcoholic, was convicted of murder following the deaths of two children of the woman with whom he was living. Following an argument between the two of them at a party, the accused had returned home, taken the babysitter home and then returned to spread lighter fluid throughout the house before setting it on fire, thus causing the death of the children. He said his objective was to destroy the woman's property. The Supreme Court held:

1. Under this subsection the element of unlawfulness necessary to qualify a

---

[42] [1983] 1 SCR 124.
[43] (2002) 162 CCC (3d) 360 (Man CA), rejecting *Brown* (1983) 4 CCC (3d) 571 (Ont HC).
[44] [1978] 1 SCR 469; (1981) 58 CCC 97.

homicide as culpable is that which is the result of the prosecution of the unlawful object by an act which is dangerous to life;

2. There is no requirement that the dangerous act be itself unlawful (though it usually is);

3. When the dangerous act is unlawful the jury must be told that there must be the prosecution of a *further* unlawful object clearly distinct from the immediate object of the dangerous act;

4. '[U]nlawful object' means the object of conduct which, if prosecuted fully, would amount to a serious crime (for example, an indictable offence requiring mens rea). (Lamer J did not make it clear whether this could cover offences where mens rea is determined objectively, although it seems more likely that he had in mind offences requiring proof of subjective mens rea). In this case the unlawful object would be the destruction of property (mischief is an indictable offence under what is now section 430 of the *Code*) and the 'dangerous act' would be resorting to the use of fire to accomplish his objective (although this was not essential, this was also an unlawful act).

5. Although section 212(c) (as it then was) was based on an objective assessment of potential consequences, it was based on a subjective test as far as the accused's knowledge of circumstances was concerned. Thus if the accused were intoxicated that should be taken into consideration in determining the accused's knowledge of the actual circumstances particularly the presence of the children.

Following the Supreme Court's decision in *Martineau*[45] it was clear that section 229(c) was problematic. In that decision the Court adverted to subsection (c), and indicated that its reasoning on the constitutionally mandated principle of subjective foresight of death cast serious, if not fatal, doubt on the constitutionality of the objective wording in the subsection.

In *Meiler*[46] the accused wanted to kill his estranged wife's boyfriend, and he went to a party with a loaded and cocked shotgun. After a scuffle in an attempt to disarm him, the gun discharged and a third party was killed. On M's appeal from his second degree murder conviction, the Ontario Court of Appeal held that there could be murder within this subsection even if a different victim was killed and not the one intended. As long as the accused had subjective awareness of the likelihood of someone's death there was no need to show that the intended victim was killed. This is obviously an extension of transferred intent within section 229(b) (which only applies where the accused does act intending to kill A and B is killed), whereas in the present case the gun discharged accidentally.

It would appear that this section might be used in the case of a terrorist bombing in a situation where it might be difficult to prove the mens rea required under section 229(a). Under section 229(c) there is no need to prove an intention

---

[45] N 22 above.
[46] (1999) 136 CCC (3d) 11 (Ont CA).

to kill or to cause bodily harm, and all that is required is proof of an unlawful object coupled with subjective *foresight* of death. Thus recklessness is enough for murder if the activity takes part in the furtherance of an unlawful object (but this is different from the old 'felony murder' provisions which did not require proof of subjective foresight of death).

At the present time there is little evidence that this section is being invoked with any regularity and it appears to have fallen out of favour. However, if an appropriate case presented itself—and terrorist bombings might well provide the necessary catalyst for its revival[47]—it could be used in cases where it is difficult to establish mens rea under section 229(a).

(v) Sentencing and Parole Eligibility

(a) Overview

In 1976 capital punishment was abolished and replaced with mandatory life sentences for high treason and first and second degree murder. Parole eligibility requirements were also established at that time; in the case of first degree murder there is an automatic 25-year period of parole ineligibility.[48] For second degree murder the minimum period of parole ineligibility is 10 years and it may be anywhere from 10 to 25 years.[49] The precise period of ineligibility is determined by the trial judge,[50] who may take into account any jury recommendations on the appropriate length.[51] Even after the accused is eligible to apply for it, parole may not be granted and the parole board will consider the risks to the public in releasing the accused. If successful in securing parole the accused is still subject to parole conditions and parole will be revoked if the accused violates those conditions or commits a new offence.

A life sentence can be broken down into three stages:

1. Ineligibility to apply for parole (which varies depending on whether the accused was convicted of first or second degree murder).
2. Eligibility to apply for parole which is not necessarily granted, and if granted is likely to be in stages – temporary absence then day parole, before full parole.

---

[47] Most situations, including those similar to the recent London bombings, could be addressed under s 229(a)(i) or (ii) since there is undoubtedly an intent (direct or oblique) to kill, or at the very least to inflict serious injury. It can be argued that in such situations recklessness about death should suffice for a murder conviction.

[48] S 745(a). This is subject to judicial review after 15 years (s 745.6(1)) (the 'faint hope clause') except in the case of multiple murders (s 745.6(2)). If granted by the review judge the application then goes to a jury (s 745.61(5)).

[49] S 745(b).

[50] S 745.2.

[51] *Code*, ss 235 and 745. The period is determined by the judge (s 745.4) but he/she must give the jury the option of recommending the requisite period. They are not obliged to make a recommendation and if they do make one the judge is not obliged to follow it.

3. The final period after parole when the accused is still subject to parole conditions.

As far as murder statistics are concerned,[52] murders count for around 3 per cent each year of total admissions to federal jails but they accumulate because of the long periods that murderers are required to serve. On 31 March 2002 there were 3,721 murderers under federal jurisdiction. 2,360 were actually incarcerated for murder and 1,361 were on some form of parole (1,182 on full parole). Most offenders (78 per cent) had been convicted of second degree murder.

(b) Section 231: First Degree Murder[53]

The following constitute first degree murder within section 231:

1. Planned and deliberate murders.[54]

The section includes planning a serious assault under section 229(a)(ii)[55] where the accused knew that the attack was likely to result in death and also includes a murder based on transferred intent within section 229(b) (accused intended to kill his wife but his plan caused the deaths of his children instead).[56]

2. Murder for consideration—murder by contract.[57]
3. Murder of a peace officer, prison guard, warden (and other similar officials).[58]

(The accused must be aware of the person's status (*Collins*)[59] but that almost certainly includes wilful blindness.)

---

[52] The National Parole Board, *Offenders Serving a Life Sentence for Murder: A Statistical Overview* (Ottawa, November 2002), available at **http://www.npb-cnlc.gc.ca/reports/pdf/pls_2002_e.pdf**.

[53] D Stuart, *Canadian Criminal Law*, 4th edn (Toronto, 2001) at 242 criticises the Canadian adoption of degrees of murder.

[54] The courts have adopted a restrictive interpretation. In *More* [1963] 2 SCR 522 for the majority Cartwright J held that both planning and deliberation must be established and both required proof of premeditation. As Culliton JA said in *Smith* (1979), 51 CCC (2d) 381 (Sask CA), '[c]learly, planning must not be confused with intention as the planning would only occur after the intent to murder had been formed. There must be some evidence the killing was the result of a scheme or design previously formulated or designed by the accused and the killing was the implementation of that scheme or design. It is obvious a murder committed on a sudden impulse and without prior consideration, even though the intent to kill is clearly proven, would not constitute a planned murder.' However the Supreme Court stated, obiter, that a murder might have been 'planned and deliberate' in a case where the intent was formed very shortly before the plan was carried out (*Harbottle*, n 18 above).

[55] *Nygaard and Schimmens*(1989) 51 CCC (3d) 417 (SCC).

[56] *Droste*, n 40 above.

[57] S 231(3).

[58] S 231(4).

[59] (1989) 32 OAC 296 (Ont CA). This ruling, although understandable, seems contrary to the Supreme Court's decision in *Farrant* above which held that s 231 is a sentencing classification provision and does not create a separate offence of first degree. The finding that s 231(4) requires proof of subjective mens rea seems contrary to that conclusion.

4. Murder[60] caused[61] in the course of committing or attempting to commit one of the named offences: hijacking an aircraft, sexual assault,[62] aggravated forms of sexual assault, kidnapping and forcible confinement,[63] or hostage taking.[64]

5. Murder committed during or while attempting to commit

   (i) an offence under section 264 (criminal harassment), where the person committing the offence intended to cause the person murdered to fear for the safety of the person murdered, or the safety of anyone known to the person murdered;[65]

   (ii) an indictable offence where the offence also constitutes a 'terrorist activity' (defined in section 83.01);

   (iii) an offence under section 81 (use of explosives) for the benefit of, or under the direction of, or in association with, a criminal organisation;[66]

   (iv) an offence under section 423.1 (intimidation of a justice system participant or a journalist)).[67]

All of the subsections noted in this paragraph were added relatively recently (between 1997 and 2002).

---

[60] S 231(5). This subsection was challenged, unsuccessfully, under s 7 of the Charter on the basis of a lack of a coherent underlying rationale. *Arkell* [1990] 2 SCR 695: ('Parliament's decision to treat more seriously murders that have been committed while the offender is exploiting a position of power through illegal domination of the victims accords with the principle that there must be a proportionality between a sentence and the moral blameworthiness of the offender').

[61] See *Harbottle*, n 18 above: 'murder caused by that person' includes a party to the murder but only if the actions of the accused were a substantial and integral cause of the death.

[62] Contemporaneity can be problematic. If it is clear from the evidence that the victim was already dead before the 'sexual assault' began, there cannot be a sexual assault on a dead victim and it would only constitute interference with a dead body. However in many cases the sexual assault may be seen to be part of one continuing transaction with some acts occurring before and others immediately after the death. See, eg, *Westergard* (2004) 185 OAC 281 (Ont CA).

[63] Confinement may occur in the course of the commission of another offence, eg robbery, though robbery is not necessarily accompanied by confinement: *Hein* (2004), 189 CCC (3d) 381 (Sask CA).

[64] *Russell* [2001] 2 SCR 804. The accused sexually assaulted X and then beat and killed Y, another occupant of the house. The Supreme Court held that s 231(5) applies even where the victim of the murder and the victim of the enumerated offence are not the same.

[65] The s reflects Parliament's intent to restrict this s to those who murder the victim being harassed: dicta in *Russell* (above at para 34).

[66] 'Criminal Organization' is defined in s 467.1(1)—a group of three or more persons which has as its main purpose or main activity the facilitation or commission of one or more serious offences that if committed would likely result in receipt of a material benefit by the group or individuals in the group. It was passed primarily because of problems arising from a turf war over drugs between biker gangs in Quebec where use of a car bomb led to the death of a young child.

[67] Passed because of the shooting of a journalist who specialised in investigating organized crime.

(c) Second Degree Murder

All murders, other than those listed above, are classified as second degree murder[68] and, while still attracting an automatic sentence of life imprisonment, have a lower period of parole ineligibity (as discussed above).

2. Liability of Accomplices to Murder

(i) Section 21(1) Perpetrators, Aiders and Abettors

(a) General Considerations

The provisions dealing with the liability of perpetrators and parties are found in sections 21 and 22 of the *Code*. The former section deals with both perpetration and aiding or abetting (the terms are used separately under the *Code*) and the latter with counselling. In the context of murder only the former (section 21) has played any significant role and section 22 is seldom invoked, perhaps because of the broad scope of section 21.

Section 21(1) provides as follows:[69]

Everyone is a party to an offence who

(a) actually commits it;

(b) does or omits to do anything for the purpose of aiding any person to commit it; or

(c) abets any person in committing it.

For most purposes it is irrelevant whether an accused is a perpetrator (or co-perpetrator), or an aider or abettor; under section 21 all are parties to the offence that was committed. Sometimes it may not be clear what role was played by a party. For example, in the Colin Thatcher case[70] the Crown actually relied on two theories to explain the accused's participation in his wife's murder. The first was based on Thatcher actually killing his wife, while the second scenario was based on his having hired the killer. The Supreme Court held that the two modes of participation were legally indistinguishable and it was not necessary for the jury to be unanimous on which it had accepted.

---

[68] S 231(7).

[69] The provision on parties contained in the first Criminal Code of 1892 was substantially similar except that it also covered counselling. The intent of the provision was to abolish the common law distinction between principals in the second degree and accessories before the fact. In 1955 for no obvious reason counselling was put under a separate s (see Martins Criminal Code 1955, referred to in D Stuart, *Canadian Criminal Law*, 4th edn (Toronto, 2001) at 602).

[70] *Thatcher* [1987] 1 SCR 652.

There may be more than one principal offender, and where the accused were acting in concert or jointly involved in a fatal attack, they are all co-principals even though it is not possible to establish who actually struck the fatal blow.[71] Occasionally, however, it may be important to determine the level of participation of the particular accused. For example in determining whether duress is available as a defence[72] it may be important to determine whether the accused was a perpetrator or simply an aider .

Section 23.1 of the *Code* makes it clear that there can be a conviction under sections 21–23 (of aiders, abettors, counsellors or accessories after the fact) even though the principal offender cannot be convicted of the offence.

(b) Actus Reus of Aiding or Abetting

Aiding can take a variety of forms: for example, providing an instrument for use in the crime, driving the getaway car, or acting as a lookout. Abetting has its own separate subsection and involves acts done to encourage or support the actions of the perpetrator, and it appears to overlap with counselling under section 22. Although there can be aiding by omission there are few cases on point and those have involved manslaughter rather than murder.[73] Presence at the scene is not a prerequisite for liability as an aider and, conversely, mere presence at the scene does not constitute aiding and abetting, but presence can be construed as providing evidence of encouragement, for example if the party had prior knowledge of the offence to be committed.[74]

(c) Mens Rea—Aiding or Abetting

Under section 21(1)(b) or (c) a party to murder must have a similar level of mens rea to that of the perpetrator—that is he must intend to aid or abet the principal in killing the victim, or intend to aid the perpetrator in causing bodily harm of a kind likely to result in death and be reckless whether death ensues or not. The aider must do the acts of assistance for the purpose[75] of assisting the principal offender to commit murder (explicit in section 21(1)(b) and read in by the courts under (c) (abetting)), so abetting must also be for the purpose of assisting the

---

[71]   *H(LI)* (2003) 176 CCC (3d) 526 (Man CA); *McMaster* [1996] 1 SCR 740.

[72]   A perpetrator of one of the excluded offences in s 17 of the *Code* (and murder is one of them) will not be able to use the defence of duress, but an aider or abettor of an excluded offence can use the common law defence of duress (*Paquette* [1977] 2 SCR 189 (SCC)). Canadian courts have yet to determine whether murder is also an excluded offence at common law. That issue is discussed below in sect 4(ii)(c).

[73]   *Popen* (1981) 60 CCC (2d) 232 (Ont CA).

[74]   *Dunlop and Sylvester* [1979] 2 SCR 881.

[75]   But 'purpose' does not require that the accused view the commission of the offence he is aiding as desirable. In this context purpose is equivalent to intention, and so the mens rea under s 21(1)(b) is not negated by duress: *Hibbert* (1995) 99 CCC (3d) 193 at 214 (SCC).

principal.[76] Intoxication may provide a defence because murder is a crime of specific intent. Presumably, if A assists B to murder C but by mistake B hits D, A ought also to be liable by extension of the transferred intent principle.

(ii) Section 21(2)—Extended Liability

Section 21(2) expands the liability of accomplices and makes them liable for *further* offences that are committed by the principal offender. For that section to apply:

1. Two or more persons must form an intention common to carry out an unlawful purpose;
   and
2. To assist each other therein;
3. One of them must commit a further offence in carrying out that common purpose;
4. The party must know (or ought to have known) that the commission of that offence would be a probable consequence of carrying out the common purpose; and
5. If 1 to 4 are satisfied that person is a party to the further offence committed by the perpetrator.

As McIntyre J explained in *Simpson*,[77] the purpose of the two subsections (1) and (2) is rather different:

> Subsection 1 applies to make everyone a party to an offence who commits it or aids and abets in its commission. Subsection (2) covers the case where in the absence of aiding and abetting a person may become a party to an offence committed by another which he knew or ought to have known was a probable consequence of carrying out an unlawful purpose in common with the perpetrator. *Thus it addresses the situation where the perpetrator goes beyond the original agreed unlawful purpose.*[(emphasis added)].

While liability under section 21(1) is based on the full subjective standard of mens rea, section 21(2) is more problematic. As noted above, section 21(2) contains objective language 'ought to know', and it was not surprising that the Supreme Court found this to be contrary to Charter standards. In *Logan*[78] (a case involving attempted murder and the liability of parties to the offence) the Supreme Court, based on its reasoning in the earlier decision in *Martineau*,[79] held that if the offence is 'a stigma offence' with a constitutionally required level of mens rea for the perpetrator (as is the case with murder or attempted murder) then a party to that offence must also have a similar level of mens rea and cannot

---

[76] *Curran* (1977) 38 CCC (2d) 151 (Alta CA).
[77] *Simpson* [1988] 1 SCR 3.
[78] [1990] 2 SCR 731.
[79] Discussed above, in sect 1(iii).

be convicted on the basis of an offence that contains significant objective elements. The Court held that attempted murder was a 'stigma' offence and that subjective mens rea was constitutionally mandated for both the perpetrator and any parties to the offence under section 21(2).

The courts have been reluctant to extend the 'stigma' analysis in *Martineau* to other offences, and have found that very few offences have a *constitutionally mandated* minimum level of mens rea.[80] Consequently murder is one of the few offences where a subjective level of mens rea (foresight of death) is mandated by the Charter. While the Crown can rely on section 21(2) in a murder case, the words 'ought to know' must not be used and the accomplice will only be liable under that section if he *actually knew* that the commission of the further offence was a probable consequence of carrying out the common unlawful purpose. If A and B agree to rob a shop and A knows that B is carrying a loaded gun and will use it, if needed, to kill or to cause serious harm that he knows is likely to cause death, then A will also be liable for murder using a combination of sections 21(2) and 229 because he had subjective foresight that B might commit murder. It is no longer sufficient to show that he *ought* to have known of the consequences of their joint enterprise.

(iii) Perpetrators and Other Parties: Liability for Different Offences?

The principal offender may be convicted of murder, while a party may be convicted of either murder or manslaughter. The party may be guilty of murder either as a co-perpetrator (under section 21(1)(a)) or as an aider or abettor (section 21(1)(b) or (c)), but this will only be possible if the Crown can establish the requisite mens rea for murder. If the perpetrator went beyond the common unlawful purpose the party will be liable for murder under section 21(2) if the party knew[81] that the principal offender was likely to commit murder (as defined in section 229) in carrying out the common unlawful purpose.

On the other hand, if the Crown cannot establish the requisite mens rea for murder then the accomplice can be convicted of manslaughter. For example if the accused knew that the perpetrator would commit bodily harm—less than harm likely to cause death—then the party can be convicted of manslaughter rather

---

[80]   So far the courts have decided that murder, attempted murder, accessory liability to an offence that constitutionally requires a subjective test, and war crimes and crimes against humanity fall within the 'stigma' category *requiring* subjective mens rea. In dicta it has been suggested that theft is also included (*Martineau*). It would appear that *Martineau* represents the high water mark of this development. The courts often read in subjective mens rea, even when it is not expressly required, but this is done as a matter of interpretation and not because there would be an infringement of the *Charter* if they did not do so.

[81]   A subjective standard is required as a result of *Logan* (n 78 above).

than murder. In *Kirkness*[82] A and B broke into the home of a frail 83-year-old woman. A sexually assaulted and then suffocated the old woman while B ransacked the house, having placed a chair at front door to prevent entry during the sexual assault. At trial A was convicted of first degree murder but B was acquitted. On appeal to the Manitoba Court of Appeal the acquittal was set aside and a new trial ordered because there was a possibility that B might be liable for manslaughter. The Supreme Court allowed the appeal and restored the acquittal. The evidence failed to show that the accused had the intent to aid or abet murder or that the accused knew that A would sexually assault or kill the victim in the course of the breaking and entering. The death occurred as a result of strangulation that occurred after the sexual assault. At that time B gave A timely notice not to strangle the woman, and from that time A was acting on his own. A manslaughter verdict would have been possible for B if the jury had found that the accused was a party to the sexual assault and the death was the result of the sexual assault (eg if the unlawful act which was aided or abetted was one that he *knew* was likely to cause some harm short of death). There was a strong dissent from L'Heureux-Dubé and Wilson JJ who supported the possibility of a manslaughter conviction. B had assisted by placing the chair during the sexual assault and he did not alter his behaviour when the violence escalated. He had not done enough to dissociate himself from the killing of the victim.

In a subsequent decision, the Supreme Court revisited its earlier ruling in *Kirkness* and expanded the limits of liability of an aider in light of its ruling in *Creighton* that the mens rea for manslaughter is objective foreseeability of bodily harm. In *Jackson (sub nom Davy)*,[83] D and J were charged with first degree murder following the killing of R, who was J's employee and lover. J was found guilty of first degree murder, and D of second degree murder. On appeal to the Ontario Court of Appeal D's conviction was set aside, a new trial was ordered and a subsequent Crown appeal to the Supreme Court was unsuccessful. The Court confirmed that a principal offender can be guilty of murder while an aider or abettor is guilty only of manslaughter (if he lacks the mens rea for murder) and that the test is an objective one. Where someone is involved as a party in the offence of murder but does not possess the mens rea for murder, he can be convicted of manslaughter if a reasonable person in all the circumstances would have appreciated that non-trivial bodily harm was a foreseeable consequence of the dangerous act. Because manslaughter is not a 'stigma' offence with a constitutionally mandated subjective level of mens rea it was quite appropriate to convict an aider of manslaughter based on an objective standard. Similarly if the situation fell within section 21(2) (extended liability) the party could be guilty of manslaughter if the perpetrator in carrying out a common unlawful purpose (robbery or arson, to take but two examples) killed the victim and the party,

---

[82] (1990) 60 CCC (3d) 97, reversing 51 CCC (3d) 444.
[83] (1991) 68 CCC (3d) 385 (Ont CA), affirmed 86 CCC (3d) 385 (SCC); see also *Portillo* (2003) 176 CCC (3d) 467 (Ont CA).

although he did not participate in the homicide, ought to have known that bodily harm was a probable consequence of carrying out the common purpose.

Is the converse true and can a party be convicted of a more serious offence than the perpetrator? If the perpetrator has a valid defence or did not have the capacity to commit the offence (section 16—mental disorder) then there seems every reason to convict the party who had full mens rea and realised what would ensue from the actions of the perpetrator. In such a case it should be possible to convict the party of murder.[84]

(iv) Counselling

Section 22 of the *Code*, which addresses counselling an offence, provides as follows:

(1)

Where a person counsels another person to be a party to an offence and that other person is afterwards a party to that offence, the person who counselled is a party to that offence, notwithstanding that the offence was committed in a way different from that which was counselled.

(2)

Every one who counsels another person to be a party to an offence is a party to every offence that the other commits in consequence of the counselling that the person who counselled knew or ought to have known was likely to be committed in consequence of the counselling.

This section deals with offences counselled by the accused and actually committed. If the offence is counselled but not committed, the appropriate section is section 464 which expressly provides for that eventuality. There are hardly any cases of counselling murder,[85] and in most cases where the accused has encouraged the offence the Crown would rely on section 21 rather than section 22.

Section 22 makes it clear that the person counselling is liable 'notwithstanding that the offence was committed in a way different from that which was counselled'. That raises the issue of whether section 21 should be interpreted similarly. What if A supplies a gun to commit murder and the perpetrator uses a knife instead? Has A aided the murder? A has certainly provided encouragement to B even though a different weapon was used, but since section 22 expressly adverts to this situation while section 21 does not, it might be argued as a matter of statutory construction that section 21 does not cover this situation. On the other hand the *Code* provisions are often out of kilter, having been added to and revised at different points over the past century, and differences in wording are

---

[84] *Hebert* [1986] NBJ No 32 (CA). See too *Remillard* (1921) 62 SCR 21.
[85] *McNulty* (1910) 17 CCC 26 (Ont CA) is a rare example where the putative father of a child counselled the mother to drown the child.

often downplayed. The courts may assume that section 21 should be similarly interpreted for the sake of consistency. What if A counsels the murder of X and B instead kills Y? If the killing is by mistake then transferred intent should ensure liability, but if B deliberately deviates from the advice then the only possibility should be liability for counselling an offence not committed (section 464).

Section 22(2), like its counterpart, section 21(2), provides for extended liability where the perpetrator commits further offences that the counsellor knew or ought to have known were likely to be committed. Clearly the objective aspect cannot stand in the light of decisions on objective liability under section 21(2) in the case of murder or attempted murder (*Logan*), and the objective component will be omitted in such cases.

(v) Accessories After the Fact

An accessory after the fact is one who, knowing that a person has been a party to the offence, receives, comforts or assists that person for the purpose of enabling that person to escape. In *Duong*[86] the accused was charged with being an accessory after the fact to murder. The court pointed out that there is little Canadian authority on the knowledge requirement in section 23, and went on to hold that the Crown must prove actual knowledge of the offence or wilful blindness.

(vi) Conclusion

The present provisions on party liability have been described as 'unduly complex and illogical'.[87] It is not clear why we retain the distinction between aiders and abettors and between aiders or abettors and counselors, but there seem to be few practical problems arising from these distinctions. The major problem is in dealing with party liability for murder and manslaughter, an area which is particularly complex and extremely difficult for jurors to comprehend. Unfortunately, there does not appear to be an easy solution. When there are so many permutations of possibilities in the murder/manslaughter context (a jury is often directed on murder, manslaughter and party liability under section 21(1)(a) and (b) and section 21(2)), simplification may not be an attainable goal.

---

[86] (1998) 124 CCC (3d) 392 (Ont CA).
[87] D Stuart, *Canadian Criminal Law*, 4th edn (Toronto, 2001) at 619.

3. Infanticide[88]

(i) General Considerations

Section 233 provides:

> A female person commits infanticide when by a wilful act or omission she causes the death of her newly-born child.[89] if at the time of the act or omission she is not fully recovered from the effects of giving birth to the child and by reason thereof or of the effect of lactation consequent on the birth of the child her mind is then disturbed.

Infanticide, a form of culpable homicide (section 222(4)), is an indictable offence carrying a maximum of five years' imprisonment. The offence was added to the *Code* in 1948[90] and assumed its present form in 1955. It appears that the objective was to prevent women being convicted of murder of their infants while in a state of mental impairment after their birth. It is one of few gender-specific offences in the *Code* and is not open to men who kill their offspring. Nor is it open to women who kill children other than the 'newly-born' infant. It is anomalous and is in reality a defence framed as an offence. The section seems to be based on assumptions that no longer hold water: for example it is doubtful whether anyone would accept that lactation by itself might cause some form of mental disturbance.

(ii) Actus Reus

Although it is not easy to separate the actus reus and mens rea components it would appear that the following actus reus components must be established by the Crown:

1. The accused was a female person;
2. She did or omitted to do an act;
3. The child died;
4. The death was caused by the act or omission;
5. The child was 'newly-born' as defined in section 2, for example a child under one year of age;
6. At the time of the act or omission the accused had not fully recovered from the effects of giving birth;
7. As a result of the lack of recovery from those effects, or as a result of lactation after the birth, her mind was disturbed. (This requires proof of a causal link

---

[88] See I Grant, D Boyle and C Chun, *The Law of Homicide* (Toronto, 1999). Updating of this looseleaf ceased in 1999.
[89] S 2: 'newly born child' means a person under the age of one year.
[90] 1948 (Can), c 39, s 7.

between the birth or lactation and the mental disturbance but does not require proof that the disturbance caused her to kill the child.)

But what does it mean to say that a woman has not fully recovered from effects of giving birth or that her mind was disturbed as a result of lactation? This surely requires proof of something less than the full blown mental disorder defence within section 16 and seems to involve a form of diminished responsibility. In any event it does seem strange that the Crown is required to prove mental disturbance as part of the offence.

The new offence created in 1948 was soon perceived as having problems, and it was necessary to add a definition of 'newly born' in 1955 amendments. Another difficulty also highlighted in *Marchello*[91] was the very difficult burden imposed on the Crown—the need to prove a negative—for example, that the mother had not recovered from the effects of the birth, and a positive, for example, that by reason of the birth or effect of lactation her mind was disturbed. McRuer J described this burden as 'almost impossible'. All an accused had to do was to raise a reasonable doubt about either and she would be entitled to an acquittal, even though she had wilfully killed her child.

It was that anomaly that led to the passing of what is now section 663.[92] Under this rather odd provision a woman may be convicted of infanticide even if the evidence does *not* establish that she was not fully recovered from the effects of the birth, or from the effect of lactation, and the balance of her mind was at that time disturbed by reason of the effect of the birth or of the effect of lactation! Despite the absence of these key elements the woman may still be convicted of infanticide unless the evidence establishes that the act was not wilful!! The section is not without its own problems. When does it come into play? Does it render much of the offence redundant? The authorities are conflicting.[93]

The offence of infanticide is obviously based on a medical model; that the woman's mind has been disturbed and essentially the issue relates to diminished capacity and that the woman because of the birth (or lactation) is less culpable. However it has been pointed out by several critics that in the nineteenth century, when juries were extremely reluctant to convict mothers, the predominant

---

[91] (1951) 100 CCC 137 (Ont HC).

[92] The *Code* provisions on infanticide were amended in 1953–4.

[93] In *Smith* (1976) 32 CCC (2d) 224 (Nfld Dist Ct), the court was of the opinion that the two ss are to be applied in sequence. What is now s 663 does not have any significance if all the elements of the infanticide provisions are satisfied. But if all the elements save those relating to a disturbed mind are established then s 663 takes effect to prevent a female who was of sound mind when she caused the death of her child from going free. However in *Lalli* [1993] BCJ No 2010 (BC Prov Ct), the court was of the view that s 663 applies only where she is actually charged with infanticide (not murder), and that in such a case the Crown need not establish mental disturbance or that the mother had not recovered from the birth. It is only where she is charged with murder and infanticide is being considered as an included offence that the Crown must then prove all the elements in s 233.

factors were socio-economic rather than medical, but when a number of jurisdictions chose to enact infanticide provisions in the twentieth century[94] the draftsmen focused on 'the barely perceived medical reasons for such behaviour which had the apparent advantages of being scientific and individually rooted'.[95] The Law Reform Commission of Canada, in its Working Paper on Homicide[96] which supported the repeal of the provision, also notes the lack of medical evidence to support this offence.

(iii) Mens Rea

What is the mens rea of the offence? While it is clear that the act or omission must be 'wilful', it is not clear whether the death must be caused wilfully. In other words is infanticide only applicable in cases that would otherwise be murder, or is it also available in cases that might otherwise be manslaughter?

According to *Smith*[97] the act must be done with a bad motive or purpose,[98] or with evil intent. In that case the mother (a 17-year-old girl who did not believe that she was pregnant), after giving birth, put her hand across child's mouth to stop it from crying which would have alerted the household to the birth. It was held that the accused did not cause the death 'wilfully'. This reasoning seems to treat infanticide as mitigating murder and that it may not be available in a case that otherwise would be manslaughter (the English legislation is clear that infanticide converts murder to infanticide, the Canadian legislation is not). However in *Lalli*[99] the court held that it was sufficient that the accused 'ought to have realized that what she did might be harmful' and this extends infanticide to cases that would otherwise be manslaughter.

In cases where the accused is mentally disturbed but there is no causal link between the birth or lactation and the mental disorder, the accused may be able to rely on the ordinary mental disorder defence under section 16 of the *Code*.[100] In *Irwin*[101] the accused was charged with murder after she killed her 7-month-old child. She had a history of mental problems, was an alcoholic and after the birth of the child had been suffering from post partum depression. She was found not guilty by reason of insanity (after 1992 the verdict would be not criminally

[94]   The English Infanticide Act of 1922 was one of the first.

[95]   JA Osborne, 'The Crime of Infanticide: Throwing Out the Baby with the Bathwater' (1987) 6 *Canadian Journal of Family Law* 47; and see also CB Backhouse, 'Desperate Women and Compassionate Courts: Infanticide in 19th Century Canada' (1984) 34 *University of Toronto Law Journal* 447; K O'Donovan, 'The Medicalization of Infanticide' [1984] *Crim LR* 259.

[96]   Law Reform Commission of Canada Working Paper No. 33 (Homicide) (1864).

[97]   (1976) 32 CCC (2d) 224 (Nfld Dist Ct).

[98]   This seems to take motive into account in determining mens rea.

[99]   N 93 above.

[100]   While the Canadian provisions on mental disorder are based on the McNaghten Rules, they are somewhat wider in scope. For a discussion see D Stuart, *Canadian Criminal Law*, 4th edn (Toronto, Carswell, 2001) Ch 6(B).

[101]   (1977) 36 CCC (2d) 1 (Ont CA).

responsible on account of mental disorder—NCRMD: see section 672.34). Until 1992 such a verdict would have resulted in indefinite detention with few safeguards for the accused, but all that was changed in 1991 (this is explored more fully in section 3(iv) below).

(iv) Related Offences

There are related offences involving unborn or newly born children and they are noted briefly. Section 238 provides for the killing of an unborn child in the act of birth (before it has become a 'human being' as defined in section 223) in such a manner that if it were a human being it would have been murder (maximum of life imprisonment).

Section 242 covers a mother's neglect to obtain assistance in childbirth where that failure results in permanent injury or death (a maximum of five years' imprisonment). Disposal of the dead body of a child in order to conceal the birth is an offence under section 243 and carries a maximum of two years' imprisonment.

(v) Charter Issues and Possible Reforms

It may be that the offence of infanticide will be subject to scrutiny under the *Charter* and, because of its gender specificity, it may be found to infringe the equality provisions in section 15(1) of the *Charter*. To the extent that the offence/defence is predicated on a medical model (and it is clear that it is), it is based on issues that are only applicable to women (hormonal imbalance, post partum depression following birth), and it almost certainly would be upheld under section 15 as not infringing equality concerns or, if it is held to infringe section 15, a strong argument could be made that it could be justified under section 1 of the *Charter*. If the offence were reformed in such a way that the focus became socio-economic, rather than medical, the exclusion of fathers would certainly be more problematic.

There have been calls for reform or abolition of this anomalous offence.[102] One option is simply to repeal the section and deal with these cases as sentencing issues, but this would only be feasible if we were to abolish the fixed sentence for second degree murder (which seems unlikely). Otherwise abolition of the offence, without change in the fixed penalty for murder, would leave the section 16 mental disorder defence as the only viable option. The other option is to

---

[102] See, eg, The Law Reform Commission of Canada Working Paper No 33, *Homicide* (1984) at 74. The Commission advocated abolishing the fixed penalty for second degree intentional homicide which would provide flexibility in sentencing. There is a very good discussion in I Grant, D Boyle and C Chun, *The Law of Homicide* (Toronto, Carswell, 1999) at 4–80. The authors, although critical of the offence, are concerned about the impact of its repeal.

employ a form of diminished responsibility which would have the advantage of also providing a defence to a mother who kills children other than the 'newly-born'. To date Canadian courts have only been willing to use a somewhat similar concept to question whether the Crown has established the mens rea of murder. It does not apply in cases of intentional killing.[103]

It must be acknowledged that this is a very complex, multi-faceted issue, and it is impossible to do justice to it in this Chapter.

4. Defences

In a chapter of this size it is simply impossible to do justice to all defences that might be relevant in the context of murder, and I have focused, primarily, only on those raised in the recent Law Commission Consultation Paper on Homicide.[104] I have omitted a discussion of mental disorder, automatism and intoxication.

(i) Defences Specific to Murder: The Partial Defence of Provocation

Professor Ives has reviewed the criticisms of the Canadian defence of provocation and canvassed a number of options for reform.[105] I am in the camp that would abolish the defence should we eventually depart from the mandatory sentence for murder. Since this is unlikely, I am reluctantly in favour of retaining some form of the defence, but it does need to be more strictly applied, particularly in the area of spousal or similar homicides where it has been successfully invoked in a number of very questionable circumstances. *Thibert*[106] provides an obvious example of the potential abuses. A man who was told by his wife that she was leaving him followed her round, took a sawn-off shot gun and eventually shot her boyfriend after he uttered a somewhat ill-advised comment. The Supreme Court held that the defence of provocation was a viable one and approved a very generous use of the 'ordinary person' standard which takes into account a plethora of individual factors (in this case the 'ordinary person' was a married man facing the break-up of his marriage). It also had the effect of downplaying the requirement of 'suddenness' (*Thibert* seems to ignore the fact that the accused was stalking his wife with a loaded shotgun).

---

[103] See sect 4(iii) below.

[104] UK Law Commission, Consultation Paper No 177, 'A New Homicide Act for England and Wales?' (London, TSO, 2005)

[105] Law Commission for England and Wales, *Partial Defences to Murder*, Consultation Paper No 173 (London, TSO, 2003) (Overseas Studies Consultation Paper, Appendix B, at 73 and following), available at http://www.lawcom.gov.uk/docs/cp173apps.pdf

[106] [1996] 1 SCR 37.

There is a fear that use of an expanded range of personal factors, including cultural ones, would be problematic. Take, for example, the case of the fanatically religious father who kills his daughter because she is promiscuous or dating someone of another race. Surely such factors should not be considered under the 'ordinary person'[107] test, and we should reject the injection of cultural values in this context. Racial insults are one thing (and should be acknowledged within the provocation defence), but it would be dangerous to permit an expansion of the ordinary or reasonable person standard to take into account such cultural values. The legal system should set its face against honour and other similar killings which are driven by cultural considerations that do not prevail in the host country.

(ii) Other Defences

(a) Diminished Responsibility

Canada does not have a provision similar to the English diminished responsibility provision that operates to reduce murder to manslaughter on the basis of an abnormality of the mind substantially impairing the accused's responsibility for the offence. The only special statutory provision that does recognise a lesser form of impairment is the offence of infanticide (discussed earlier). There are some decisions, however, that appear to have recognised mental impairment less than that required under the section 16 mental disorder defence. First, the Supreme Court has recognised a form of 'diminished responsibility' in determining whether a murder was 'planned and deliberate' which, prior to 1975, would have been a capital offence and now constitutes first degree murder (without eligibility for parole for 25 years).[108] However, this is not really a recognition of 'diminished responsibility' because section 231 is simply a sentence-classifying provision and does not create a separate offence with mens rea requirements.[109] Indeed the Supreme Court in its later decision in *Chartrand*[110] states quite clearly that diminished responsibility is not recognised under Canadian law.

While *More* is relatively uncontroversial (and simply serves to reduce first to second degree murder), there are other statements approving of a defence based on lack of mens rea and stemming from mental impairment short of the mental disorder defence under section 16, which seem to fly in the face of the clear ruling

---

[107] The Canadian equivalent of the reasonable person.

[108] *More* [1963] 2 SCR 522. Cartwright J held that evidence of impaired mental function had a direct bearing on the question whether the killing had been deliberate. Fauteux J, dissenting, was of the view that admitting evidence of mental impairment short of the s 16 defence would be 'tantamount to introducing in Canadian law a new and secondary test of legal irresponsibility' (at 529).

[109] *Farrant* [1983] 1 SCR 124.

[110] [1977] 1 SCR 314 at 318.

in *Chartrand*. Most significantly the Supreme Court in the later decisions *Swain*[111] and *Jacquard*[112] has acknowledged that mental impairment short of section 16 is relevant in determining whether the accused actually formed the intent for murder. In *Swain* Lamer CJ, for the majority, states:

> [I]f. . .evidence of mental impairment is, in the view of the trier of fact, insufficient to meet the requirements of s 16, the accused is still entitled to have such evidence considered with respect to the essential element of *mens rea*. This accords with the current practice wherein an accused has been able to deny the element of planning and deliberation or the specific intent required for murder, despite the fact that s. 16 has not been satisfied.[113]

Although Lamer CJ speaks of the 'current practice' as if this principle were routinely applied, he cites no authority on the point, and it is clear that most of the decisions which support that proposition seem to involve dicta or are brief judgments in which few relevant authorities are cited.[114] this development has been welcomed by some commentators[115] because it is seen as evidence of 'a commendable judicial concern to take the subjective *mens rea* inquiry seriously',[116] it is not without its problems. The law provides that certain accused are not to be found criminally responsible and sets out the criteria in the mental disorder defence under section 16. It would seem that if an accused fails at that hurdle it should not be possible to adopt a different tactic and plead lack of mens rea. Is it appropriate to provide an 'escape route' from section 16[117] which is likely to create further uncertainty? If there are some accused suffering from a mental impairment to the point where they could not form the intent for murder, but who fall outside the section 16 defence, then the solution should be to expand section 16 rather than to fudge the issue by permitting arguments based on lack of mens rea.

There also appears to be growing acceptance of the combined use of other failed defences (frequently a combination of provocation, self defence and intoxication) where the accused may not be able to satisfy any particular defence, but the cumulative effect of the defences is sufficient to raise a doubt about the existence of the mens rea for the offence. This will be explored more fully below.[118]

---

[111] [1991] 1 SCR 933 at 987.
[112] [1997] 1 SCR 314 at 333.
[113] [1991] 1 SCR 933 at 987.
[114] See, eg, *Browning* (1976) 34 CCC (2d) 200 (Ont CA).
[115] See, eg, D Stuart, *Canadian Criminal Law*, 4th edn (Toronto, 2001) at 403.
[116] *Ibid.*
[117] See DB Bayne, 'Automatism and Provocation in Canadian Case Law' (1975) 31 *CRNS* 257 at 271.
[118] Under sect 4(iii).

(b) Necessity

In *Perka*[119] the Supreme Court acknowledged that there is a common law defence[120] of necessity 'preserved' by section 8(3) of the *Code*. More recently, in *Latimer*,[121] the Supreme Court had occasion to return to the formulation of the defence. In that case a father was charged with the murder of his 12-year-old severely disabled daughter, who had a mental capacity of a 4-month-old baby, and who had frequent seizures. She had already experienced numerous medical procedures, was often in pain and was facing the prospect of additional major surgery, and the father decided to end her life by the use of carbon monoxide gas.

At the first trial the judge refused to put the defence of necessity to the jury, a decision that was upheld by the Saskatchewan Court of Appeal. The Supreme Court ordered a new trial (on a different issue), and at the second trial the judge again withdrew the issue of necessity from the jury and L was convicted of second degree murder. The jury recommended a one year sentence,[122] which was accepted by the judge, but which was upset on further appeal to the Saskatchewan Court of Appeal. Under the *Code* the only option was life imprisonment with a minimum of 10 years' imprisonment without eligibility for parole, a sentence which was upheld on further and final appeal to the Supreme Court.[123] The Court held that there was no air of reality to the defence of necessity, a defence which they indicated is narrow and of limited application.

Building on the foundations laid down in *Perka* the Court held that there are three elements of the defence:

1. There is a requirement of imminent peril or danger;
2. The accused must have had no reasonable legal alternative to the course of action he or she undertook;
3. There must be proportionality between the harm inflicted and the harm avoided.

The first and second requirements are to be determined on a modified objective basis, for example, one that takes into account the situation and characteristics of the particular accused, as long as the accused's subjective perceptions are based on reasonable grounds. The third requirement, proportionality, is to be measured on a purely objective standard.

Here, the trial judge was correct to remove the defence from the jury since there was no air of reality to any of the three requirements for necessity. The

---

[119] [1984] 2 SCR 233.

[120] Characterised as an excuse rather than a justification, and based on the principle of 'normative involuntariness' advocated by GP Fletcher, *Rethinking Criminal Law* (Toronto and Boston, 1978) at 803 ff.

[121] [2001] 1 SCR 3.

[122] Apparently they were quite astonished when asked to recommend a period between 10 and 25 years without eligibility for parole as required under s 745.2 and instead recommended 1 year.

[123] (2001) 150 CCC (3d) 129 (SCC).

accused did not himself face any peril, and the daughter's ongoing pain did not constitute an emergency in this case. Her proposed surgery did not pose an imminent threat to her life, nor did her medical condition. It was not reasonable for the accused to form the belief that further surgery amounted to imminent peril, particularly when better pain management was available. Moreover, the accused had at least one reasonable legal alternative to killing his daughter; he could have struggled on with what was unquestionably a difficult situation, by helping her to live and by minimising her pain as much as possible, or by permitting institutional care. Leaving open the question whether the proportionality requirement could ever be met in a murder case, the Court noted that the harm inflicted in this case was immeasurably more serious than the pain resulting from the impending operation which the accused sought to avoid. Killing a person in order to relieve the suffering produced by a medically manageable physical or mental condition is not a proportionate response to the harm represented by the non-life-threatening suffering resulting from that condition.

The Court also rejected an argument based on section 12 of the *Charter* ('cruel and unusual punishment') and refused the remedy of a constitutional exemption from the operation of the mandatory sentence.

(c) Duress[124]

In *Carker No 2*[125] the Court adopted a very restrictive interpretation of the requirements of 'presence' and 'immediacy' which are found in section 17 of the *Code*, which defines the defence of duress.[126] It also held that the defence of duress is exhaustively defined in section 17. However, in its later decision in *Paquette*[127] the Court held that section 17 is *not* exhaustive and that there are two separate defences of duress—one under section 17 that applies to perpetrators, and the other, the common law defence, that applies to other parties to the offence. Section 17 contains a list of 22 excluded offences where the statutory defence of duress cannot be used. However if the accused is a party (for example an aider) to the offence, even one of the excluded offences within section 17, then he can use the common law defence which is much less restrictive than its statutory counterpart. (In *Hibbert*[128] the Supreme Court also held that duress will negate the mens rea of an offence only in very exceptional cases.)

---

[124] [1977] 2 SCR 189
[125] [1967] SCR 114
[126] S 17 provides: '[a] person who commits an offence under compulsion by threats of immediate death or bodily harm from a person who is present when the offence is committed is excused for committing the offence if the person believes that the threats will be carried out and if the person is not a party to a conspiracy or association whereby the person is subject to compulsion, but this section does not where the offence committed is. . .' (there follows a list of 22 excluded offences which includes murder and attempted murder).
[127] [1977] 2 SCR 189.
[128] [1995] 2CR 973.

Thus, following *Paquette*, Canada had a bifurcated defence of duress, one statutory and the other common law based, until developments came to a head in the recent Supreme Court decision in *Ruzic* which considered the effect of the *Charter* on the statutory defence in section 17. In *Ruzic*[129] (involving a charge of importing drugs), the Supreme Court, adopting the principle of normative involuntariness as a principle of fundamental justice (it is contrary to the *Charter* to find an accused liable for an offence where his or her actions were normatively involuntary[130]) found the presence and immediacy requirements in section 17 to be unduly restrictive, since they might exclude some accused persons whose conduct was normatively involuntary from using the defence, and the Court struck down those requirements. While that aspect of the judgment is clear, the remainder is not; for example, it is *not* clear whether the Court simply excised the restrictive words from section 17, or whether it went even further and struck down the whole of section 17 (with the exception of the list of excluded offences). Looking at the judgment as a whole, and considering the fact that the trial judge directed the jury on the common law defence (even though Ruzic was in fact a perpetrator, not an aider), it seems clear that the Court intended to substitute the common law defence of duress and to make it available for all offenders (whether parties or principals).

One thing is quite certain, though, and that is that the list of excluded offences, all 22 of them, were not struck down in *Ruzic* and await further *Charter* challenge.[131] At the present time if the accused is the perpetrator of one of the named offences, for example, murder or sexual assault, he cannot use section 17 or the common law defence, and his only remedy will be to challenge the list of excluded offences as contrary to the *Charter*, and invoke arguments similar those already accepted in *Ruzic* on the issue of moral involuntariness.

It is assumed that as a result of *Ruzic* the common law defence of duress has now become the only defence available and that section 17 (apart from the list of excluded offences) is a dead letter. It is generally acknowledged that the common law defence is broader than the defence in section 17, but its exact contours are still far from clear. So far the requirements appear to be as follows:

1. Threats of death or serious harm to himself or others;
2. That the accused had no safe avenue of escape—judged on a combined objective/subjective standard—the reasonable person in the shoes of the accused;

---

[129] [2001] 1 SCR 687.

[130] Based on work of George Fletcher (GP Fletcher, *Rethinking Criminal Law* (Toronto and Boston, 1978)), first adopted by the Supreme Court in the context of necessity (*Perka*), then applied in *Hibbert* in the context of the common law defence of duress, and used by the Supreme Court in the context of a constitutional challenge under s 7 of the *Charter* to the restrictively defined defence of duress within s 17. The example given by Fletcher is that of the lost alpinist on the point of freezing to death, who breaks open a mountain cabin. His 'choice' to break the law is no true choice: it is remorselessly compelled by normal human instincts (cited in *Perka*).

[131] See, eg, *Fraser* [2002] NSJ No 400 (Prov Ct), where a lower court authority struck down 'robbery'.

3. In some decisions there is mention of a proportionality requirement;[132]
4. The absence of prior involvement with those likely to exert pressure on the accused: for example membership in a gang prior to the use of the threats;[133]
5. Higher courts have yet to deal with the issue of excluded offences. As noted above section 17 contains a list of 22 offences that are excluded. Many will be challenged under the *Charter*, but the most difficult issue will be whether murder should remain an excluded offence. This is yet to be determined, but a strong argument can be made for denying the defence in murder cases, both to perpetrators and to parties. That would certainly be in line with the law in England and other jurisdictions.

(d) Self-defence and 'Battered Woman Syndrome'

The Code provisions on self-defence (sections 34–37 of the Code) have been the subject of unrelenting judicial criticism (for example, see *Pintar*[134]), but the repeated calls for reform have fallen on deaf ears. The provisions are so complex, confusing and overlapping that little is to be gained from a review of them in this study. However there is one point which is of more general interest, and that is the treatment of 'battered woman syndrome' under our self defence provisions.

The key decision is *Lavallee*.[135] The accused, a woman with a history of abuse from her husband, killed him by shooting him in the back of the head. He had made threats on the day in question but at the time was walking out of the room. The traditional concept of self-defence involves a response to an immediate threat to one's safety, but this case involved a pre-emptive strike in self-defence. The Supreme Court addressed the appropriateness of the use of expert evidence in this case, evidence that was based on the work of Lenore Walker on the 'cycle of violence' experienced by battered women. This is a landmark decision because Wilson J's judgment broke new ground in expanding the self-defence provisions. As the shooting of the husband was deliberate, the accused relied on section 34(2) of the *Code*.[136] In the past, the requirement that the attack be imminent had been read into the section and would have precluded the use of the section in this case.

The Ccourt held that expert evidence can be useful in these cases in explaining a number of factors for the jury

---

[132] *Li* (2002) 162 CCC (3d) 360 (Ont CA) (kidnapping case).
[133] *Ibid.*
[134] (1996) 110 CCC (3d) 402 (Ont CA).
[135] [1990] 1 SCR 852.
[136] Everyone who is unlawfully assaulted and who causes death or grievous bodily harm in repelling the assault is justified if (a) he causes it under reasonable apprehension of death or grievous bodily harm from the violence with which the assault was originally made, or with which the assailant pursues his purposes; and (b) he believes, on reasonable grounds, that he cannot otherwise preserve himself from death or grievous bodily harm. This s (unlike s 34(1)) applies even where there is an intention to kill or cause grievous bodily harm.

1. It can dispel myths and stereotypes about abused women and can help to explain why the accused's beliefs were reasonable, given her circumstances of abuse (in particular her increased sensitivity to an impending attack by the husband).
2. It also explains why it is very difficult for battered women to leave their spouses, thus explaining why leaving the husband may not be a viable option ('learned helplessness') and in explaining why an accused believed that killing the spouse was the only way to save herself.

As a result of *Lavallee* battered women have been able to fit within the self-defence provisions, even in cases where there is no immediate attack,[137] and it has in effect sanctioned pre-emptive strikes in self-defence at least where an attack was anticipated within a short interval of time.

While the decision has been welcomed it has also been criticised from a number of perspectives, feminist and otherwise. Feminists have criticised the 'syndromization' of what is in essence a social problem. Battered women are responding to a terrible reality of abuse that was largely ignored by the social system, and the focus should be on social factors rather than on 'learned helplessness'.[138] It is also pointed out that increased funding and resources, while addressing some of the more immediate concerns of abused spouses by providing shelter and other services, have still left the essential problem of male violence against intimate partners largely unresolved.

The *Lavallee* decision has been extended to cover what has been called 'prison environment syndrome' *(McConnell)*.[139] The Supreme Court, however, seems to have become aware of the dangers of adopting too liberal an interpretation of self-defence and has refused to accept pre-emptive strikes against fellow criminals or gang members.[140]

The reasoning in *Lavallee* has had far-reaching implications outside self-defence and it has been in the vanguard of an increasing trend towards the contextualisation of defences with objective criteria. Increasingly 'reasonableness' has come to be determined on the basis of the accused's personal characteristics (the reasonable person in the shoes of the accused).[141] While this is an interesting

---

[137] Prior to that decision such women had no defence: see *Whynot* (1983) 37 CR (3d) 198 (NS CA).

[138] See comments of L'Heureux-Dubé J and McLachlin J (as she then was) in *Petel* [1994] 1 SCR 3. Both women indicated that we should focus on the reasonableness of the response of battered women, given their social circumstances, rather than on the pathology of 'learned helplessness'.

[139] [1996] 1 SCR 1075. The Supreme Court adopted the dissenting judgment of Conrad JA in the Alberta CA. 'Prison environment syndrome' is similar to 'battered woman syndrome' in that it was a situation of kill or be killed. There was a history of assault, earlier threats and escalating activity with present ability to carry out the threats. A pre-emptive strike was justified.

[140] *Cinous* [2002] 2 SCR 3; *Charlebois* [2000] 2 SCR 674.

[141] See, eg, *Petel* [1994] 1 SCR 3 (self-defence and impact of prior threats); *Hibbert* [1995] 2 SCR 973 (common law defence of duress); *Ruzic* [2001] 1 SCR 687 (duress); *Thibert* [1996] 1 SCR 37 (characteristics of an ordinary person in the context of provocation); *Latimer* [2001] SCR 3 (necessity).

development, it is not without its dangers. After all, the tests are objective and the focus should be on the reasonableness of the accused's action. Too generous an injection of subjectivity into essentially objective standards might well lead to an increasing slide into subjectivity. If we attach too much weight to the particular circumstances of the accused the objective standard will become meaningless.

(iii) Intent and the Impact of 'Failed Defences'—the 'Rolled-up Charge'

I have already discussed the use of mental impairment short of mental disorder within section 16 above, and it was noted that Canadian courts have shown some willingness to allow evidence of such impaired mental functioning to be considered in determining whether the accused in fact had the requisite intent for murder.[142] There has also been acceptance of what has become known as a 'rolled-up charge'. The accused raises a number of defences, typically intoxication, self-defence and provocation. The question is should the jury also consider the impact of the *cumulative* effect of such defences on the issue of intent, even if the evidence, considered separately, would not be capable of supporting any of those defences? In the particular context of this Chapter the question is might the cumulative effect of the separate failed defences be sufficient to raise a reasonable doubt about whether the accused had the requisite intent for murder?

The answer is not clear. The Supreme Court seems to have rejected such an approach in *Perrault*[143] (if accused falls outside the provocation provisions, he cannot argue that because of provocation he did not form the intent for murder), but there are several Court of Appeal decisions which seem to accept the possibility. For example in *Campbell*[144] Martin JA noted that provocation might produce in the accused a state of excitement, anger or disturbance as a result of which he might not contemplate the consequences of his actions and not intend those consequences. In *Nealy* Cory J (as he then was) noted that all the circumstances surrounding the act of killing must be taken into account in determining whether or not the accused has the requisite intent for murder:

> It may well be that the evidence does not give rise to a reasonable doubt as to whether there was provocation or whether the accused lacked the ability to form that intent as a result of consuming alcohol or drugs. Nevertheless, the evidence adduced on those issues, viewed cumulatively, may be of great importance in determining the crucial issue of intent and so the jury must be instructed to considered the cumulative effect of alcohol or drugs, provocation and excessive force in self defence.[145]

---

[142] Discussed in sect 4(ii)(a) above.
[143] [1971] SCR 196.
[144] (1977) 17 OR (2d) 673 (Ont CA). See also *Clow* (1985) 44 CR (3d) 228 at 231, and *Nealy* (1986) 17 OAC 164.
[145] *Ibid*, at 170.

There is also Supreme Court support for the 'rolled up charge'. In *Robinson*,[146] a case involving murder (specific intent) and the impact of intoxication, the Court expressly acknowledged that while the jury might reject individual defences it might still have had a reasonable doubt about intent and it could still consider the cumulative effect of intoxication, provocation and self defence on the issue of intent. In the earlier decision in *Faid*,[147] a case involving excessive force in self-defence, the Court acknowledged that in a failed case of self-defence the evidence might still be relevant in determining whether the accused lacked the intent for murder.

However, the whole development may have been halted by the more recent SCC decision in *Parent*.[148] P was charged with murder after he shot his estranged wife at an auction to dispose of their business assets. At trial he relied on lack of intent to kill and the defence of provocation (he alleged that she had uttered provocative words prior to the shooting). The jury returned a verdict of man-slaughter. When the matter reached the Supreme Court the Court was clear that anger is not a stand-alone defence (the judge had instructed the jury that anger might negate intent). The Court held that outside the defence of provocation anger has no role to play in reducing murder to manslaughter. However in extreme cases anger may lead to a state of automatism.

The rejection of anger as relevant to the issue of intent certainly seems contrary to earlier authority. However it may be that in *Parent* the Court was dealing only with the issue of anger and was acknowledging that in that context only the defence of provocation (with its attendant limitations) can be consid-ered. It would be dangerous to permit evidence of anger without the objective requirements of the provocation defence. The Court did not deal with other aspects of the rolled up plea, but simply with the issue of anger, and it could be argued that in general the rolled-up plea has survived the decision.

While it is not without its problems (and the prospect of side-stepping the ordinary person requirements of provocation are potentially problematic) the 'rolled-up plea' is certainly consistent with generally accepted principles of mens rea. The accused should be entitled to raise a reasonable doubt about intent by tendering any evidence that might raise such a doubt, but the fact that it is tendered and considered by the trier of fact is no guarantee of its acceptance.

5. Conclusion

The Canadian law of homicide is itself in need of further examination and does not provide a good model for reform. The homicide provisions have been the

---

[146] [1996] SCR 683.
[147] [1983] 1 SCR 265.
[148] [2001] 1 SCR 761.

subject of considerable criticism, and in 1984 the then Law Reform Commission of Canada,[149] having drawn attention to the illogical location of General Part provisions (for example, the causation rules) within a Special Part, the tortuous structure of the homicide provisions and their unnecessary detail, proposed extensive revisions. The Working Paper recommended, inter alia:

—that homicide should no longer be classified as culpable and non-culpable;
—that the causation sections should be replaced by a general provision;
—that 'intentional' homicide should apply only to cases of actual intent to kill;
—that 'reckless' homicide should be included in a separate category and should apply only to the causing of death by knowingly exposing another to a serious and socially unacceptable risk of death;
—if there is an offence of 'negligent' homicide it should carry a lower penalty than reckless homicide;
—that there should be two degrees of intentional homicide and the second degree offence should carry a *maximum* of life imprisonment, thus allowing judicial discretion in sentencing;
—only the first degree offence should carry a minimum penalty and be defined in principle as comprising intentional homicide involving the deliberate subordination of the victim's life to the offender's purpose;
—infanticide should be abolished and the matter dealt with under second degree murder where there is flexibility in sentencing.

The LRCC Paper was very critical of the Canadian 'felony murder' provisions and recommended their abolition. While Parliament did nothing it fell to the courts to deal with the matter and, as noted above, the Supreme Court has found those provisions to be an infringement of the *Charter* and thus unconstitutional. While that problem has been addressed, other proposals have not been implemented and it is unlikely that they will be, given the amount of time that has elapsed and the lack of any political will to engage in reform (particularly one that would involve restricting murder to intentional killing). In any event the Working Paper is now very much out of date and a new study, which takes into account vitally important *Charter* jurisprudence which has evolved since the Working Paper was published, is now called for. However, many of the LRCC comments remain pertinent, especially the conclusion that Canadian homicide rules are, without a doubt, badly organised, tortuous and at times tautologous. The barnacle-encrusted homicide rules would certainly benefit from the type of study conducted by The Law Commission for England and Wales.

---

[149] LRCC Working Paper No 33, above n 96. The Law Reform Commission of Canada (which focused on reforming specific areas of law (particularly criminal law)) was disbanded in the 1990s and replaced by the Law Commission, which had a very different mandate.

7

Recklessness and Moral Desiccation in the Australian Law of Murder

IAN LEADER-ELLIOTT

1. Introduction

AUSTRALIAN CRIMINAL LAW is an aggregate of diverse elements. Four jurisdictions adopted criminal codes based, with varying degrees of fidelity, on Sir Samuel Griffith's Draft Criminal Code of 1899. Four get by on admixtures of common law and statute. They are conventionally known as 'common law' jurisdictions though most of their offences and many defences are defined by statute. Federal criminal law has been codified. The Commonwealth Criminal Code is based on the Model Criminal Code,[1] which was compiled by the Model Criminal Code Officers Committee, a body consisting of representatives of each of the nine Australian jurisdictions.[2] As its name suggests, the Model Criminal Code was originally intended to provide a pattern for consistency, if not uniformity, in the principles of criminal liability and formulation of the major offences in Australian criminal law. At this time the prospect of consistency, let alone uniformity, across the nine jurisdictions is distant and perhaps unattainable. But two jurisdictions, the Australian Capital Territory and Northern Territory, are currently engaged in codifying their criminal laws in accordance with the Model Criminal Code pattern.

---

[1] The Model Criminal Code consists of 9 chs, published in the form of a series of Reports, which include legislative drafts and commentary, between 1992 and 2001 by the Australian Commonwealth Attorney General's Department. The most significant of the Code Chs, for the purposes of this Ch, are Ch 2: *General Principles of Criminal Responsibility* (Final Report 1992) and Ch 5: *Fatal Offences Against the Person* (Discussion Paper 1998). The Model Criminal Code can be found on the Attorney General's website at:_www.ag.gov.au/agd/www/Agdhome.nsf/Page/RWPA93DBE7859B79635CA256BB20083B557?OpenDocument.

[2] The history of the codification process has been written by M Goode, 'Constructing Criminal Law Reform and the Model Criminal Code' (2002) 26 *Crim LJ* 152.

Murder and manslaughter are recognised as distinct offences in Australian federal criminal jurisdiction and in all state and territorial jurisdictions. As one would expect, there are substantial similarities in the way the offences are defined. The differences are of more interest. In two states, South Australia and Victoria, common law determines the fault elements[3] for murder and man-slaughter. Such differences as may arise from time to time can be dissolved or reconciled by an appeal to the High Court, for there is only one common law in Australia.[4] Elsewhere, in the other seven jurisdictions, murder is defined by statute and there are substantial differences in the various definitions of the offence and in the location of the borderline between murder and manslaughter. In this Chapter I will be concerned primarily with the differences that arise from the diversity of approaches to the concept of recklessness in the law of murder. Other areas of diversity, as for example in the incidence and formulation of doctrines of constructive murder and the provision of complete and partial defences to murder, are ignored for the most part.

The offence of manslaughter is recognised in all jurisdictions, supplemented by an expanding list of ancillary homicides. In New South Wales and Victoria where manslaughter is not defined by statute, there has been a recurring tendency for a minority of judges to take the position that manslaughter requires proof that the offender realised that their conduct created a risk of death or serious injury, unless liability is based on proof of a dangerous and unlawful act.[5] In *Lavender*[6] the High Court rejected that contention and reiterated the position that manslaughter can be committed by gross inadvertent negligence. On that point at least, the High Court has imposed uniformity on federal, state and territorial definitions of the offence.[7] Recognition of gross negligence as a fault element for manslaughter is consistent, of course, with the likelihood that many

---

[3] The vocabulary of element analysis used in this Ch is drawn from the Commonwealth Criminal Code. Intention, knowledge, recklessness and negligence are 'fault elements'. Other fault elements can be found in the Code, 'belief' for instance, but they are rare. Conduct, circumstances and results—an exhaustive list—are 'physical elements'. See: Criminal Code 1995 (Cth), Ch 2: *General Principles of Criminal Responsibility*. Current Australian usage in statutes, case law and texts is confusing. The older terms, 'actus reus' and 'mens rea' persist, but they have been largely displaced by references to 'external elements' and 'mental elements' which are likely, in turn, to be displaced by the Code terminology. The most recent general text on Australian criminal law, S Bronitt and B McSherry, *Principles of Criminal Law,* 2nd edn (Pyrmont, 2005) Ch 3, entitled 'Principles of Criminal Responsibility', adopts the Code vocabulary.

[4] See, eg, *Lipohar v the Queen; Winfield v The Queen* (1999) 200 CLR 485 (HC Aust).

[5] Adams J provided a recent and eloquent statement of that position in *Lavender* [2004] NSWCCA 120 (NSW Court of Criminal Appeal). In Victoria the controversy was brought to an end by the decision in *Nydam* [1977] VR 430 (Sup Ct of Victoria).

[6] (2005) 222 CLR 67.

[7] Gross or criminal negligence is not, at the time of writing, a fault element for the offence of manslaughter in the Northern Territory Criminal Code. The statement in the text anticipates the effect of the recent *Criminal Reform Amendment Act 2006 (No 2)*, as amended by the *Criminal Reform Amendment Act 2006*, neither of which has yet been proclaimed. The Acts reformulate the offence of manslaughter, in s 160 of the *Criminal Code,* so as to require proof of recklessness or criminal negligence with respect to the death of another.

who are guilty of that offence were aware that their conduct risked death or serious injury. The decision in *Lavender* merely states the threshold requirement for negligent manslaughter.

I have referred to 'recklessness' as if it had a commonly accepted meaning in relation to murder. There is, however, an absence of unanimity about the meaning of the concept. There is also a persuasive argument that it should not be called 'recklessness' except, perhaps, in New South Wales and the Australian Capital Territory, where the statutory definitions of murder refer to 'reckless indifference'.[8] I will avoid the issue of nomenclature for the moment. An exhaustive definition of the concept will not be attempted: it will be assumed that it is a necessary condition for proof of recklessness with respect to a result that the accused person knew or was aware that the result could follow as a consequence of his or her conduct. In murder the result in question may be restricted to death or it may extend to include grievous bodily harm, depending on the jurisdiction. The degree of the defendant's awareness of the risk required for recklessness in murder—whether of likelihood, probability or possibility—is the subject of unresolved tension.

Six jurisdictions accept recklessness as a fault element sufficient to support a conviction for murder; three do not (see below, Table 7.1). Among those that do accept that recklessness is a sufficient fault element for murder some might baulk at calling the concept by that name.

The opening section of the Chapter charts the diversity of Australian laws on the distinction between murder and manslaughter. The central section explores judicial and academic discussions of the concept of recklessness in its applications to murder as a perpetrator and as an accessory to a murder committed by another. The concluding sections examine the role of the jury in determining the difference between murder and manslaughter before proposing a simple reform that would permit the jury to make a relatively unguided moral choice between the offences.

The descriptive sections of the Chapter provide the basis for the suggestion that Australian courts have failed to articulate a morally coherent explanation of the concept of recklessness or its relationship to intentional harms. Moral incoherence is compounded by the diversity of Australian laws determining the difference between murder and manslaughter. If a Victorian and a New South Welshman shoot each other across the Murray River,[9] which divides their States, the question whether murder has been committed can depend, among other fortuities, on which side of the river the shot takes fatal effect and who recovers from his or her wound. So also if a South Australian and a Queenslander shoot each other across their shared border. That does not exhaust the possibilities of cross border differences, but it is unnecessary to multiply examples.

---

[8] *Crimes Act* 1900 (NSW), s18; *Crimes Act* 1900 (ACT) s12.
[9] Compare *Ward* [1979] VR 205; *Ward* [1980] VR 209; (1980) 142 CLR 308. Strictly speaking, it is not necessary for the shot to cross the river, for the common border is on the Victorian side.

2. The Meaning of 'Intention' with Respect to Incriminating Results

In his monograph, *Fault in Homicide*,[10] Stanley Yeo opens his discussion of Australian law with the remark that 'Australian courts have largely avoided the difficulties that their English counterparts have had over the meaning of intention as a fault element for murder'.[11] In most Australian jurisdictions a defendant's realisation that his or her conduct will probably result in death is accepted as equivalent in blameworthiness to intention to cause death or grievous bodily harm. In some jurisdictions, realisation that conduct will probably result in grievous bodily harm is accepted as equivalent in blameworthiness to an intention to cause grievous bodily harm (see below, Table 7.1). Since intention in murder is supplemented in this way by a fault element conventionally described as recklessness, Yeo asserts that Australian courts 'have not felt the same need to define intention' to cause death or injury as their English counterparts.[12]

That cannot be a complete explanation, however, for the near absence of judicial consideration of the concept of intention when liability for results is in issue. Some jurisdictions do not recognise recklessness with respect to death as equivalent in blameworthiness to intention to kill when murder is in issue. In those jurisdictions there can be an issue over the meaning of intention with respect to death or grievous bodily harm. And, murder aside, modern codifications of the law relating to non-fatal offences against the person characteristically distinguish between harms inflicted recklessly and harms inflicted intentionally.[13] So far, however, courts in the common law jurisdictions have had little to say about the meaning of intention in the offences against the person. The issue has received more considered attention in the jurisdictions that adopted Sir Samuel Griffith's Queensland Code.[14] Consistent with its nineteenth century origins, the Code makes no reference to recklessness. It was one of the more significant achievements of the Code that it eliminated all references to 'malicious' wrongdoing—the nineteenth century precursor to recklessness—in the formulation of offences. The fault elements in the Griffith Code are restricted to intention, knowledge and occasional references to 'willful' wrongdoing. Recent case law, in particular the decisions of the Queensland Court of Criminal Appeal, has rejected any suggestion that recklessness is equivalent to intention with

---

[10] S Yeo, *Fault in Homicide: Towards a Schematic Approach to the Fault Elements for Murder and Involuntary Manslaughter in England, Australia and India* (Sydney, 1997).

[11] *Ibid*, 52.

[12] *Ibid*, 55.

[13] As, eg, in the Victorian Crimes Act 1958, s 16: causing serious injury intentionally; s 17: causing serious injury recklessly.

[14] See G Taylor, 'The Victorian Criminal Code' (2004) 23 *University of Queensland Law Journal* 170.

respect to an incriminating result.[15] The extended meaning that intention sometimes bears in other Australian jurisdictions has been characterised as a development of common law doctrine that has no place in the Code, which is taken to refer to intention in its 'ordinary or natural' meaning. When an act is intentional, it is what the person meant to do; when a result is intentional, it is his or her purpose or design to bring about that result. Since ordinary usage governs the meaning of the concept, the courts have said that it is both unnecessary and undesirable to 'set about explaining an ordinary and well understood word in the English language'.[16] It is a curious and perhaps unexpected consequence of codification that it has led Queensland courts to make a sharp distinction between ordinary language and legal terminology and to criticise courts in common law jurisdictions for confusing them. Queensland courts have declined to consider the question whether intention with respect to a result extends to those results of conduct that were known to be certain. In what may seem a strange reversal of roles, the appellant in *Laycock and Stokes*[17] sought to overturn his conviction for murder on the ground that the trial judge had not given a *Woollin*[18] direction to the jury in explanation of the requirement of intention to kill or cause grievous bodily harm. The Queensland Court of Appeal simply reiterated its view that intention required no definition or explanation. So far as the law of murder is concerned, the significance of these decisions lies in the fact that the jury's sense of the meaning and applications of 'intention to cause death' and 'intention to cause grievous bodily harm' will determine the limits of murder in most of the jurisdictions that adopted the Griffith Code. Unless, of course, the case is one in which a statutory equivalent of the felony murder doctrine or other provisions that impose constructive guilt is applied.

Elsewhere in Australia, as Stanley Yeo points out, there have been few occasions in recent decades when courts have given considered attention to the meaning of intention with respect to results. The High Court made passing reference in *Crabbe*[19] to the view that 'a person who does an act knowing its probable consequences may be regarded as having intended those consequences to occur'.

---

[15] Compare the earlier High Court decision, on the Tasmanian Criminal Code, in *Vallance* (1961) 108 CLR 56, in which Dixon CJ argued that references to 'intention' in s 13 of the Code extended to include the defendant's awareness of the likely consequences of their conduct. That suggestion was vigorously promoted in the first and succeeding editions of Colin Howard's *Australian Criminal Law* (Sydney, 1965), 5, 113–15, 356. More recent case law, cited in the following footnotes, decisively rejects the equation of intention with recklessness.

[16] *Laycock and Stokes* [1999] QCA 307, at para [65], citing *Wilmot (No 2)* [1985] 2 Qd R 413 (Qld CA). See I Campbell, 'Recklessness in Intentional Murder under the Australian Codes' (1986) 10 *Crim LJ* 3.

[17] [1999] QCA 307. The same curious reversal is apparent in *Reid* [2006] QCA 202. The argument for the appellant appears to rest on the mistaken view that one cannot intend a result unless one believes it to be certain or at least likely. See, in addition, *Sancar* [1999] NSWCCA 284, to the same effect, declining to consider *Woollin* in circumstances where oblique intention had no possible application.

[18] [1998] 4 All ER 103.

[19] (1985) 156 CLR 464.

The Court took care, however, to avoid expressing approval of that view, and it has not been adopted in subsequent case law.[20] On another occasion, McHugh J suggested that intention should be taken to extend to results that were known to be certain,[21] but his suggestion was obiter, unsupported by authority and given in a case where the issues were far removed from the crime of murder.

There is legislative support, however, for the concept of oblique intention. The Commonwealth Criminal Code, which does provide a definition of intention, declares that a person 'has intention with respect to a result if he or she means to bring it about or is aware that it will occur in the normal course of events'.[22] So far as the Commonwealth is concerned, occasions for the application of that definition in cases involving violent crime may become increasingly and distressingly common. The Commonwealth Code includes a complete set of offences against the person. They include the murder of UN personnel and the murder of Australian citizens and residents, whether abroad or at home, resulting from conduct in other countries.[23] The definition may also find applications in the law of murder in the Australian Capital Territory and Northern Territory, both of which are currently engaged in adopting the Commonwealth Criminal Code.

---

[20] See, eg, *Grant* (2002) 55 NSWLR 80 (NSW Court of Criminal Appeal) at 523–4. Though Brennan J lent support to the passage in *He Kaw Teh* (1985) 157 CLR 527, 570, his discussion in *Boughey* (1986) 161 CLR 10, 43, distinguishes between intention in murder and foresight of the probability of death or grievous bodily harm. In Queensland, the remarkable decision in *T* [1997] Qd R 623 (Qld CA) entails a firm distinction between intention and foresight of probable consequences. The Appendix to the judgment of Fitzgerald P provides a useful compendium of divergent judicial usage.

[21] *Peters* (1998) 192 CLR 493, at para [68]: 'a person may intend to do something even though it is the last thing that he or she wishes to bring about…. Intention in this context is broader than a person's inclination to act to achieve a result that he or she believes is desirable. If a person does something that is virtually certain to result in another event occurring and knows that that event is certain or virtually certain to occur, for legal purposes at least he or she intends it to occur…. In *R v Moloney*…and *R v Hancock and Shankland*…, however, the House of Lords held that foresight of a consequence, even foresight that the consequence was virtually certain, was merely evidence of intention. But if this is so, a jury would be bound to acquit a person accused of murder if the jurors believed that the accused had not committed the fatal act in order to bring about the death of the deceased even though the accused knew that death was the certain result of his or her actions.' The concluding reflection, which provided the punchline for the argument, has potential application only in those jurisdictions where recklessness is not recognised as a fault element for murder. Recent cases in those jurisdictions indicate that the courts will leave the issue of intentionality to the jury, without an extended definition.

[22] Ch 2: General Principles of Criminal Responsibility; Ch 5.2: Intention.

[23] See *Criminal Code (Cth)*, 71.4: Intentionally causing serious harm to a UN or associated person; 115.1: Intentionally causing serious harm to an Australian citizen or resident of Australia.

3. The Australian Law of Murder: Common Law, Statute and Code

In two states, Victoria and South Australia, the fault elements of murder are governed by Australian common law. It will be apparent from the discussion that follows that there is now considerable divergence between Australian and English common law. Divergent statutory definitions of the fault elements for murder have been enacted in New South Wales[24] and the Australian Capital Territory.[25] In the remaining five jurisdictions—Queensland, Northern Territory, Western Australia, Tasmania and the Commonwealth— substantive criminal law has been completely codified. No two codes define homicide in the same way. The table that follows summarises the differences in fault elements:

Table 7.1: Fault Elements in Murder in Australian Law					
Jurisdiction	Intend to kill	Intend GBH	Reckless as to death	Reckless as to GBH	Constructive murder
Commonwealth[26]	YES	NO	YES	NO	NO
Aust Cap Territory[27]	YES	NO	YES	NO	NO
New Sth Wales[28]	YES	YES	YES	NO	YES
Nth Territory[29]	YES	YES	NO	NO	YES
Queensland[30]	YES	YES	NO	NO	YES
Sth Australia[31]	YES	YES	YES	YES	YES
Tasmania[32]	YES	YES	YES	NO	YES
Victoria[33]	YES	YES	YES	YES	YES
1. West Australia[34]	YES	NO	NO	NO	NO
2. West Australia[35]	YES	YES	NO	NO	YES

---

[24] *Crimes Act 1900* (NSW), s 18: Murder and manslaughter defined.

[25] *Crimes Act 1900* (ACT), s 12: Murder. The ACT has embarked on codification of its criminal law, following the model provided by the *Commonwealth Criminal Code 1995*. See *Criminal Code 2002* (ACT). The ACT law of homicide awaits codification.

[26] See *Criminal Code* (Cth) 71.2: Murder of a UN or associated person; 115.1 Murder of an Australian citizen or resident of Australia.

[27] *Crimes Act 1900*, s 12.

[28] *Crimes Act 1900*, s 18.

[29] *Criminal Code 1983*, s 162; *Charlie* (1997) 199 CLR 387.

[30] *Criminal Code 1899*, s 302.

[31] Common law.

[32] *Criminal Code, 1924*, s 157(1). Subs (1) requires (a) proof of intention to cause death or (b) intention to cause 'bodily harm which the offender knew to be likely to cause death' or, switching to the constructive mode, (c) an unlawful act or omission that 'the offender knew or ought to have known, to be likely to cause death in the circumstances, though he had no wish to cause death or bodily harm to any person'. These provisions envisage a rather narrower ambit for reckless murder than other Australian jurisdictions though they also, in para (c), abandon the requirement of subjective realisation of risk. S 157 was the subject of exhaustive consideration by the High Court in *Boughey* (1986) 161 CLR 10.

[33] Common law

[34] The Western Australian *Criminal Code* 1913, exceptionally, distinguishes two grades of the offence of murder: 'willful murder', s 278 and s 279 'murder'.

[35] *Ibid*. It seems likely that the references to intention in these provisions are not meant to extend to instances of recklessness with respect to death or bodily harm. See *Draper* [2000] WASCA 160 (WA Court of Criminal Appeal).

In all jurisdictions evidence of self-induced intoxication, of whatever degree, is admissible on the issue of intention in murder and, in jurisdictions where the concept of recklessness is recognised, on the issue of awareness of risk.[36] Evidence of self-induced intoxication is also admissible, in the common law states, on the issue of voluntariness in murder. In *Hawkins*,[37] the High Court held that mental illness is also admissible on the issues of intention and recklessness in murder. Evidence of mental illness, unlike evidence of intoxication, is not admissible when the question is whether the conduct of the offender was voluntary.[38]

In general, a person is taken to be criminally responsible for an intended result of his or her conduct, even if the result occurs by an unexpected causal path.[39] The same rule may apply when liability is based on recklessness.[40] It is possible, however, that courts will distinguish between results intended and results merely foreseen, when issues of remoteness in causation arise.

4. Punishment for Murder—The Variations

Sentencing options for murder vary from jurisdiction to jurisdiction (see below, Table 7.2). In most, life imprisonment is not mandatory. The distinction between jurisdictions that continue to impose a mandatory life sentence and the remainder is not, however, of great significance. In all jurisdictions the sentencing court is permitted to set a non-parole period that will, in normal circumstances, result in release before the entire sentence is served. It is exceptional for sentencing courts to impose a life sentence in jurisdictions where the sentence is not mandatory, and exceptional to decline to set a non-parole period in jurisdictions where the life sentence is mandatory.

---

[36] *O'Connor* (1980) 146 CLR 64 (HC Aust). For an uncontroversial application of *O'Connor* in a case of 'reckless murder' see *Faure* [1999] 2 VR 537.

[37] (1994) 179 CLR 500.

[38] *Hawkins* (1994) 179 CLR 500 discussed in S Bronitt and B McSherry, *Principles of Criminal Law*, 2nd edn (Pyrmont, 2006) 240–1; I Leader-Elliott, 'Cases in the High Court: *Hawkins v The Queen*' (1994) 18 *Crim LJ* 347.

[39] *Royall* (1991) 172 CLR 378 (HC Aust).

[40] *Ince* (2001) 127 A Crim R 517 (Vict CA), at para [46] (Callaway J): '[a]ll that is required is that an act of the accused that was done with the requisite intent or recklessness was a cause of death, even if not in the manner intended or foreseen'.

In most, if not all, jurisdictions courts are under continuing governmental pressure to increase the severity of sentences. In some—New South Wales is a notable example—the judicial discretion to specify a parole date or the length of the non-parole period is subject to legislative guidelines that set standard non-parole periods for different categories of murder.[41]

With the exception of Western Australia, where willful murder and murder are separate offences, statutory guidelines that define or constrain courts' sentencing discretion draw no distinctions between intentional killings, intention to cause grievous bodily harm, or reckless or constructive murders.[42] Case law on sentencing for murder, or determining a non-parole period in jurisdictions where the life penalty is mandatory, does discriminate between intentional and reckless killings. There is, however, no rule or presumption that murder by recklessness must draw a lesser sentence than a murder that involved intention to kill or caused grievous bodily harm. Instances of murder by recklessness can occupy the same 'worst cases' category as intentional killings.[43]

---

[41] Crimes (Sentencing Procedure) Act 1999 (NSW). These guidelines appear in Pt 4, Div 1A of the Act

[42] In Western Australia, offenders convicted of willful murder, unlike those convicted of murder, are liable, but not required, to be sentenced to 'strict security life imprisonment' rather than 'life imprisonment': Criminal Code 1913, s 282, Penalty for willful murder and murder.

[43] See n 77 below.

Table 7.2: *Murder and Manslaughter— Forms of Sentence*							
Jurisdiction	**Murder**					**Manslaughter**	
	Manda-tory Life	Life or term of years	Courts may set a non parole period	Legislative guidelines for non parole period	Courts may refuse to set non parole period	Maxi-mum Life	Period of years
Commonwealth[44]	NO	YES	YES	NO	YES	/	25
Aust.Cap. Territory[45]	NO	YES	YES	NO	YES	/	20
New Sth Wales[46]	NO	YES	YES[47]	YES	YES	/	20
N.Territory[48].	YES	NO	YES	YES	YES	YES	/
Queensland[49]	YES	NO	YES	YES	YES	YES	/
Sth Aust[50]	YES	NO	YES	NO	YES	YES	/
Tasmania[51]	NO	YES	YES	NO	YES	/	21
Victoria[52]	NO	YES	YES	NO	YES	/	20
1. West Aust[53]	YES	NO	YES	YES	YES	/	20
2. West Australia[54]	YES	NO	YES	YES	YES	/	20

[44] *Criminal Code (Cth)* 71.2 Murder of a UN or associated person; 104.1 Murder of an Australian citizen or resident of Australia; *Crimes Act 1914*, s 19AB

[45] *Crimes Act 1900*, ss 12, 15; *Rehabilitation of Offenders (Interim) Act 2001*, s 31.

[46] *Crimes Act 1900,* ss 18, 19A; *Crimes (Sentencing Procedure) Act 1999*, ss 21A, 44, 45, 54D, 61. For discussion of these sentencing provisions, with excerpts from the Second Reading Speech of the NSW Attorney-General (New South Wales, Parliamentary Debates, *Legislative Assembly*, 23 Oct 2002, 5813 (Bob Debus, Attorney General), see *Way* (2004) 60 NSWLR 168.

[47] A person sentenced to life imprisonment for murder in NSW is sentenced to life without the possibility of parole: *Crimes (Sentencing Procedure) Act 1999*, s 61(1); *Harris* [2000] NSWCCA 469. For a recent application see *Knight v R* [2006] NSWCCA 292 (NSW Court of Criminal Appeal) In other jurisdictions where life imprisonment is a maximum rather than mandatory penalty, courts do have power to determine a non-parole period when imposing a life sentence.

[48] *Criminal Code Act 1993*, ss 164, 167; *Sentencing (Crime of Murder) and Parole Reform Act 2003*, s 53A; *Sentencing Act* s 65.

[49] *Criminal Code 1899*, ss 305, 310; *Penalties and Sentences Act 1992*, Pt 10—Indefinite sentences.

[50] *Criminal Law Consolidation Act 1935*, ss 11, 13; *Criminal Law (Sentencing) Act 1988*, s 32.

[51] *Criminal Code Act 1924*, s 158; *Sentencing Act 1997*, s 18.

[52] *Crimes Act 1958*, ss 3, 5; *Sentencing Act 1991*, s 18A, B.

[53] *Criminal Code 1913*, ss 282, 287; *Sentencing Act 1995*, ss 90, 91, 96. The State of Western Australia distinguishes between wilful murder and murder. The sentence for both is mandatory life imprisonment. The sentencing court may, however, set a non-parole period. The Sentencing Act specifies mandatory non-parole guidelines for willful murder at 15–19 years and murder at 7–14 years.

[54] N 53 above.

5. Intention and Recklessness in the Australian Common Law of Murder

In the common law states the evolution of the law of murder over the last 50 years has been marked by judicial insistence on subjectivity combined with an increasingly desiccated set of distinctions that delineate the borderland between murder and manslaughter. Subjectivity is no guarantee of moral coherence. The desiccation of the law is a consequence of the growing significance of recklessness in Australian criminal law theory, case law and recent codifications of the criminal law. The rise of recklessness can be traced, in part at least, to the influence exerted by successive editions of Colin Howard's *Australian Criminal Law*, which first appeared in 1965.[55] The states and territories that adopted the Griffith Code have largely avoided both the insistence on subjectivity and the moral desiccation that characterise the homicide case law of the common law states. The Code was originally intended to set the threshold of criminal liability by reference to the limits of the reasonable man's foresight of likely results and his susceptibility to reasonable mistakes about circumstances. Recklessness receives no overt recognition in the Code. It does, however, have two inconsistent uses in Griffith Code case law. Recklessness is sometimes used as a synonym for criminal negligence[56] and it has a sequestered role in the definition of the fault element of 'wilful' wrongdoing in offences involving damage to property.[57] Liability for this offence requires proof of intention to damage property or recklessness, in the sense that the defendant knew it was more likely than not that property would be damaged.[58]

Recklessness is the central fault element in the Commonwealth Criminal Code, which adopted the general provisions of the Model Criminal Code without significant change. Chapter 2—*General Principles of Criminal Responsibility*—was intended by the Model Criminal Code Officers Committee (MCCOC) as a statement of common law principles of criminal responsibility amalgamated, to the limited extent that amalgamation was possible, with the corresponding principles found in the various versions of the Griffith Code. It was hoped that a model code would provide the 'best mechanism for achieving uniformity in the important and complex area of criminal law'.[59] Uniformity in matters of basic

---

[55] See P Brett, *An Inquiry Into Criminal Guilt* (Sydney, 1963) at 94 ff, on recklessness.

[56] See, eg, *Stottand & Van Embden* [2002] 2 Qd R 313 (Qld Court of Criminal Appeal); *Agnew* [2003] WASCA 188 (WA Court of Criminal Appeal). Compare the remarks on 'reckless indifference' in the judgment of Deane and Dawson JJ in the High Court decision in *Royall* (1991) 172 CLR 378 at para [29].

[57] *Criminal Code*, s 469: Wilful damage.

[58] *Thomson* [1996] QCA 258 (Qld CA; Fitzgerald P and McKenzie J). Fitzgerald P provides an exhaustive examination of authorities, most of which have to do with the definition of the fault element of murder in English and Australian common law jurisdictions. Pincus J declined to express an opinion on the degree of knowledge of probability.

[59] Model Criminal Code, Ch 2: 'General Principles of Criminal Responsibility' (Final Report Dec 1992), Preface, iii.

principle has not been achieved. The Code was conceived and drafted, for the most part, as a statement of common law principles of criminal responsibility, and it has so far proved unacceptable to the Griffith Code states.[60]

The definition of recklessness is a stripped down version of the one in the American Model Penal Code. A person is reckless with respect to a result:

> when he or she is aware of a substantial risk that it will occur and it is, having regard to the circumstances known to him or her, unjustifiable to take the risk.[61]

Recklessness with respect to circumstances was defined in identical terms. Omitted from this formulation of the concept was the additional defining qualification in the American version:

> The risk must be of such a nature and degree that, considering the nature and purpose of his conduct and the circumstances known to him, its disregard involves a gross deviation from the standard of conduct that a law abiding person would observe in the actor's situation.

The omission is surprising; MCCOC conceded, in its commentary to the Model Criminal Code, that there would be instances where negligence with respect to a result would be *more* blameworthy than recklessness with respect to the same result.[62] Justification for taking a risk is a demanding standard and it is quite possible to imagine circumstances in which taking an unjustifiable risk does not involve a gross deviation from the standard of the reasonable person. Failure to realise a risk, on the other hand, may result from gross and inexcusable disregard for consequences. There appear to have been two reasons for the omission of the Model Penal Code qualification. First, because MCCOC took the view that its definition was an accurate reflection of Australian common law and, secondly, because recklessness marks the threshold of criminal responsibility in the Code. Recklessness is the universal fault element in the Code, unless displaced by a provision that specifies another form of fault or one that simply eliminates fault elements. Omission of the qualification requiring a gross deviation enhanced the versatile negotiability of the concept. A requirement of gross deviation might be appropriate for some offences but inappropriate for others. Among serious offences, rape is an obvious example where the additional requirement would distort the offence: any conscious deviation at all from reasonable standards of law-abiding conduct must be sufficient for guilt.[63] In minor offences, where any

---

[60] The Northern Territory is an exception. Common law prevailed in the Territory until 1983 when a bowdlerised version of the Griffith Code was enacted. It is anticipated that the Northern Territory *Criminal Code* provisions on the general principles of criminal responsibility will be displaced by the *Criminal Reform Amendment Act 2006 (No2)*, as amended by the *Criminal Reform Amendment Act 2006*. Neither Act has been proclaimed at the time of writing.

[61] Model Criminal Code, Ch 2: 'General Principles of Criminal Responsibility' (Final Report Dec 1992), 203 (fault elements).

[62] See *ibid*, Commentary 31.

[63] Recklessness is the fault element for rape in common law jurisdictions and in the Northern Territory and Australian Capital Territory. See *Banditt* (2005) 157 A Crim R 420, where the High

advertent deviation from reasonable standards of conduct should be sufficient for guilt, a requirement of gross deviation might be considered equally inappropriate.

The twin themes of formal insistence on subjectivity and moral desiccation are even more apparent when the definitions of murder in the Model Penal Code and the Commonwealth Criminal Code are compared. They are discussed below.[64]

Though the evaluative component in recklessness is slender—absence of justification—the Commonwealth Code preserves the memory at least of recklessness as a concept that combines a state of mind and a criterion for moral evaluation of the defendant's risk-taking conduct. With a few fleeting exceptions in minority judgments, the courts in common law jurisdictions have sought to eliminate the evaluative component in recklessness. They have sought instead to express the moral distinction between murder and manslaughter, when recklessness marks the boundary between the offences, by an exquisite concern with verbal formulae expressing the *degree* of risk perceived by the accused.

6. Murder and Manslaughter: Unquantifiable Degrees of Difference

If constructive murder is put to one side, the unanimous High Court decision in *Crabbe*[65] provides a canonical statement of the fault elements of common law murder:[66]

> If an accused knows when he does an act that death or grievous bodily harm is a probable consequence, he does the act expecting that death or grievous bodily harm will be the likely result, for the word 'probable' means likely to happen. That state of mind is comparable with an intention to kill or to do grievous bodily harm....a person who, without lawful justification or excuse, does an act knowing that it is probable that death or grievous bodily harm will result, is guilty of murder if death in fact results.[67]

The facts of the case provided a plausible basis for the conclusion that Crabbe's conduct might have been accompanied by the knowledge that it could cause death or grievous bodily harm rather than by an intention to do so. Crabbe was a B Triple road train driver who was thrown out of an outback motel bar in the Northern Territory after he became drunk and quarrelsome. Some time later, in the early hours of the morning, he unhooked two trailers from the B Triple and returned to the motel at the controls of his prime mover and remaining trailer. He drove this rig through the wall of the motel and into the bar, killing five people and injuring many others. It is possible, perhaps likely, that he intended to

---

Court decisively rejected the appellant's argument that there may be circumstances in which it is reasonable to take a small risk that the other person has not consented to sexual penetration.

[64] Text accompanying nn 119–140 below.

[65] (1985) 156 CLR 464.

[66] Though the case arose in the Northern Territory, which has codified its criminal law, the events occurred in 1983, before the *Northern Territory Criminal Code* came into effect.

[67] (1985) 156 CLR 464 at 469: Gibbs CJ, Wilson, Brennan, Deane and Dawson JJ.

kill some of the people inside. It is also possible, however, that he intended a spectacular act of destruction of the building rather than death or injury to patrons who might be inside. The trial judge gave a recklessness direction, which the High Court accepted as adequate and upheld Crabbe's conviction for murder.

The case law that followed the decision in *Crabbe* is essentially exegetical: no court has doubted the authority of the High Court's formulation of the fault elements in murder. There has been an interpretive drift, however, away from the requirement that the offender must have known that death or grievous bodily harm was a *probable* result of his or her conduct.

A few points of clarification are necessary before examining the concept of recklessness in more detail. It is accepted that the recklessness direction should only be given in cases where the facts provide a foundation for it and that the trial judge must explain the potential application of recklessness to the facts of the case.[68] Australian courts are alive to the risk that an unfounded direction can confuse the jury about the distinction between recklessness and negligence. For the same reason, courts tend to avoid specific reference to 'recklessness' in jury directions, referring instead to knowledge, foresight, awareness or realisation of the likelihood of death or grievous bodily harm. There appear to be no restrictions on the kind of conduct that may provide the grounds for a recklessness direction: no distinctions are drawn between act and omission[69] and there is no requirement of hostility.[70] There is no requirement that the reckless conduct be aimed at any particular individual, though the more notable cases involving the concept do tend to involve conduct that was intended to threaten another[71] or to induce fear, as in mutual Russian roulette.[72]

The second point of clarification has to do with recklessness as to grievous bodily harm. The High Court accepted this as a fault element 'comparable' with an intention to cause grievous bodily harm when common law liability for murder is in question. In most Australian jurisdictions, the common law has been displaced on this particular issue. Only in Victoria and South Australia is recklessness as to grievous bodily harm accepted as a fault element for murder.[73] The declaration in *Crabbe* that intention and recklessness with respect to grievous bodily harm are 'comparable' is curiously evasive. They are certainly not

---

[68] See *Royall* (1990) 172 CLR 378 (HC Aust), 414–6, Deane and Dawson JJ, and authorities cited; *Pemble* (1971) 124 CLR 107 (HC Aust); *Cooke* (1985) 39 SASR 225 (Sup Ct SA), 237; *Craig Allan Williamson* (1996) 67 SASR 428 (Sup Ct SA). For a recent example of a court refraining from giving a recklessness direction on the ground that it was more likely to confuse than assist the jury see *Murphy and Watson* [2001] VSC 523 (Sup Ct Vict; Flatman J). See, in addition, I Leader-Elliott, 'Recklessness and Murder—The Facts of the Case' (1986) 10 *Crim LJ* 359.

[69] *Lawford and Van Der Wiel* (1993) 61 SASR 542 (Sup Ct SA), 549–50.

[70] *Boughey* (1986) 161 CLR 10, 23–7 (HC Aust; Mason, Wilson and Deane JJ).

[71] As, eg, in cases involving fatal shootings, where the defendant maintained that his intention was merely to frighten another: *Pemble* (1971) 124 CLR 107 (HC Aust); *Sergi* [1974] VR 1 (Sup Ct Vict); *La Fontaine* (1976) 136 CLR 62 (HC Aust).

[72] *Faure* [1999] 2 VR 537 (Vict CA).

[73] Victorian courts now refer to 'really serious injury' rather than 'grievous bodily harm' when directing juries. See, eg, *Franklin* [2001] VSC 79 (Victorian Court of Criminal Appeal). South Australian courts have been more cautious: *Griffiths* [1999] SASC 70, though the practice seems to

equivalents. The most likely instances of recklessness as to grievous bodily harm are those in which the offender has made a physical attack on another with the intention of inflicting something *less* than grievous bodily harm. If *Crabbe* is taken literally on this particular point recklessness will displace intention. The trial judge may direct the jury that it is unnecessary to consider whether the defendant's attack on the victim was meant to cause grievous bodily harm: it is sufficient if the defendant was aware that grievous bodily harm was the likely or probable result of an intentional attack.[74] In practice, trial courts in Victoria and South Australia seem to have avoided this obvious implication of *Crabbe*. The recklessness direction is reserved for more exotic scenarios than those involving a simple, brutal attack with fists, boots, knife or other weapons of variable lethality. The many problems inherent in the acceptance of intention to cause, and recklessness as to, grievous bodily harm as fault elements for murder will be skirted in the remainder of this Chapter, which is primarily concerned with intention to cause death and recklessness as to that result.

In general, courts in Australian common law jurisdictions have accepted the statement in *Crabbe* that a person who acts in the knowledge that death or grievous bodily harm is a probable or likely result of his or her conduct, 'can be regarded for the purposes of the criminal law as just as blameworthy as one who intended to kill or do grievous bodily harm'.[75] That proposition is reinforced by the practice of sentencing courts when determining non-parole periods for murderers. Sentencing courts accept that cases of reckless murder will be less likely than instances of intentional murder to fall within the category of 'worst cases' where a penalty in the maximum range will be imposed. But exceptional cases of murder by recklessness can fall within the worst case category[76] and draw sentences equivalent to those for utterly unmitigated instances of murder where the offender intended death or grievous bodily harm.[77] As a consequence, there is

have been accepted in more recent cases. The High Court refrained from expressing disapproval in *Meyers* [1997] HCA, available at www.austlii.edu.au/au/cases/cth/high_ct/unrep342.html, para 1, per curiam.

[74] Discussed in I Elliott, 'Recklessness in Murder' (1981) 5 *Crim LJ* 84.

[75] *Crabbe* (1985) 156 CLR 464 at 469.

[76] The maximum sentence is appropriate when a murder falls within the 'worst case category': *Veen* 1988 164 CLR 465 (HC Aust). For discussion see *Leach* (2004) 145 NTR 1 (NT Sup Ct); *Clarke* [2005] NSWSC 413 (Sup Ct NSW).

[77] R Fox and A Freiberg, *Sentencing: State and Federal Law in Victoria*, 2nd edn (Melbourne, 1999) 880–1, citing *Aiton* (1993) 68 A Crim R 578 (Vict Court of Criminal Apeal); *Chan* (1994) 76 A Crim R 252 (Sup Ct Vict); *Ainsworth* (1994) 76 A Crim R 127 (NSW Court of Criminal Law). See also *Grant* (2002) 55 NSWLR 80 (NSW Court of Criminal Appeal), at paras [72]–[73]; *Holton* [2004] NSWCCA 214 (NSW Court of Criminal Appeal), at para [59]; *Crabbe* (2004) 150 A Crim R 523, at para [137]. In *Holton*, Grove J took the point that recklessness as to the probability that conduct will cause *death* can exceed, in blameworthiness, death resulting from conduct intended to cause *grievous bodily harm* [120–1]. Compare, however, *Clarke* [2005] NSWSC 413 (Sup Ct NSW) at paras [35]–[36]. The decisions on sentencing when felony murder provided the route to conviction are to similar effect: see *Robinson* [2001] NSWCCA 180, at para [12], 'one must not draw a distinction between felony murder and murder with a pre-ordained intention'; *Jacobs and Mehajer* (2004) 151 A Crim R 452 (NSW Court of Criminal Appeal).

a conflict of principle between the case law governing sentences for murder and the many statutory provisions that create lesser offences against the person, which do distinguish between injuries inflicted intentionally and injuries inflicted recklessly, and impose lesser maximum penalties for the latter class of offences.[78]

There is much to be said for the view that intentional and reckless killing can occupy the same category of 'worst case' murders, deserving of the highest penalties. Intentional killing does cover a broader spectrum of human wickedness than causing death by recklessness. There are so many more reasons for killing intentionally than there are for continuing a course of conduct in the knowledge that it is likely to result in the death of another person. Reckless murder has no equivalents for the depravity involved in killing for the sake of killing or taking the life of another in order to exact vengeance or terrorise a community. But intentional murder and murder by recklessness can be matched in moral depravity in one dimension at least—that of callousness—when the conduct of the offender displays utter indifference to the value of the victim's life. That level of indifference may be uncommon in cases of recklessness: in most instances of reckless murder one might surmise that the offender would not have persisted in the conduct had they realised that the fatal outcome was certain.[79] There are, however, cases where reckless and intentional killings are matched in callousness, when the reasons for killing intentionally or persisting in conduct known to be likely to cause death are equally trivial and equally indicative of contempt for the value of human life.

The conclusion that reckless killing can, on occasion, match or approach the degree of blameworthiness associated with death caused intentionally leaves the central problem posed by *Crabbe* untouched. Murder by recklessness has no readily definable lower boundary of seriousness that can mark the difference between murder committed in this way and manslaughter. The difficulty of articulating the distinction might perhaps be of less significance if the courts enjoyed an unfettered discretion to determine the penalty for murder when setting the head sentence or the period of imprisonment to be served prior to parole. There is, in practice, a substantial statistical overlap in the penalties imposed for

---

[78] See, eg, s 16: 'Causing serious injury intentionally', and s 17: 'Causing serious injury recklessly', in the Victorian *Crimes Act 1958*; *Commonwealth Criminal Code*, 104.3: 'Intentionally causing serious harm to an Australian citizen or resident' (20 years maximum), and 104.4: 'Recklessly causing harm to an Australian citizen or resident (15 years maximum). Similar examples can be found in all other jurisdictions. For an instance where the Court insists on the distinction between intention and recklessness see *McKnoulty* (1995) 77 A Crim R 333 (NSW Court of Criminal Appeal). See also *Livingstone* [2004] NSWCCA 122 (NSW Court of Criminal Appeal).

[79] See, for discussions bearing on this issue, B Mitchell, 'Culpably Indifferent Murder' (1996) 25 *Anglo-American Law Review* 64, 72, on the 'value-deficit killer'; A Halpin, 'Intended Consequences and Unintended Fallacies' [1987] *OJLS* 104; A Michaels, 'Acceptance: the Missing Mental State' (1998) 71 *Southern California Law Review* 953; K Huigens, 'Homicide in Aretaic Terms' (2003) 6 *Buffalo Criminal Law Review* 97; K Simons, 'Does Punishment for "Culpable Indifference" Simply Punish for Bad Behaviour?' (2002) 6 *Buffalo Criminal Law Review* 219.

murder and manslaughter. In general, however, an offender who is convicted of murder rather than manslaughter can expect a far heavier penalty as a consequence of that characterisation of his or her offence. In New South Wales, sentencing legislation sets out presumptive non-parole periods for different categories of murder. The presumptive sentence can be varied, but variation can only occur after a determination of the existence of listed aggravating and mitigating factors.[80] The list of aggravations and mitigations is exhaustive and it makes no reference to the fault elements for the offence of murder. Nor do the courts enjoy unfettered discretion in other jurisdictions where similar though less rigid constraints militate against a seamless merger of the penalties for murder and manslaughter.

The decision in *Crabbe* makes liability for murder depend on proof of intention to kill or cause grievous bodily harm or on knowledge that those were 'probable or likely' results of the defendant's conduct. No distinction appears to have been intended between likelihood and probability: 'the word "probable" means likely to happen'.[81] There is no indication that the Court meant to imply that the defendant is only guilty of murder if death or grievous bodily harm is known to be more likely than not.[82] It became very clear that probability did not bear that meaning in the subsequent High Court decision in *Boughey*[83] in which a majority of the Court held that it was sufficient if the prosecution established that the accused knew that there was a 'substantial or real chance, as distinct from a mere possibility' that his conduct might result in death or grievous bodily harm.[84] The facts of the case are illustrative of that statement of principle. The defendant, who was a medical practitioner, caused the death of his sexual partner by manual strangulation. There was evidence that he meant to kill her. He maintained, however, that her death was an accidental consequence of pressure applied to her carotid arteries, with her consent, in an endeavour to heighten her sexual pleasure by what he called his 'carotid artery technique'. That alternative account of events prompted the trial judge to direct the jury that they were to convict even if Boughey meant no harm, if he realised that there was 'a good chance' that death might result or that death was 'something that might well happen'. The majority of the Court found no fault with the direction. Those expressions were an acceptable jury explanation of the requirement of knowledge

---

[80] *Crimes (Sentencing Procedure) Act 1999*, s 54B.

[81] *Crabbe* (1985) 156 CLR 464, [8].

[82] There were earlier indications in Victorian case law that recklessness did require realisation that a result was more likely than not: *Sergi* [1974] VR 1 (Sup Ct Vict), 10. See G Maloney, 'Case and Comment: *Nuri*' (1990) 14 *Crim LJ* 363. Queensland courts have consistently taken the view that these expressions were to be taken as meaning that a person is reckless only if the result was known to be more likely than not: *Hind and Harwood* (1995) 80 A Crim R 105 (Sup Ct Qld); *Deemal-Hall, Darkan and McIvor* [2005] QCA 206 (Qld CA); *Thomson* [1996] QCA 258 (Qld CA). But those expressions of opinion occurred in cases that involved issues far removed from the fault element of recklessness in common law murder.

[83] (1986) 161 CLR 10.

[84] *Ibid*, Mason, Wilson and Deane JJ, at para [15]. See, in addition, the subsequent High Court decision in *Wilson* (1992) 174 CLR 313.

that the conduct was 'likely to cause death'. Gibbs CJ thought it would have been better to avoid the reference to 'chance', which suggested that realisation of a mere possibility might be enough for murder, but concurred with the majority. Consideration of the dissent by Brennan J will be deferred for the moment; his judgment raises deeper questions than these slippery issues of chance, likelihood and possibility. So far as current Australian common law is concerned, *Boughey* can be taken to have established the propriety of a direction, in an appropriate case, that it is murder if the defendant knew that there was a substantial or real chance, as distinct from a mere possibility, that the conduct in question would cause death or grievous bodily harm.

The High Court was unanimous in its rejection of the appellant's suggestion that the jury might be directed to quantify the risk in mathematical terms. That was, in any event, impossible in the circumstances of the *Boughey* case. The issue of quantification took a more palpable form in *Faure*,[85] where the Victorian Court of Appeal expressed the view that a man who said that he killed his girlfriend while playing Russian Roulette with her might be convicted of murder though the odds of causing death were considerably less than 50/50.[86] *Faure's* conviction was quashed on other grounds and the Court's expression of opinion on the question was not essential to the appeal: it was addressed to the possibility of a retrial.[87] It does, however, represent the current state of the law on the issue. The Court paraphrased *Boughey* and *Crabbe* in a compendious formula:

> '[P]robable' as contrasted with 'possible but not likely' (*Crabbe* at 469–70) means a substantial, or real and not remote chance, whether or not it is more than 50% (*Boughey* at 21 per Mason, Wilson and Deane JJ)....[88]

---

[85] [1999] 2 VR 537.

[86] Faure said that he and his girlfriend agreed to a couple of rounds of Russian Roulette. He said that he placed a single cartridge in the chamber of a six shot revolver and that they agreed that they were each to pull the trigger twice, taking it in turns to hold the muzzle of the pistol to the other's head. The chamber was spun each time. The fatal shot occurred when Faure took his fourth and final turn. The Court appears to confuse the estimate of the odds that the cartridge might be discharged with the chance that discharge of the cartridge might kill the girlfriend rather than Faure: 'The probability of getting a six in four throws of a die is 671/1296: RM Eggleston, *Evidence, Proof and Probability*, 2nd edn (London, 1983), 16.' The Court accepted, however that a jury would be entitled to convict even if the trigger was only pulled once and only one chance of killing the girlfriend was to be taken.

[87] In the event, Faure pleaded guilty to murder at his second trial: *Faure* [2000] VSC 208.

[88] See *ibid*, at para [36]. In *Crabbe*, the High Court suggested an alternative route to the conclusion that a person who plays Russian Roulette with another's life might be guilty of murder: A person who realised that his or her conduct might possibly cause death or grievous bodily harm could be convicted of murder if 'the act was done with the intention and for the sole purpose of creating a risk of death or grievous bodily harm'. The suggestion was not elaborated and it has been ignored in subsequent cases. A similar suggestion is made by W Wilson in 'Murder and the Structure of Homicide' in A Ashworth and B Mitchell (eds), *Rethinking English Homicide Law* (Oxford, 2000) 21 at 39–43.

The last word, for the moment, is to be found in the June 2006 decision of the High Court in *Darkan*,[89] where it was said that a 'substantial or real chance' that a result will occur is something less than a 'probable consequence'. There appears to have been a retreat, of unquantifiable dimensions, from the original position that recklessness required proof that death or grievous bodily harm was 'likely or probable'.[90] The case was concerned with the fault elements required for an accessory to be guilty of a murder arising out of a joint enterprise. Accessorial liability will be discussed towards the end of this Chapter. The case law on recklessness and awareness of risk appears to have reached a dead end. Nothing in these permutations of probability, likelihood, real and substantial chances offers any determinate guidance for a jury that must decide whether an accused who did not intend death or grievous bodily harm is to be convicted of murder or manslaughter. One might guess that members of the jury are more likely to be guided by a global view of the circumstances of the death and their intuitive sense of what it takes, morally speaking, for a killing to amount to murder rather than a lesser form of unlawful homicide.

7. Murder and the Unnameable Fault Element

I have followed the conventional practice of state and territorial courts, and text writers, in referring to murder by 'recklessness'.[91] In fact, the joint judgment of the High Court in *Crabbe* made no reference to the concept. Their formulation was drawn from the definition of malice aforethought in Stephen's *Digest*, which includes 'knowledge that the act which causes death will probably cause the death of or grievous bodily harm to, some person...although such knowledge is

---

[89] *Darkan, Deemal Hall and McIvor* [2006] HCA 34.
[90] Compare the decision of the NSW Court of Criminal Appeal in *Annakin* (1987) 37 A Crim R 131, quashing a conviction for murder on the ground that the jury was misdirected when they were instructed that they could convict if they were satisfied that the defendants knew that their conduct 'might well result' in death.
[91] Among textbooks see: S Bronitt and B McSherry, *Principles of Criminal Law*, 2nd edn (Sydney, 2005), 180–1, 470–2; L Waller and CR Williams, *Criminal Law: Text and Cases*, 10th edn (Sydney, 2005) 161; D Brown, D Farrier, S Egger and L McNamara (eds), *Brown, Farrier Neal and Weisbrot's Criminal Laws: Materials and Commentary on Criminal Law and Process in New South Wales*, 3rd edn (Sydney, 2001) 524–5; B Fisse, *Howard's Criminal Law*, 5th edn (Sydney, 1990) 58–612; S Yeo, *Fault in Homicide: Towards a Schematic Approach to the Fault Elements for Murder and Involuntary Manslaughter in England, Australia and India* (Sydney, 1997). Case law in Victoria, South Australia and ACT commonly refers to recklessness when describing the fault element in murder. See, eg, the important decision of the Sup Ct of Victoria in *Faure* [1999] 2 VR 537, which speaks of 'willful murder' and 'reckless murder'. In New South Wales, s 18 of the *Crimes Act* 1900 further compounds the problem of nomenclature by defining the fault element of murder by reference to 'reckless indifference'. Compare Gray J in the South Australian Court of Criminal Appeal, who avoids referring to recklessness in *Foster* [2001] SASC 20.

accompanied by indifference whether death or grievous bodily harm is caused or not, or by a wish that it may not be caused'.[92]

There appear to have been two reasons for the omission of any reference to recklessness. The first was to avoid the possibility of confusion between reckless-ness and negligence. In an earlier High Court decision Gibbs CJ had expressed concern about the general practice of 'judges and textwriters alike' in describing this form of fault as recklessness.[93] In his view, this invited confusion between murder and manslaughter, since many earlier authorities referred to 'recklessness' when explaining the degree of negligence required for manslaughter. Reckless-ness continues to be used as a synonym for criminal negligence in the Griffith Code states. The second reason goes deeper. In *Pemble*,[94] some years before the decision in *Crabbe*, Barwick CJ had defined common law recklessness in murder as realisation that death or grievous bodily harm might possibly result, coupled with indifference to the consequences. Barwick CJ did not carry the Court with him on that occasion; his fellow judges did not insist on indifference and Gibbs J, who was to succeed him a Chief Justice, disputed his view that awareness of a mere possibility was sufficient. In *Crabbe*, the Court quoted Stephen's *Digest* and declared that the common law did not require proof of indifference in addition to knowledge of the risk of death or grievous bodily harm. The Court was of the view that knowledge of likelihood or probability was equivalent to intention as a fault element in murder: 'indeed, on one view, a person who does an act knowing its probable consequences may be regarded as having intended those conse-quences'.[95] The offender's attitude of acceptance, indifference or regret as to the consequences was irrelevant, whether culpability was based on intention or on knowledge of the risk.

Three members of the High Court recently affirmed, in passing, their view that 'recklessness' was a misnomer when a person was charged with murder unless statute required reference to the concept.[96] It may be that their continued insistence on the issue of nomenclature will induce lower courts and text writers to abandon their habit of referring to 'reckless murder'. The more significant question is whether the High Court has at last managed to eliminate the fugitive evaluative component in reckless murder. In New South Wales and the Australian Capital Territory, where statutory definitions refer specifically to 'reckless indif-ference' as a ground for a conviction of murder, courts have accepted that the *Crabbe* and *Boughey* formulations of the supplementary fault element in murder

---

[92] *Crabbe* (1985) 156 CLR 464 at 467–8, quoting from Stephen's *Digest of Criminal Law* (London, 1877), art 223. Earlier Victorian cases drew on the same passage: *Jakac* [1961] VR 367 (Sup Ct Vict); *Sergi* [1974] VR 1 (Sup Ct Vict).

[93] *La Fontaine* (1976) 136 CLR 62, Gummow J, at para [76].

[94] (1971) 124 CLR 107.

[95] *Crabbe* (1985) 156 CLR 464, at para [8].

[96] *Banditt* (2005) 157 A Crim R 420, Gummow, Hayne and Heydon JJ.

provide an adequate translation of the statutory expression.[97] A similar approach may be taken when it becomes necessary to elucidate the meaning of recklessness in the Commonwealth Criminal Code offences of murder of Australians and UN personnel. The Code requirement that the risk be 'unjustifiable' as well as 'substantial' could be dismissed as nothing more than a cross reference to the Code defences of duress, sudden or extraordinary emergency, self-defence or lawful authority.[98]

8. Murder, Recklessness and the Elusive 'Moral Element'

The Australian law of murder could have developed differently. There are three paths not taken that appear to be closed, for the present at least, to judicial traffic. They are worth consideration, if only to provide a vantage point for a critical appreciation of the current state of the law of murder. The first is an intriguing suggestion in a judgment by Jacobs J, in the High Court, that the *attitude* of the defendant towards the anticipated death of the victim might make the difference between murder and manslaughter. The second draws on the influential text by Colin Howard and Brent Fisse, *Howard's Criminal Law*,[99] which suggested that there was a 'moral element' in the attribution of recklessness. Their text appears to have exerted a pervasive influence on the formulation of the fault elements and homicide offences in the Commonwealth Criminal Code. If the Code provisions are given a literal interpretation they may extend liability for reckless murder beyond common law limits. Though Howard and Fisse insisted on the 'moral element' it remains elusive, both in their text and in the Code. The third draws on the far older statutory definition of murder in New South Wales that permits conviction of murder on proof of 'reckless indifference to human life'.[100] This was the most overt of the attempts to articulate a distinctive moral element that would justify the equation of reckless and intentional murder. It has been traduced, however, by judicial interpretation and transformed, after the decision in *Crabbe*, into the familiar fault element of knowledge of a substantial or real chance of death.

---

[97] *Solomon* [1980] 1 NSWLR 321 (NSW Court of Criminal Appeal); *Royall* (1991) 172 CLR 378 (HC Aust).

[98] Ch 2, 'General Principles of Criminal Responsibility'; Div 10: 'Circumstances involving external factors'.

[99] (5th edn Sydney, 1990). The fifth and last edn of Prof Howard's text, prepared by Prof Fisse, was published under the title *Howard's Criminal Law*.

[100] Crimes Act 1900 (NSW), s 18: 'Murder and manslaughter defined'.

(i) Expecting Death: Is 'Acceptance the Missing Mental State'?[101]

The possibility that recklessness in murder may include an evaluative component runs like an occasionally discernible thread through the case law. It surfaces briefly in *Crabbe*, when the Court said that it is murder if the accused person 'does the act *expecting* that death or grievous bodily harm is a probable consequence' (my emphasis).[102] It is the reference to 'expectation' that is significant here, though nothing is said in the judgment to explain its significance and it has been almost entirely ignored in the cases that followed the decision in *Crabbe*.

In *Woollin*[103] the House of Lords accepted the view that realisation that a result was certain was equivalent, in culpability to an intention to cause that result. Realisation of a certainty is equivalent in blameworthiness to intention, one might say, because it is evident that the agent who knows what the result of his or her action will be has accepted that result, whether willingly or unwillingly. The result is the price he or she is prepared to pay and, in that sense, not unlike the means to an intended objective. There is no need to go on to consider whether it can be said that the foreseen result was intended or intentional, if acceptance is the missing mental state that links awareness of risk and intention to cause a result as equivalents in culpability.

To take realisation of a certainty and intention as equivalents is a small extension of culpability, even if one speaks of 'practical certainty' or an expectation that the result 'will occur in the ordinary course of events'.[104] If the result was less than certain, however, it may still be the case that the agent was prepared, if it came to the point, to accept that result. It may be apparent—the agent may readily concede—that they would not have desisted from their course of conduct even if some prescient vision of the future had revealed that the death of another would inevitably follow. Drawing on Alan Michaels, I will call this state of mind 'counterfactual acceptance'.[105]

Counterfactual acceptance of a result, as a bridge that links intentional killings and some instances of reckless killing, can be identified with the thread of judicial authority on 'expectation' as a ground for culpability in the Australian common law of murder. One who continues a course of conduct in the expectation that it will result in the death of another can be said to accept that outcome or to be reconciled to its occurrence. The attitude of a person who is indifferent to the

---

[101] The reference is to A Michaels, 'Acceptance: the Missing Mental State' (1998) 71 *Southern California Law Review* 953. See also K Huigens, 'Homicide in Aretaic Terms' (2003) 6 *Buffalo Criminal Law Review* 97; K Simons, 'Does Punishment for "Culpable Indifference" Simply Punish for Bad Behaviour?' (2002) 6 *Buffalo Criminal Law Review* 219.

[102] *Crabbe* (1985) 156 CLR 464.

[103] [1999] 1 AC 82.

[104] *Criminal Code* (Cth), 5.2: Intention.

[105] Michaels, n 100 above. It is assumed, for the purposes of discussion of reckless murder, that the defendant is aware, to some unspecified degree, of the risk. The question whether counterfactual acceptance should extend to situations in which the person is not aware of the risk will not be pursued. For an exploration of that possibility, see Huigens, n 100 above.

result of his or her conduct—who could not care less whether the result occurs—belongs to the same family, though there are some obvious distinctions among these attitudes of expectation, acceptance and indifference to results.

The reference to expectation in *Crabbe* had its origin in the dissenting judgment of Jacobs J in the High Court decision in *La Fontaine*.[106] The case involved a fatal gunshot that may have been fired to frighten rather than kill the victim. When reckless murder was in issue, Jacobs J insisted that it was the defendant's *expectation* that his or her conduct would result in death or grievous bodily harm that justified a conviction. His judgment is at once the most subtle and the most neglected of the Australian judicial attempts to elucidate the meaning of recklessness in murder.[107] Like other members of the Court, Jacobs J rejected any attempt to quantify the degree of risk in recklessness. He did insist, however, that nothing less than an awareness that death or grievous bodily harm was 'probable' would do, when liability for murder was in issue. One could hardly be said to *expect* one or other of those results if one thought it merely possible. Jacobs J linked expectation of a result with an attitude of 'positive indifference' to that result. That was both unnecessary and misleading, for one can expect a result, just as one can accept a result, which is unwanted and unwelcome.

The references to expectation recur throughout his judgment, as if insistence on the word alone was sufficient to carry the idea: the quotation that follows is the nearest that Jacobs J came to explaining what he had in mind:

> [W]e are dealing with the state of a man's mind, with that state of mind which the word 'malice' connotes. To say that a man knows in his mind that a consequence of his act is probable is to say that he expects that it will happen even though he would be prepared to concede that it is not certain that it will happen. To say that a man who knows in his mind that a consequence of his act is possible though not probable is to say that he believes the consequence is not certain or that he expects it will not happen even though he would be prepared to concede that it may happen. There is a great difference in moral and social content between the first state of mind and the second....The difference...should be preserved in the law of murder.[108]

The sense that Jacobs J sought to give to 'expectation' is elusive. Brennan J, who dissented in *Boughey*, appears to have been the only member of the High Court to have perceived the significance of his insistence on the offender's expectations as the critical factor that distinguishes murder from manslaughter. Like Jacobs J, he does not attempt to elucidate the idea: his formulation is equally gnomic:

> Knowledge that there is a good chance that an event may happen is a different state of mind from knowledge (or foresight) that the event will probably happen. One state of

---

[106] (1976) 136 CLR 62. Jacobs J dissented on the facts: he considered the recklessness direction to be unnecessary and inappropriate.

[107] With the notable exception of Stanley Yeo, *Fault in Homicide: Towards a Schematic Approach to the Fault Elements for Murder and Involuntary Manslaughter in England, Australia and India* (Sydney, 1997), ch 3: 'The Fault Elements for Murder Under Australian Law', who provides an extended consideration of the High Court decision in *La Fontaine*.

[108] (1976) 136 CLR 62, 96.

mind is an appreciation of a risk, perhaps a substantial risk; the other state of mind is an expectation. I do not put this on any basis of mathematical odds. It is simply that one form of words conveys the meaning of a state of mind different from the state of mind meant by the other form of words.[109]

The effect of the distinction between knowledge of a risk and an expectation that it will eventuate only becomes apparent towards the end of his judgment in *Boughey* when Brennan J formulates the question that, in his opinion, the trial judge should have asked the jury. It is a blunt question and one that eliminates any reference to the offender's 'appreciation of a risk'. If the jury was not satisfied that Dr Boughey intended to kill his sexual partner or cause her grievous bodily harm, Brennan J says that they should have been directed to consider whether, 'when he applied pressure to the carotid arteries...he knew that his action would probably kill her'.[110]

Neither the majority judgment in *Boughey* nor subsequent case law lends support to Brennan J's suggestion that trial judges are required to direct juries in this blunt and uncompromising fashion when recklessness is in issue in a prosecution for murder. On a realistic consideration of the evidence in the case it is not easy to see what ground there could be for a recklessness direction in these terms. By far the most likely inference is that Dr Boughey meant to kill his victim and that he lied when he said that her death resulted from a mutually agreed use of his 'carotid artery technique' to heighten their sexual pleasure. If Boughey did tell the truth about his reasons for pressing on the carotid arteries of his victim, it would be utterly unlikely that he would do so in the knowledge that his use of the technique would probably kill her.[111] Evidence of a quite different sort of depravity from that involved in a simple instance of intentional murder would be necessary to support that hypothesis and provide justification for a recklessness direction.

For Jacobs J, an expectation of death or grievous bodily harm could count as a fault element in murder because it was equivalent in moral culpability to an intention to cause either of those results. Formulation of the fault element in that way had the additional advantage that liability for murder was based on the defendant's state of mind: his or her realisation of risk and his or her attitude about the anticipated result, should the risk eventuate. Jacobs J did concede that it might in the end prove impossible to exclude consideration of the moral turpitude of the defendant's conduct—or 'popular indeterminate connotations of malice'—when reckless murder was in issue, but the object of his emphasis on 'expectation' was to avoid that expedient.[112]

---

[109] *Boughey* (1986) 161 CLR 10 (Brennan J) at para [26].

[110] *Ibid*, at para [32].

[111] Compare *Maurice* (1992) 61 A Crim R 30 (NT Court of Criminal Appeal) for an all too believable instance of death by misadventure, during 'blackout sex', resulting in a guilty plea and conviction for a lesser form of homicide under s 154 of the Northern Territory *Criminal Code*.

[112] *La Fontaine* (1976) 136 CLR 62 (Jacobs J) at para [17]

It may be objected that a requirement of proof of an 'expectation' that death or grievous bodily harm would result pitches the fault requirement for reckless murder at altogether too demanding a level—pitches it, indeed, at a point not far short of foresight of a practical certainty. Counterfactual acceptance, which also combines attitude and appreciation of risk, is a less demanding criterion for guilt. The magnitude of the risk, whether large or small, may have been a matter of indifference to the defendant, who would have pursued the same fatal course even if the fatal outcome had been known for certain. If counterfactual accept-ance can link intentional murder and certain instances of reckless murder in a relationship of equivalent culpability, there is no justification in principle for a requirement that the fatal outcome be expected as well as accepted or that the defendant realise that it is probable. Some such view probably accounts for another fugitive theme in the Australian case law. In *Pemble*[113] and again in *La Fontaine*,[114] Barwick CJ suggested that reckless indifference required no more than the realisation that death or grievous bodily harm was a possible conse-quence of conduct.

Is acceptance the 'missing mental state' that could provide an appropriate moral foundation for reckless murder? Almost certainly not, if moral culpability is taken to be determinative. The test is still too restrictive. The family resem-blance that links counterfactual acceptance, expectation and reckless indifference to results lies in the fact that the defendant would have continued the same fatal course of action, even if the outcome had been known for certain. That requirement of counterfactual acceptance of the consequences would exclude some individuals who seem no less deserving of conviction of murder. A comparison of two hypothetical torturers , one sadistic and one avaricious, makes the point:[115]

Sadistic Torturer

Sadistic torturer [ST] gets pleasure from inflicting pain. The form of torture involved will cause little physical injury. ST knows, however, that the pain may kill his victim, who has a weak heart. The torture victim suffers a fatal heart attack. ST admits that he would not have desisted from inflicting pain, even if he had known that the victim would certainly die.

Sadistic Torturer accepts the death. He may also expect the death and he may even be indifferent to it.

Avaricious Torturer

Avaricious torturer [AT] wants his victim to reveal the combination of a safe containing diamonds. Other means of gaining the information have been tried and failed, so AT

---

[113]   (1971) 124 CLR 107 (HC Aust).
[114]   (1976) 136 CLR 62.
[115]   Compare the discussion of the hypothetical torturer in K Simons, 'Does Punishment for "Culpable Indifference" Simply Punish for Bad Behaviour?' (2002) *6 Buffalo Criminal Law Review* 219 at 265–7.

tries torture though he knows that the pain may kill his victim, who has a weak heart. Once again, the torture causes intense pain resulting in death. As a consequence, AT's plan fails and he is left empty handed.

There is, in this second variation, no counterfactual acceptance of death. Had Avaricious Torturer known the outcome he would have desisted from torture. There is, however, no moral distinction worth taking between Sadistic Torturer and Avaricious Torturer when liability for murder is in issue.[116]

The case of the avaricious torturer and others that might be devised, where the offender gambles against death, suggest that it is not the defendant's counterfactual acceptance of the outcome that should determine guilt; it is his or her reasons for risking the life of the victim. The 'cognitive counterfactual criterion', as Kenneth Simons calls it, is an under-inclusive criterion for murder. If the offence is not to be arbitrarily limited by considerations of subjective probability, along the lines suggested by Jacobs J,[117] consideration of the moral turpitude of the defendant's conduct or its lack of social value may be unavoidable.

(ii) Risk, Social Value and Subjectivity in the Criminal Code: The American Comparison

Four editions of Colin Howard's text on Australian criminal law between 1965 and 1981 vigorously promoted the view that attribution of recklessness required a consideration of both the 'social value' of the defendant's conduct and his or her appreciation of the degree of risk of harm.[118] There was, he argued, an 'element of moral judgment' in the attribution of recklessness.[119] The argument was presented, essentially unaltered, in Brent Fisse's reworking of Howard's text in 1990.[120] Howard and Fisse argue that it is not reckless to disregard a risk if the conduct has a 'social value that outweighs the social harm of the danger inherent in the risk'.[121] If the risk is unjustified, however, 'its degree of probability or substantiality need be only very slight to suffice for recklessness, no more than enough to move from the apparently impossible to the apparently possible'.[122]

[116] *Ibid.*

[117] Compare S Yeo, *Fault in Homicide: Towards a Schematic Approach to the Fault Elements for Murder and Involuntary Manslaughter in England, Australia and India* (Sydney, 1997), 66 and 298, who draws the line at 'high probability' and would hold the Russian Roulette player guilty of manslaughter rather than murder.

[118] *Australian Criminal Law* (Sydney, 1965); *Australian Criminal Law*, 2nd edn (Sydney, 1970); *Criminal Law*, 3rd edn (Sydney, 1977); *Criminal Law*, 4th edn (Sydney, 1982).

[119] *Australian Criminal Law* (Sydney, 1965) 319.

[120] *Howard's Criminal Law*, 5th edn (Sydney, 1990) 486–94. Some degree of doubt is apparent in Prof Fisse's additions to the original text at 491: '[i]t may be argued that murder is a distinctively egregious offence…&c'

[121] *Ibid*, 490.

[122] *Ibid*, 490–1.

Later, it is said that the defendant's realisation of a 'bare possibility' of harm is sufficient[123] if the conduct creating the risk is without social value.

Justification is a demanding standard and one that is not readily divisible by reference to degrees of departure from a norm. The social value involved in taking the risk either outweighs the danger or it does not. If it does not outweigh the danger, anything beyond a 'bare logical possibility' is a 'substantial' risk.[124] Fisse and Howard went on, however, to add a further requirement. It is not reckless to take the risk unless it is a 'gross deviation from accepted standards of conduct' to do so.[125] That additional requirement was taken from the definition of recklessness proposed by the American Law Institute in the Model Penal Code.[126] The requirement of a gross deviation was introduced by Fisse and Howard in the chapter dealing with 'General Concepts of Responsibility'. It was ignored or forgotten, however, in their substantive chapters, on murder and other offences that can be committed by recklessness. Though the chapter on murder opens with the statement that 'foresight of the mere possibility of causing death is insufficient for reckless murder',[127] the discussion ends with the bland conclusion that the degree of risk is unquantifiable and that one can only say that reckless-ness requires realisation of a 'substantial' risk.[128] The 'moral element' in reckless-ness, if it survives at all, is effectively concealed by that conclusion.

Two quite different things have been confused in their exposition. The first has to do with the idea that the justifications for taking a risk that proves fatal are different from and more extensive than the justifications for intentionally causing death.[129] That is not to say, however, that there are degrees of justification. Howard and Fisse are correct in their conclusion that the risk is either justified or it is not. It is a quite separate question, however, whether conduct that is not justified can be said to involve a 'gross deviation from accepted standards'. Absence of justification is a necessary but not a sufficient ground for that conclusion. Glanville Williams, whose discussion of the question of social value provided the source for Howard and Fisse, made the point in a neat paradox: 'recklessness should be classified as a species of the genus negligence, rather than

---

[123] *Ibid*, 493.

[124] *Ibid*, 490; and at 491: '[t]he point can be put differently by saying that if the degree of probability of the event…in question is such as to render the word "risk" at all meaningful in the context, the requirement of substantiality is satisfied'.

[125] *Ibid*, 486. See also at 493–4 and 495.

[126] Proposed Official Draft 1962 (Philadelphia), s 2.02(2).

[127] *Howard's Criminal Law*, n 119 above, 59. Compare the 1st edn, n 117 above, 50.

[128] 5th edn, n 119 above, 61. Compare the 1st edn, n 117 above, 51: '[o]ne can only say that the risk must be, in the view of the jury, substantial'.

[129] Stanley Yeo discusses the issue of justification in *Fault in Homicide: Towards a Schematic Approach to the Fault Elements for Murder and Involuntary Manslaughter in England, Australia and India* (Sydney, 1997) n 117 above, 79–90. He agrees that 'unjustifiable risk taking should be a necessary requirement of reckless murder'. His discussion of the issue is more nuanced and the differences between his eventual position and that adopted in *Howard's Criminal Law*, n 120 above, are more significant than their superficial agreement that the risk must be unjustifiable.

as a form of intention'.[130] The requirement of gross departure from acceptable standards of conduct should qualify both fault concepts in their application to serious offences of causing physical harm.

Recent cases on the Australian common law of murder provide no support for the contention that there is an 'element of moral judgment' in the attribution of recklessness. In *Crabbe* the High Court rejected the suggestion that the prosecution must prove something more than realisation of risk: 'lack of social purpose is not an element of the mental state with which we are here concerned'.[131] It appears that an accused would have to adduce evidence in support of a recognised defence before a jury direction would be required. Moreover the trial judge would be required to formulate the elements of the defence for the jury's consideration. The Court does concede that a competent surgeon who 'performs a hazardous but necessary operation is not criminally liable if the patient dies, even if the surgeon foresaw that...death was probable'.[132] The judgment can be taken, perhaps, to imply that the range of justifications would be more extensive when the prosecution case was based on knowledge that a result was probable, rather than intention to cause that result.[133] Necessity is not a defence to murder, in most Australian jurisdictions, when death is intended. It was, however, a passing suggestion by the Court and it was not amplified.

The Commonwealth law of murder is different. Recklessness is a fault element for two of the exotic varieties of murder in the Criminal Code.[134] This is the same, all-purpose variety of recklessness that is established by proof that the accused was aware of a substantial and unjustifiable risk of causing a specified result.[135] In Chapter 2 of the Code, which sets out the general principles of criminal responsibility, MCCOC followed Howard and Fisse and accepted that the degree of risk and the justification for taking it were linked in a reciprocal relationship.[136] As I mentioned earlier, however, the Code definition of recklessness omits the American Model Penal Code qualification that the defendant's disregard of the risk must involve a gross deviation from the standard of a law abiding person.

Even when augmented by that requirement of gross deviation, Model Penal Code recklessness is not sufficient for murder. That Code distinguishes between

---

[130] G Williams, *The Mental Element in Crime*, (Oxford, Jerusalem at the Magnes Press, The Hebrew University, 1965), 32.

[131] *Crabbe* (1985) 156 CLR 464 470.

[132] *Ibid.*

[133] Discussed by S Yeo, *Fault in Homicide: Towards a Schematic Approach to the Fault Elements for Murder and Involuntary Manslaughter in England, Australia and India* (Sydney, 1997), 85–7.

[134] See 71.2: Murder of a UN or associated person; 115.1: Murder of an Australian citizen or a resident of Australia. There are other offences of murder, in Ch 8: Offences against humanity and related offences, but these do not require or permit proof of recklessness as a fault element.

[135] *Criminal Code 1995* (Cth), 5.4: Recklessness.

[136] MCC, Ch 2, 'General Principles of Criminal Responsibility'; Final Report 1992 (Canberra, 1993), 29: '[t]he Committee has defined recklessness in terms of a "substantial" risk rather than in terms of probability or possibility because those terms invite speculation about mathematical chances and ignore the link between the acceptable degree of risk and unjustifiability of running that risk in any given situation.'

recklessness when it determines the threshold of criminal liability and the more restricted use of the concept when it marks the difference between murder and lesser grades of unlawful homicide. In murder, the conduct that causes death must be accompanied by recklessness and, in addition, by 'circumstances manifesting extreme indifference to the value of human life'.[137] In the absence of proof of extreme indifference to the value of human life, the offender is guilty only of manslaughter.[138] Recklessness and indifference are presumed, however, and the offender is guilty of murder when the victim's death results from the commission of certain major offences. The Model Penal Code retains a statutory version of the felony-murder rule.

Consistent with its commitment to subjectivity, the Commonwealth Criminal Code rejects constructive guilt. There is no felony murder rule; the prosecution must prove that the offender intended death or was reckless as to causing death.[139] Manslaughter requires proof of recklessness as to serious harm.[140] There are no equivalents in these offences of the additional requirements of gross deviation and extreme indifference that qualify the definitions of murder and manslaughter in the Model Penal Code. If the intentions of those who wrote Commonwealth Code provisions were to guide their interpretation, the fault element for murder requires nothing more than proof that a risk of causing death was taken consciously in circumstances where the risk was unjustifiable or 'unacceptable'.[141] Any risk beyond a bare possibility will count as substantial if it is unacceptable or unjustified.

The concept of recklessness, as defined in the Commonwealth Code, does not mark a rational or morally coherent distinction between murder and manslaughter. That should have been obvious from the outset, when MCCOC conceded that instances of causing harm recklessly may be less culpable than instances of

---

[137] N 125 above, 210.2: Murder.

[138] *Ibid*, 210.3: Manslaughter.

[139] 71.2: Murder of a UN or associated person; 115.1: Murder of an Australian citizen or resident of Australia. The Code provisions were based on the offence of murder in the Model Criminal Code, Discussion Paper, Ch 5: Fatal Offences Against the Person (5.1.9 *Murder*) discussed at 53–7. It is assumed, for the purposes of discussion, that the prosecution must prove that the defendant perceived the risk to be substantial. The commitment to subjectivity may be qualified however. Though it is quite clear that the prosecution must prove that the defendant was aware of the risk of death, it is at least arguable that the defendant's assessment of the *substantiality* of the risk is not determinative. In the Criminal Code, 5.4 (Recklessness), 5.4(2) states that D is reckless with respect to a result 'if he or he is aware of a substantial risk that the result will occur' and 'having regard to the circumstances known to him or her, it is unjustifiable to take the risk'. It is evident that D's views on justification are not determinative. It is arguable that D's evaluation of the substantiality of the risk is to be treated in the same way

[140] 71.3: Manslaughter of a UN or associated person; 115.2: Manslaughter of an Australian citizen or resident of Australia. A lesser offence of 'dangerous conduct causing death', requiring proof of negligence, was proposed in the Model Criminal Code but not adopted in the *Commonwealth Criminal Code*.

[141] MCC, Ch 2, 'General Principles of Criminal Responsibility'; Final Report 1992 (Canberra, 1993), 29:

causing the same harm by criminal negligence.[142] The Committee's insistence that proof of recklessness should determine the threshold of criminal responsibility, in the absence of express legislative reversal of the requirement, was salutary and enactment of that threshold requirement for liability in the Code is a significant achievement. The concept is quite unsuited, however, to determining the difference between the most serious and a less serious form of unlawful homicide. Trial judges and juries must work with a desiccated set of distinctions between risks that the accused might have considered 'substantial' and risks that might have been considered less than substantial, if they were considered at all.

(iii) Depraved Hearts and Malignant Spirits

Jacobs J allowed that it might in the end prove impossible to avoid reliance on overtly moral criteria in the definition of murder. He referred in passing to Blackstone's explanation of malice aforethought as a state of mind that expresses the 'dictate of a wicked, depraved and malignant heart'.[143] If considerations of moral turpitude were to intrude, however, he thought that there could be no better formulation of the necessary element of depravity than that given by Traynor J, in the Californian Supreme Court, when he said that it is murder when death results from conduct undertaken 'for a base, anti-social motive and with wanton disregard for human life'.[144] Though the reference to motive is omitted, similar statutory formulations can be found in the Model Penal Code requirement of 'extreme indifference to the value of human life' and the far earlier definition of reckless murder in New York as conduct that causes death in 'circumstances evincing a depraved indifference to human life'.[145]

Though the language is laconic by comparison, New South Wales statute law has defined murder in similar terms for well over a century:[146] It is murder if death results from conduct that was accompanied by 'reckless indifference to human life' or by an intention to kill or cause grievous bodily harm. There are indications in the reports that the requirement of 'reckless indifference' was once taken to require something more than a finding that the defendant was aware that his or her conduct might cause death.[147] In more recent times, since the High

---

[142] *Ibid.*

[143] *La Fontaine* (1976) 136 CLR 62 (HC Aust) (Jacobs J) at para [17].

[144] *Ibid*, citing *People v Thomas* (1953) 261 P 2d 1, 7.

[145] Penal Law (NY) Section 125.25 (murder in the second degree), s (2).

[146] *Crimes Act* 1900 (NSW) s 18. The original provision, which has remained unaltered, was introduced in 1883 by 46 Vic, No 17. The history of the provision is recounted in GD Woods, *A History of Criminal Law in New South Wales: The Colonial Period 1788–1900* (Sydney, 2002). See also Begg J in *Solomon* (1980) 1 NSWLR 321 (NSW Court of Criminal Appeal), 339; Windeyer J in *Parker* (1962) 111 CLR 610 (HC Aust), 655–7.

[147] Extracts from the trial direction in *Royall* (1991) 172 CLR 378, 394 stress the attitudinal implications of the requirement: '[b]y reckless indifference to human life is meant that the accused was aware that the act contemplated carried a risk to the life of the human being concerned, that

Court decision in *Royall*,[148] it is accepted that *Crabbe* provides authoritative guidance on the meaning of the statutory provision. Reckless indifference to life is taken to be the equivalent of knowledge of a 'likely or probable' risk of death.[149]

What New South Wales courts might have made of 'reckless indifference to human life', had they been permitted to develop a more literal and imaginative interpretation of their murder statute, is uncertain. The definition does not speak of indifference to a *risk* of *death*, though recent cases read it in that way. It speaks more generally of reckless indifference to 'human life', which must be taken to mean indifference to the *value* of human life. It is accepted that the prosecution must prove that the defendant was aware that his or her conduct might cause death rather than grievous bodily ham.[150] That does not, however, exhaust the meaning of the statute. Reckless indifference to life is additional to realisation of a risk of death. On a literal reading, the New South Wales definition of murder suggests the following distinction between the threshold fault requirement for an unlawful homicide and the more culpable level of fault required for conviction of murder:

a. *It is manslaughter* if a person causes death by criminal negligence, which includes conduct that is accompanied by:
    i. failure to have regard to an unjustifiable risk of death or serious harm; or conscious disregard of an unjustifiable risk of death or serious harm;
    ii. in circumstances evincing so great a falling short of the standard of care that a reasonable person would exercise as to deserve criminal punishment.[151]
b. *It is murder* if a person causes death by:
    iii. conduct that is intended to cause death or grievous bodily harm; or
    iv. conduct that is accompanied by conscious awareness of an unjustifiable risk that it will cause the death of another; in circumstances evincing reckless indifference to [the value of] human life.

It would be pointless to pursue the interpretation further. The problem about overt reference to a moral criterion, such as 'reckless indifference to [the value of]

---

accused did not care whether his act threatened the life concerned, that is he was indifferent to whether or not his act took that life and he committed the act with such an attitude of mind to its result that you, as jurors, should consider it to be reckless indifference'. See, too, the remarks of Barwick CJ in *Pemble* (1971) 124 CLR 107, 120–1.

[148] See, eg, *Royall* (1991) 172 CLR 378, 431 (Toohey and Gaudron JJ): 'reckless indifference involves a willingness to run the risk of the probability, as distinct from the possibility of death ensuing'.

[149] See, eg, *Grant* (2002) 55 NSWLR 80 (NSW Court of Criminal Appeal) 243; *Katarsynski* [2005] NSWCCA 72 (NSW Court of Criminal Appeal). The *Criminal Courts Bench Book*, published by the Judicial Commission of New South Wales and available at http://www.judcom.nsw.gov.au/sisdemo/ ctbb.htm, at para [5–1140] provides the written form of instruction: '[a]n act is done with reckless indifference to human life if the accused foresaw or realised that his act would probably cause the death of the deceased but he continued with that act regardless of the risk of death'.

[150] *Solomon* (1980) NSWLR 321 (NSW Court of Criminal Appeal). It is certainly arguable that the requirement of realisation of risk is a modern graft on the statutory stock.

[151] This formulation of criminal negligence is standard in Australian common law. See *Nydam* [1977] VR 430 (Vict Court of Criminal Appeal).

human life', is that it adds very little to one's intuitive understanding of the difference between murder and manslaughter. Nor is the problem solved if it is said that the indifference must be 'extreme' or 'depraved'. Glanville Williams, in a critical review of the Model Penal Code formulation of reckless murder, remarked that there are no degrees of indifference.[152] Experience in the United States suggests that a requirement of 'extreme' or 'depraved' indifference to the value of human life does not guarantee a morally defensible distinction between murder and manslaughter. In 2005 the New York Court of Appeals remarked a tendency for the standard to drift downwards and embarked on a re-evaluation of 'depraved indifference' murder. The Court declared that a direction to the jury allowing conviction on this ground was only applicable to a 'small and finite category of cases where the conduct is at least as morally reprehensible as intentional murder' involving 'wanton cruelty, brutality or callousness'.[153] It is apparent from experience in other US jurisdictions that the Model Penal Code criterion of 'extreme indifference to the value of human life' can drift to a point where it is indistinguishable from gross negligence.[154]

It is worth asking why we continue to distinguish between murder and manslaughter. There is no reason to suppose that Australians at large or Australian juries have an intuitive understanding of the difference: our homicide laws subvert the possibility of intuitive understanding. The definition of murder varies from jurisdiction to jurisdiction both in the fault elements required for guilt and in the provision of available defences and partial defences. One or other or all of the defences of provocation, excessive self-defence, duress, necessity and diminished responsibility are recognised in some jurisdictions as complete or partial defences. In others, some or all of these are factors that can only mitigate a sentence. Penalties for murder and manslaughter overlap substantially. In all jurisdictions, by one means or another, courts impose a sentence that is proportionate to the facts of the murder and the murderer's culpability.

Fitzjames Stephen thought that the great reason why murder is considered so dreadful is that men are hanged for it.[155] When they are no longer hanged, the standard drifts. It seems likely that a moral criterion that distinguished between murder and manslaughter—whether of reckless indifference, wanton disregard or wicked and malignant depravity—could be sustained only if it was linked to determinate, retributive penal consequences.

---

[152] G Williams, *The Mental Element in Crime* (Oxford, Jerusalem at the Magnes Press, The Hebrew University, 1965) Lionel Cohen Lectures, 1965, 92–3. He is equally critical of the Model Penal Code reference to extreme indifference to 'value of human life', which he describes as 'a dodge that creates more difficulties than it solves': *ibid*, 95.

[153] *People v Suarez* [2005] NY SlipOp 09811 (NY CA), available at www.courts.state.ny.us/reporter/3dseries/2005/2005_09811.htm. See also *People v Mancini* [2006] NY SlipOp 05235 (NY CA), available at www.courts.state.ny.us/reporter/3dseries/2006/2006_05235.htm.

[154] *State v McKnight* [2003] South Carolina Supreme Court, Opinion No 25585, available at www.judicial.state.sc.us/o inions/displayOpinionPF.cfm?caseNo=25585.

[155] JF Stephen, 'Capital Punishments' (1864) 69 *Fraser's Magazine* 753, 761: '[t]he fact that men are hung for murder is one great reason why murder is considered so dreadful'.

I labour the point because there has evolved in New South Wales a case law of 'worst case' murder that is explicitly based on considerations of moral turpitude.[156] It is, however, a sentencing category that is sustained by the collective experience of the judiciary, rather than by jurors' intuitive understanding of moral depravity. A similar, though more rudimentary, evolution of worst case jurisprudence is apparent in a number of other jurisdictions. The development is most evident, however, in New South Wales, where it is sustained by a large annual crop of murderers and an unusually rigid sentencing structure for the worst among them. Life imprisonment is the maximum penalty for murder in New South Wales. The penalty is not often imposed; perhaps 10 per cent of New South Wales murderers will receive a life penalty. A court that sentences a murderer to gaol for life cannot set a non-parole period and there is no administrative procedure for review of these sentences. It is anticipated that those who receive the life penalty will die in gaol. The life penalty is a quite exceptional sentence, reserved for murderers whose offence the courts cannot define but only indicate by a string of vituperative epithets: 'heinous', 'atrocious, detestable, hateful, odious, gravely reprehensible and extremely wicked'.[157] There is no determinate list of criteria for these worst case murderers, only a list of instructive examples of moral enormity that illustrate, but do not circumscribe, a category that is sustained by the irrevocable severity of the penalty.[158] Worst case murderers may have killed once or many times. They may have killed professionally for money or killed because they enjoyed it. The deaths of their victims may have been inflicted intentionally or as a consequence of callous indifference to human suffering or to the value of human life. The category exists as a consequence of successive determinations by the judiciary that the murderers found in this gallery of types are so far removed in the degree of their depravity from other murderers that life in prison is the only appropriate penalty for them.

---

[156] The discussion that follows draws on the invaluable resources of the New South Wales Public Defenders' Office and, in particular, various 'Papers by Public Defenders' and 'Sentencing Tables, available at www.lawlink.nsw.gov.au/lawlink/pdo/ll_pdo.nsf/pages/PDO_index. See in addition the following publications of the Judicial Commission of New South Wales, available at www.judcom. nsw.gov.au; J Kean and P Poletti, *Sentenced Homicides in New South Wales 1994–2001* (Sydney, 2004), J Kean, P Poletti and H Donnelly, 'Common Offences and the Use of Imprisonment in the District and Supreme Courts in 2002' (2004) 30 *Sentencing Trends and Issues* (Judicial Commission of New South Wales).

[157] *Arhurell* [1997] NSWSC (unreported 3 Oct 1997; Hunt CJ at CL) (Sup Ct NSW); cited with approval: *Leonard* [1990] NSWSC 510 (Sup Ct NSW), 25–6; *Harris* [2000] NSWCCA 469 (NSW Court of Criminal Appeal) at para [85], Wood CJ at CL; *Hyland, Parry and Yates* [2001] NSWSC 470 (NSW Sup Ct) at para [35].

[158] Though courts cannot consider the possibility, it is unlikely that the legislature will allow the existing laws governing the punishment of worst case murderers to continue unchanged for the next half century, during which the existing population of worst case murderers is expected to serve its time.

9. Elaborations of Subjective Probability: The Problem of Complicity

In the common law jurisdictions, the characteristically Australian judicial preoccupation with subjective perception of degrees of risk is apparent when the liability of the accessory or joint offender is in issue. In Queensland, Western Australia and Tasmania, which adopted the Griffith Code, the liability of the accessory or joint offender is extended to offences that were a probable consequence of the venture, whether or not the offence was foreseen by the accessory.[159] That jurisdictional division between objective and subjective criteria for accessorial guilt has resulted in a further judicial elaboration of the degrees of inculpative probability.

People who band together in a joint criminal enterprise are guilty of any offence that is within the scope of their criminal plan. That will include offences that may have seemed highly unlikely at the outset. Burglars may have taken every precaution to ensure that they timed their break-in to occur when the householder was absent. Their plan, let us say, required one to do the breaking and entering and the other to drive the getaway car. Suppose, however, that the householder appeared quite unexpectedly and was shot and killed intentionally by the burglar who broke into the house. If the burglars had resolved to shoot the householder, in the remote eventuality that she might unexpectedly return, the getaway driver would be equally guilty with the burglar who fired the shot. It does not matter that the chance that the householder would be shot was remote, for their plan envisaged this contingency. The liability of the accessory is not limited, however, to planned contingencies: it extends to offences that were neither planned[160] nor incidental to the plan. The driver may have made it quite clear to his fellow burglar that he wanted no part in violence. Australian common law would hold the driver guilty of murder if the prosecution could prove that he knew that his fellow burglar might use his gun to shoot the householder. This is the 'extended' joint enterprise or common purpose rule. There is no requirement in this case of proof that the driver knew that a shooting was likely or probable. It is sufficient if the driver foresaw the shooting 'as a possible incident of the venture'.[161] And, if that eventuality was foreseen by the driver, it would make no

---

[159] *Darkan, Deemal-Hall and McIvor* [2006] HCA 34.

[160] In principle, there is no reason why the liability of the accessory should not extend to include crimes that were quite beyond the contemplation of either offender. We combine in ventures, legal and illegal, in order to take advantage of the creative responses that our fellow venturers will make to unexpected obstacles.

[161] *Gillard* (2003) 219 CLR 1, 31, Hayne J: 'the contemplation of a party to a joint enterprise includes what that party foresees as a possible incident of the venture. If the party foresees that another crime might be committed and continues to participate in the venture, that party is a party to the commission of that other, incidental, crime even if the party did not agree to its being committed'. Hayne J's statement of the principle is uncontroversial and accepted by other members of the Court.

difference if it were to turn out that he was a dupe who had been tricked into believing that he was engaged in a burglary by the perpetrator, who was in fact a contract killer hired to shoot the householder.[162] If the driver realised that she might be shot, that would be sufficient for guilt of murder. So also, apparently, if the perpetrator took opportunistic advantage of the occasion and raped the returning householder. If the driver was aware that this was something his partner in crime might do, though it was no part of their plan, he is equally guilty of rape.[163]

This extended liability for the consequences of joint criminal[164] ventures has been subjected to academic criticism[165] and appellate attack in the High Court. It is now clear, however, that the Court will not resile from its earlier decisions.[166] What is of interest, for present purposes, is a strange bifurcation of the law on subjective probabilities in the law of complicity that has taken place since *Johns*,[167] which was decided by the Court in 1980. Though the course of that development is complex, the story can be quickly told. Stephen J, in what appears to have been a passing remark in *Johns*, suggested that an accessory to an armed robbery who 'contemplated "a substantial risk"' that the killing would occur' would be guilty of murder.[168] The suggestion was supported by a quotation from the third edition of Howard's *Criminal Law*.[169] Later that year, in *Miller*,[170] the Court repeated the quotation from Howard's text and said that the accessory who contemplated a substantial risk that the perpetrator would commit murder was equally guilty of that offence. Across the Tasman Sea, the New Zealand Court of Criminal Appeal relied on the same quotations from Stephen J in *Johns* and

---

The case is the most recent of a series in which the High Court has enunciated the same rule. See *Johns* (1980) 143 CLR 108, which was a precursor, and *McAuliffe* (1995) 183 CLR 108, which settled the law.

[162]   *Gillard* (2000) 219 CLR 1.

[163]   *Miller* (1980) 32 ALR 321.

[164]   The High Court held in *ibid* that the same inculpatory rule applies when the joint venturers are engaged in a lawful activity and the accessory is aware that the other may take advantage of his assistance to commit a murder. The Court's holding on the point was based on a barely credible factual hypothesis that is unlikely ever to be duplicated.

[165]   C Cato, 'Foresight of Murder and Complicity in Unlawful Joint Enterprises where Death Results' (1990) 2 *Bond Law Review* 182; S Odgers, 'Criminal Cases in the High Court of Australia (*McAuliffe v McAuliffe*)', (1996) 20 *Crim LJ* 43; S Gray, '"I Didn't Know, I Wasn't There": Common Purpose and the Liability of Accessories to Crime' (1999) 23 *Crim LJ* 201.

[166]   In *Gillard* (2003) 219 CLR 1, Kirby J indicated his willingness to reconsider existing doctrine: at 26. Other members of the Court did not share his views. See, in particular, Gummow and Hayne JJ, at 11 and 32 respectively. The issue has now been put beyond doubt in *Clayton and Hartwick* [2006] HCA Transcript 433 (9 Aug 2006). The transcript of argument concludes with an affirmation of existing law in *Gillard* and *McAuliffe* (1995) 183 CLR 108.

[167]   (1980) 143 CLR 108.

[168]   *Ibid*, 119.

[169]   Citing C Howard, *Criminal Law*, 3rd edn (Sydney, 1977) 276.

[170]   (1980) 32 ALR 321

Howard's text in its interpretation of the common purpose rule.[171] The Court went on to add, however, that the trial judge might explain the meaning of a 'substantial risk' as something 'such as might well happen'. Five years later the Privy Council cited the same passages in *Chan Wing Sui*[172] and endorsed the suggestion that the common purpose rule might be explained by a jury instruction that guilt required a finding that the defendant was aware of a 'substantial risk', a 'real risk' or a 'risk that something might well happen'.[173] In 1990, a new edition of Howard's *Criminal Law* appeared with an extended argument in support of the proposition that the accessory was liable for a murder committed by the perpetrator if it had been authorised or if the accessory was aware of a substantial risk that the perpetrator would commit murder. The common purpose rule was explained as yet another instance where recklessness provided the necessary fault element.[174] MCCOC adopted the same rule when it drafted the provisions on criminal responsibility in the Model Penal Code and they were adopted without modification in the Commonwealth Criminal Code. The common purpose rule in the Code makes liability depend on proof that the accessory was reckless with respect to the offence committed by the perpetrator.[175]

Australian common law took a different path. Stephen J appears to have had a hand in writing the joint judgment in *Miller*. He resigned from the High Court in 1982, and the common purpose decisions that followed his resignation make no further reference to foresight of substantial risk. After his departure, the Court speaks of accessorial liability based on awareness of what the perpetrator 'might' do and of the accessory's liability for murder as a foreseen 'possible incident' of the venture.[176] In formulating the law in this way, the Court has chosen to compress two quite different grounds for accessorial liability in a single test of liability for murder:

a. An accessory is guilty of murder if the accessory and perpetrator contemplated the possibility of intentionally killing another (or intentionally inflicting grievous bodily harm) if that were to be necessary in order to complete their venture, defend themselves or prevent apprehension; and

b. An accessory is guilty of murder if the accessory contemplated the possibility that the perpetrator might intentionally kill another (or intentionally inflict grievous bodily harm) in the course of the venture, though murder would not further their common purpose and might contravene the accessory's wishes, intentions or instructions.

---

[171] *Gush* [1980] 2 NZLR 92, 94–5, Richmond P. The common purpose rule in s 66(2) of the Crimes Act 1961 (NZ) required proof that the accessory was aware that the offence committed by the perpetrator was a 'probable' consequence of the prosecution of the common purpose.

[172] [1985] AC 168.

[173] *Ibid*,179.

[174] *Howard's Criminal Law*, 5th edn (Sydney, 1990), 339–43.

[175] Ch 2: *General Principles of Criminal Responsibility*, 11.2: *Complicity and common purpose*, s (3).

[176] *McAuliffe and McAuliffe* (1995) 183 CLR 108. Brennan CJ, Deane, Dawson, Toohey and Gummow JJ refer throughout their joint judgment to murder as a 'possible incident' of what they describe as a 'venture' 'joint enterprise', 'common design' or 'common purpose'.

There can be no quarrel with the imposition of liability for murder when that was an agreed incident of the venture, no matter how remote the chance that the venture might require the commission of that offence. Concern has been expressed, however, that the imposition of liability in the second of these alternatives is an unjustifiable anomaly. If murder by a solo offender requires proof of recklessness with respect to death or grievous bodily harm, is it not inconsistent to convict the mere accessory of murder on the ground that the risk was foreseen as merely possible? It is argued that recklessness should be required in both cases, as it is in the Commonwealth Criminal Code. This particular argument against the current extended common purpose rule is a pale reflection of the argument based on the far more striking discrepancy between the fault elements for complicity and murder in English law.[177] It has been equally unsuccessful in England.

The merits of the argument that the extended common purpose rule should require proof of recklessness are not my concern. The point of interest is the elaboration of a scale of degrees of probability that has emerged in recent High Court decisions when these and similar issues have been debated. It is open to question whether there is any discernible difference between the degrees of subjective probability required to establish recklessness against the solo offender and common purpose against the accessory. The table that follows is based on the most recent of the Court's decisions on the common purpose rule in *Darkan, Deemal-Hall and McIvor*.[178] At issue in *Darkan* was the meaning of the rule in the Queensland Criminal Code, which makes an accessory liable for the 'probable consequence' of an unlawful enterprise, whether or not the accessory realised that the perpetrator might commit the offence.[179] The Court distinguished four levels of probability between more likely than not and a bare or remote possibility. Since the Queensland common purpose rule does not require proof that the accessory was aware of the risk that the perpetrator would commit murder, the Court required something more than a common law possibility of that happening before a Queensland accessory could be convicted of murder. The higher level of objective probability was supposed to compensate for the loss of subjectivity.[180] The orders of probability distinguished by the Court are set out in Table 7.3

---

[177] *Powell and English* [1999] 1 AC 1. For a defence of the rule see AP Simester, 'The Mental Element in Complicity' (2006) 122 *LQR* 578.

[178] [2006] HCA 34 (22 June 2006)

[179] Criminal Code (Qld) 8: *Offences committed in prosecution of an unlawful purpose.*

[180] *Darkan Deemal Hall and McIvor* [2006] HCA 34 (22 June 2006) at paras [74], [76].

Table 7.3: Orders of Probability in the Law of Murder[181]		
1	More probable than not	On the balance of probabilities.
2	Probable	A probability of less than 50/50, but more than a substantial or real and not remote possibility: • a 'probable or likely outcome' • 'probable as distinct from possible' • 'probable in the sense that it could well happen'[182]
3	Substantial possibility	A substantial or real and not remote possibility:[183] More than 'merely possible'[184]
4	Bare possibility	A possibility which is 'bare' in the sense that it is less than a substantial or real and not remote possibility.[185]

A 'Queensland probability' is an event that is likely to happen or probable, in the sense that it could well happen. It is more than a substantial or real possibility. It is evident that this scale of probabilities cannot be reconciled with the current law on recklessness in murder in the common law states. In *Boughey*, where the liability of a solo offender was in issue, the High Court approved a jury direction that the defendant was guilty of murder if he was aware of a 'substantial or real chance as distinct from…a mere possibility' that death was 'something that may well happen' or something that is 'likely to happen'.[186] This sounds like something less than a 'Queensland probability'.[187] It may, indeed, be identical to a 'substantial or real and not remote possibility'. If that is the case, the common law distinction between the fault element of recklessness required for a solo offender and the knowledge of a possible outcome required of the accessory to murder has faded into insignificance.

It does not really matter that *Darkan, Deemall Hall and McIvor* was a decision on the Queensland Code, where the common purpose rule does not require proof that the accessory was aware of the risk. The distinctions that the High

---

[181]   *Ibid*, at paras [27], [81]–[82] (Gleeson CJ, Gummow, Heydon and Crennan JJ). The table is compiled from the list in the majority judgment at para [27] supplemented by explanatory remarks elsewhere in their judgment.

[182]   *Ibid*, at para [79], citing *Gush* [1980] 2 NZLR 92 at 94, per Richmond P, Richardson and O'Regan JJ; *Hagen, Gemmell and Lloyd*, unreported, CA of NZ, 4 Dec 2002 at para [46] per Tipping, McGrath and Anderson JJ 1. See, in addition, *Piri* [1987] 1 NZLR 66; *Te Pou* [2004] NZCA 197.

[183]   Compare *Hartwick and Hartwick* (2005) 159 A Crim R 1 (Vict CA) at para [34] (Charles, Chernov and Nettle JJ).

[184]   *Darkan Deemal Hall and McIvor* [2006] HCA 34 at paras [81]–[82].

[185]   Compare *Powell and English* [1999] 1 AC 1, 31, Lord Hutton: a 'risk so remote that the jury take the view that the secondary party genuinely dismissed it as altogether negligible'.

[186]   *Boughey* (1986) 161 CLR 10, 22, para 18 (Mason, Wilson and Deane JJ).

[187]   The High Court certainly considered it to be less than a Queensland probability. See *Darkan Deemal Hall and McIvor* [2006] HCA 34, at paras [81]–[82].

Court endeavoured to draw among degrees of probability are not distinctions among legal concepts, and it does not really matter whether the jury is supposed to make its own objective estimate of probabilities or put themselves subjectively in the defendant's shoes: this was an attempt to calibrate a scale of probabilities in ordinary language that could be used to instruct a jury. There is every reason for scepticism about the use and, indeed, the intelligibility of such a scale when the difference between murder and manslaughter is in issue. Their incantatory quality is more obvious than their communicative content.

10. Moral Elbow Room for Juries

I have suggested that the accepted definition of reckless murder fails to articulate a coherent moral distinction between murder and manslaughter. That is not to say that juries will not make a moral judgement on the facts of the particular case. Recent High Court decisions on the role of appeal courts accept that juries make moral or strategic choices, based on reasons that cannot be formally articulated in legal criteria, when deciding whether to convict of murder or manslaughter. The moral distinction between murder and manslaughter, so rigorously excluded from the substantive law by the High Court in *Crabbe*, has been secreted in the interstices of procedure.

It has long been accepted that the jury has the power to return a verdict of manslaughter, which will be accepted by the court, though the evidence is consistent only with a verdict of murder or complete acquittal.[188] The existence of the power is accepted in both code and common law jurisdictions. The trial judge is not required to inform the jury that they can do this. Should the jury ask, the trial judge may choose, in appropriate circumstances, to direct them that the evidence provides no basis for a verdict of manslaughter. It is, however, a misdirection to tell the jury that it is beyond their power to convict of manslaughter.

There will be cases in which it is quite clear that the evidence is consistent only with conviction for murder or a complete verdict of acquittal. The nature of the weapons used or the injuries inflicted may leave no room for doubt that the person who caused death intended to do so or intended, at least, to cause grievous bodily harm.[189] Very often, however, the defendant's intentions will be open to argument. If recklessness is in issue and the question is whether the defendant was aware of a substantial and real rather than remote risk of death or grievous bodily harm, the degree of subjective probability will almost always be in issue. It now appears that it is an error for the trial judge to omit a direction

---

[188] *Gammage* (1969) 122 CLR 444.
[189] *Kanaan* (2005) 157 A Crim R 238 (NSW Court of Criminal Appeal).

that manslaughter is a possible verdict in these cases. It does not matter that the defendant's counsel may have made a tactical decision to conduct the defence on the basis that the case was one of murder or nothing. Nor does it matter that a murder verdict provides the basis for a logical inference that the jury must have been convinced beyond reasonable doubt of the elements of murder. Recent decisions in the High Court accept that juries may choose to play the role of moral arbiters and choose among the available verdicts, rather than follow the trial judge's instructions in a 'mechanistic' fashion. The Court has accepted that a jury, faced with a choice between convicting the accused of murder and outright acquittal, might choose to disregard inadequacies in the evidence and convict of murder out of compassion for the victim or his or her family.[190] It is also possible, when juries are aware of their power to return a verdict of manslaughter, that compassion for the defendant might induce them to convict of that offence, though there is overwhelming evidence that the defendant is guilty of murder.[191]

The question whether to direct the jury on manslaughter must now be made in the light of the possibility that the jury may disregard the trial judge's instructions and choose to acquit, convict of murder or convict of manslaughter on compassionate or strategic grounds. If the trial judge failed to offer the manslaughter alternative when it was open on the evidence, the murder verdict will be set aside unless the appeal court is itself convinced beyond reasonable doubt that the appellant is a murderer.[192] After a troubled series of appeals on the issue,[193] the Victorian Court of Criminal Appeal suggested that the High Court has revived, to some degree, the idea that the jury has a constitutional right, rather than an ungovernable power, to return a verdict of manslaughter in a trial for murder.[194]

When juries are permitted a choice between manslaughter and murder in marginal cases, and their instructions require them to juggle probabilities and possibilities, it seems unlikely that their choice will be 'mechanistic' and 'divorced from a consideration of the consequences'.[195] The jury will be aware that the name of the crime makes a very substantial difference to the penalty. Their understanding of the trial judge's instructions will be supplemented, and perhaps displaced, by their consciousness that the trial judge will impose a far more severe penalty if they convict the offender of murder rather than manslaughter. Moral and strategic discriminations of that order, based on the facts of the particular

---

[190] *Gilbert* (2000) 210 CLR 414, Gleeson CJ and Gummow J at paras [16]–[17], Callinan J at para [101].

[191] It is possible, in such a case, that the manslaughter verdict might be overturned. See *Mraz* (1955) 93 CLR 493 (HC Aust). Compare, however, *Tajber* (1986) 23 A Crim R 189.

[192] *Gilbert* (2000) 210 CLR 414.

[193] See, eg, *R v Kane* [2001] VSCA 153; *R v Makin* [2004] VSCA 85; *R v Gill and Mitchell* [2005] VSCA 321.

[194] *R v Gill & Mitchell* (2005) 159 A Crim R 243 at para [4].

[195] *Gilbert* (2000) 210 CLR 414 at para [16] (Gleeson CJ and Gummow J)

case, do not require a clear legal definition or even a coherent moral understanding of the meaning of murder in marginal cases.

11. Real Murderers—A Reform Proposal

There have been two profound changes in the law of murder over the past century or so. The first is the slow recession of the death penalty. The last person hanged in Australia was Ronald Ryan, whose execution took place in Victoria in 1967. Western Australia was the last state to abolish the death penalty, which it did in 1984.[196] The second and equally significant change, which ran roughly parallel to the first, was the transfer, by no means complete, of the power to determine the punishment of murderers from the executive arm of government to the courts. These changes in the consequences of conviction have had a significant though indeterminate influence on the substantive law that defines murder. A couple of instances of that influence must suffice. First, one would hope that the almost complete absence of academic interest in the continued existence of the felony murder rule is a consequence of the abolition of the death penalty and introduction of variable sentences for murder. Secondly, reformers and courts continue to be preoccupied with issues of intention and recklessness and the inadequacies of the defences and partial defences to murder. So far as the structure of defences is concerned, it is unlikely that the current trend to recommend abolition of the qualified defence of provocation would have had the same momentum and the same success, if the penalty for murder was mandatory.

It is probable that most Australians, whether or not trained as lawyers, have an idea—without form or precise factual content—of a paradigm case of murder in which the paradigmatic murderer takes the life of his or her victim intentionally and without justification, excuse or palliation. The paradigm case hangs suspended somewhere between the uncertain borders of manslaughter and the enclave within which are to be found the small minority of worst case murderers, who are sentenced to spend the entirety of their remaining years in prison. At the other end of the continuum, where murder shades into manslaughter, juries will usually determine whether the offender is guilty of murder when guilt is contested. In a small minority of cases the decision will be made by a judge alone, in jurisdictions where the accused is permitted to choose this mode of trial.

The suggestion that I will make in conclusion is that we will do better, in marking the difference between murder and manslaughter, to make the punitive consequences of the verdict determinative of the difference in marginal cases.

---

[196] On the history see I Potas and J Walker, No3 *Trends and Issues in Crime and Criminal Justice*: 'Capital Punishment', Australian Institute of Criminology (Canberra, 1987), available at www.aic.gov.au/publications/tandi/tandi03t.html.

Graduated scales of subjective probability may play a supportive, rhetorical, role, supplemented perhaps by condemnatory epithets. It is the consequences, however, that should be determinative.

Defining the borders of murder is not a new problem, though the landscape is utterly changed. In 1864, in an essay on capital punishment, Fitzjames Stephen distinguished 'real murders' from lesser homicides that counted as murder only because of what he considered to be an unnecessarily extended definition of the offence.[197] He argued that the legal definition should be narrowed to coincide with the 'popular impression' of murder[198] which is close to the paradigm sketched earlier. Real murders, for Stephen, were 'cases in which a man either means to kill, or does some act which shows a mind as reckless of human life as the actual intention to kill'.[199] Stephen's concept of 'real murder' was intended to coincide with the popular or juror's conception of an unlawful homicide that was deserving of capital punishment, which was far more restricted than the legal definition of the offence. His object was to match the mandatory death penalty to the crime. Times have changed. No Australian jurisdiction would contemplate a definition of the offence that restricted it to the paradigm case. The paradigm case no longer even matches the maximum penalty for the offence. Most murderers who kill intentionally or with reckless indifference to human life will regain their freedom after serving less than 20 years in prison. There is no longer the same discrepancy, remarked on by Stephen, between the extended definition of murder and popular impressions of the offence. The modern problem is different. At the lower end of the scale murder and manslaughter merge. A definition of murder that does not include recklessness is unacceptable, but attempts to set a limit to murder by tinkering with the definition of recklessness have failed. Though the landscape has changed, Stephen's argument is readily adaptable to the modern law of murder and manslaughter. His observation that the death penalty was 'one great reason why murder is considered so dreadful a crime'[200] made the point that the perceived severity of the penalty was parent to the moral sentiment that informed the popular impression of 'real murder'. Though murder must remain an extended category that spans a broad range of human wickedness, the lower limit could be marked by a simple and arbitrary punitive consequence, expressed in years of imprisonment, when the jury returns a murder conviction. The jury could be instructed that the penalty for murder, as distinct from manslaughter, would be augmented by a minimum fixed period of imprisonment. A conviction of murder would ensure that this fixed period, at least, would be served in prison, in addition to the penalty that would otherwise have been imposed for manslaughter. It would be inappropriate, at this late stage, to suggest a mode of calculation or, with one exception, to anticipate objections.

---

[197] 'Capital Punishments' (1864) 69 *Fraser's Magazine* 753.
[198] *Ibid*, 764.
[199] *Ibid*, 767–8.
[200] *Ibid*, 761.

The exception arises from the fact that reckless murder is really quite rare and the proposal would only apply in cases at the margin of murder. It is almost certainly the case that Dr Boughey meant to kill his victim. The fact that the jury was directed on recklessness does not mean that the trial judge must assume that this was the ground of conviction or that this was a case on the margins of murder. In the sentencing stage of the trial, the prosecution can and should argue that the defendant meant to kill if there is evidence in support of that hypothesis, and the trial judge will sentence for intentional murder if the prosecution proves its case. The proposal for an explicit distinction between the penalties for murder and manslaughter is appropriate only to mark a minimum penal consequence of conviction for murder in marginal cases.

The proposal is neither radical nor new: it is an adaptation of familiar ideas. Recent Australian case law on appeals against conviction bows to the unavoidable fact that juries do play the role of moral arbiters and make strategic choices of verdict in marginal cases. The proposal is very close to the way in which we distinguish, further down the scale of culpability, between negligent manslaughter and accidental homicide. Both at common law and in the Commonwealth Criminal Code, a finding of negligence requires a jury to conclude that the defendant's conduct was so marked or so gross a departure from reasonable standards of care as to deserve criminal punishment. A similar proposal to establish a borderline at the other end of the scale of homicidal culpability was advanced by the Royal Commission on Capital Punishment, in the mid twentieth century.[201] The Royal Commission was concerned to distinguish between capital murderers and murderers who would serve a term of imprisonment. After an extended consideration of definitional alternatives and the possibility of dividing murder into degrees, the Commission concluded that the difference should be determined on a case-by-case basis by the unguided common sense and common morality of the jury. There was no legal formula 'that would provide a reasonable criterion for the infinite variety of circumstances that may affect the gravity of the crime of murder'.[202]

The Australian problem is different of course. When trial judges sentence the worst among murderers, they can draw on their collective memory of a gallery of instances of depravity to assist in determining particular cases. It would be inappropriate to enlist a jury for this task. At the other end of the continuum, however, a persuasive case can be made for permitting a jury to decide whether the case is murder or manslaughter on criteria that will refer, specifically, to the penal consequences of their decision. The history of judicial and legislative attempts to devise more articulate criteria, that avoid moral arbitrariness, is one of consistent failure.

---

[201] Royal Commission on Capital Punishment 1949–53, *Report*, Cmnd 8932 (London, reprint 1965).

[202] *Ibid*, 208 at para 595.

8

The Scots Law of Murder

VICTOR TADROS

1. Setting the Context

PERHAPS THE OBVIOUS place to begin in thinking about the evolution of homicide offences in both Scotland and England and Wales is the issue of disposal. As has been well noted, the death penalty, and more recently the mandatory life penalty, which were consequences of a conviction of murder, provided significant motivation for the development of the distinction between murder and culpable homicide (in Scotland) or manslaughter (in England and Wales), including the availability of partial defences to murder.

The significant post-trial decision, then, is now not the nature of the sentence but rather what the relevant tariff should be before which the defendant can be considered for parole. Thus, the decision of whether to convict the defendant of murder determines that the defendant's conviction will remain permanently unspent. However, despite that, decisions concerning the time that the defendant will spend in prison will be determined post-trial at the sentencing stage when the tariff is set and at any subsequent parole hearing.

Overall, with respect to the law of murder, then, although there will be some flexibility with regard to the punishment faced by the defendant, that flexibility will be substantially diminished when compared with other offences. Hence, ensuring that the category of murder is appropriately defined does not have only fair labelling implications, which are shared amongst offences; it has powerful practical implications. This is especially stark in Scots law where in common law offences other than murder there is a very high degree of flexibility with respect to sentencing, there being no minimum or maximum sentence for common law offences other than murder.

Structurally, at least, the Scots law of homicide resembles the law of England and Wales. In common with the law of England and Wales, there are two central homicide offences in Scots law. The offences of murder and culpable homicide in Scotland closely resemble the offences of murder and manslaughter in England

187

and Wales. As in England and Wales, as noted, the offence of murder carries with it a mandatory life sentence. There is complete discretion regarding the sentence of culpable homicide.

As in England and Wales there are different kinds of manslaughter, so in Scotland there are different kinds of culpable homicide. First, a conviction of culpable homicide may arise where the victim dies as a consequence of another criminal act, normally an assault.[1] Secondly, the victim may die as a result of the reckless actions of the accused.[2] Finally, the accused may fulfil the other requirements of the offence of murder but have a partial defence. Despite some concern amongst the judiciary about this way of putting it,[3] we might still say that a charge of murder may be 'reduced' to a conviction of culpable homicide through the use of a partial defence.

As in England and Wales, there are two partial defences: provocation and diminished responsibility. Self-defence, insanity and automatism are complete defences to murder. Subject to qualifications considered below, coercion and necessity are probably not defences to murder, however, not even partial defences. There is no Scots equivalent of the offence of infanticide. If a conviction of murder is to be avoided where a mother kills her small child, diminished responsibility may, in the appropriate case, provide a defence.

Historically, Hume, whose *Commentaries on the Law of Scotland Respecting Crimes*[4] is regarded as a source of law, recognised a further distinction in the law of homicide between murder and aggravated murder. If the latter was proved it would result in 'a more rigorous mode of execution, or some indignity and suffering, beside the loss of life'.[5] Cases that Hume considers include those involving the administration of poison and those involving a close relationship between the killer and the victim such as parricide or child murder. The distinction between murder and aggravated murder appears no longer to be significant in the law of Scotland. There is now a single offence of murder.

In this Chapter I will outline the Scots law of murder. I will focus primarily on the substance of the offence, but I will also consider some evidential issues, defences to murder and the Scots law of complicity as it applies to murder. In the final section I will make some tentative proposals for reform.

---

[1] The assault may be very minor indeed. See *Bird v HMA* 1952 JC 23.

[2] Whilst many Scots lawyers have supposed Scots law to adopt an objective definition of recklessness, now see the contrast between the Scots approach and the English test for gross negligence in *Transco PLC v HMA* 2004 SCCR 1 at 35.

[3] The language of 'reducing' murder to culpable homicide was questioned in *HMA v Drury* 2001 SCCR 583. Lord Rodger in that case suggested that the 'defence' of provocation is a way of establishing lack of mens rea. However, his reasoning has been heavily criticised for failing to understand the distinction between offence and defence, on which see below.

[4] 4th edn (Edinburgh, 1844); in two volumes, hereafter Hume i and Hume ii.

[5] Hume i, n 4 above, 191.

2. Actus Reus

The actus reus of murder is the destruction of a human life. Any act that shortens life constitutes the destruction of life for these purposes, although the law has tended to turn a blind eye to the shortening of life through the provision of drugs for pain relief. If the victim dies more than a year and a day after the initial attack a murder charge may nevertheless be competent.[6] A conviction for a homicide offence is competent in cases where the victim's death came about through the voluntary ingestion of proscribed, or even possibly non-proscribed, drugs,[7] and if the accused had the mens rea, a conviction of murder would presumably be possible, although culpable homicide is the more likely offence to be charged.

3. Mens Rea

The mens rea of murder in Scots law is in a chaotic state. There is no longer any equivalent of the term 'malice aforethought' that is used in English law.[8] Until recently, the definition of murder most commonly used derived from the fifth edition of JHA Macdonald's *Criminal Law*:

> Murder is constituted by any wilful act causing the destruction of life, whether intended to kill, or displaying such wicked recklessness as to imply a disposition depraved enough to be regardless of the consequences.[9]

Recently, however, this definition has been qualified by *Drury v HMA*[10] in which it was suggested that it is not a mere intention to kill, but rather a 'wicked intent' to kill, that is required to fulfil the mens rea of murder. Neither the concept of wicked intent nor the meaning of the phrase 'displaying such wicked recklessness as to imply a disposition depraved enough to be regardless of the consequences' has been carefully developed in the law.

---

[6] *Ibid*, 186. It may be that if the victim dies several years after the assault, it will be regarded as oppressive to try the accused. See *Tees v HMA* 1994 SCCR 451.

[7] See *Lord Advocate's Reference (No 1 of 1994)* 1995 SLT 248. Scots law draws no distinction in this context between proscribed and non-proscribed drugs, as can be seen from cases involving non-fatal offences against the person such as *Khaliq v HMA* 1984 JC 23 and *Ulhaq v HMA* 1991 SLT 614.

[8] The historic Scots equivalent, 'forethocht felony', is no longer used. See D Sellar, 'Forethocht Felony, Malice Aforethought and the Classification of Homicide' in WM Gordon and TD Fergus (eds), *Legal History in the Making: Proceedings of the Ninth British Legal History Conference Glasgow 1989* (London, 1991).

[9] 5 th edn (Edinburgh, 1948) 89, cited, eg, in all 3 judgments in *Cawthorne v HMA* 1968 JC 32.

[10] 2001 SCCR 583.

4. Wicked Intent

The case law on the nature of intention is much less developed in Scots law than it is in English law, partly as a consequence of the alternative mens rea of wicked recklessness. Much of the analysis that exists is in the context of fire-raising, for the reason that there are separate offences of wilful fire-raising and culpable and reckless fire-raising in Scots law. However, the analysis of intention in that context does not provide a clear indication of the scope of intent.[11] Hence, it is not clear whether intent to kill, for these purposes, includes foresight of virtual certainty of death or foresight of a high probability of death.

In *Drury* the accused was charged with murder and attempted to use the defence of provocation. The defence is available in Scots law only if the accused was provoked either by violence or by the discovery of infidelity on the part of a person from whom he had an expectation of fidelity. A condition for the use of the defence where the accused suffers violent provocation is that his response must not have been grossly disproportionate to the provocation. The trial judge in *Drury* had directed the jury that a similar principle applied where the provocation arose from infidelity. The accused was convicted and appealed. It was decided that proportionality was not a requirement for the use of the defence in such circumstances. The High Court also took the opportunity to 'clarify' the definition of murder.

The central passage is in the judgment of Lord Justice-General Rodger, whose account was more or less followed by the other judgments in the case. He refers to the direction of the trial judge, which follows closely the standard direction from Macdonald quoted above. He then makes the following comments:

> The definition of murder in the direction is somewhat elliptical because it does not describe the relevant intention. In truth, just as the recklessness has to be wicked so also must the intention be wicked. Therefore, perhaps the most obvious way of completing the definition is by saying that murder is constituted by any wilful act causing the destruction of life, by which the perpetrator either wickedly intends to kill or displays wicked recklessness as to whether the victim lives or dies.[12]

This was motivated by the fact that a person who kills intentionally in self-defence is not guilty of murder.

Effectively, murder is redefined in a way such that the definition of the offence itself excludes cases in which the accused would be entitled to a defence.[13] The High Court, in redefining murder, supposes that if a defence is available to the defendant, he ought not to fall within the definition of the offence. This

---

[11] *Byrne v HMA* 2000 SCCR 77.

[12] 2001 SCCR 583, 588–9.

[13] See also Lord Rodger's rejection of the idea that murder is reduced to culpable homicide: 2001 SCCR 583, at 591. He objects on the ground that if there is sufficient provocation the accused has not completed the offence of murder at all.

requirement is obviously contrary to much modern criminal law scholarship, in which the separation between offence and defence is regarded as being fundamental in principle, albeit that there is disagreement as to exactly why.[14] It is also contrary to an earlier decision on the mens rea of murder, *Scott v HMA*,[15] which was not referred to in *Drury*.

A starting point for analysing the consequences of this decision is whether (a) the 'clarification' in *Drury* only alters the structure of the law by incorporating extant defence definitions negatively into the definition of the offence (so, for example, 'wicked intent' can be redefined as 'intent to kill in the absence of self-defence, provocation or diminished responsibility');[16] or (b) *Drury* introduces the possibility that the accused killed the victim intentionally, did not fall within any extant defence definition, but nevertheless is properly to be acquitted of murder.

There is some good reason to think that it is (b) that was intended. Lord Rodger claimed that provocation is effectively evidence as to whether the accused had wicked intent or was wickedly reckless as to death.[17] Furthermore, the proper procedure in provocation cases following *Drury* is to consider whether the defence was available to the accused and, if the defence fails, consider whether the accused had wicked intent or was wickedly reckless on the basis of the remaining evidence. However, there appears to be nothing in *Drury* which explicitly restricts the accused from raising 'quasi-provocation' evidence as a way of showing a lack of wicked intent or wicked recklessness.[18]

For example, in Scots law, the defence of provocation is available only if the accused responded immediately to the provoking incident. This requirement appears to exclude the possibility of cumulative provocation.[19] But, following *Drury*, there appears to be nothing to prevent the accused raising evidence of cumulative provocation as a way of showing lack of wicked intent.[20] Similarly,

---

[14] See K Campbell, 'Offence and Defence' in I Dennis (ed), *Criminal Law and Criminal Justice* (London, 1987); J Gardner, 'Justifications and Reasons' in AP Simester and ATH Smith, *Harm and Culpability* (Oxford, 1996); G Fletcher, *Rethinking Criminal Law* (Oxford, reprinted 2000); V Tadros, *Criminal Responsibility* (Oxford, 2005), ch 4. For a similar argument in the context of *Drury*, see J Chalmers, 'Collapsing the Structure of Criminal Law', 2001 *SLT (News)* 241; M Christie, 'The Coherence of Scots Criminal Law: Some Aspects of *Drury v H.M. Advocate*' (2002) *Juridical Review* 273.

[15] 1996 SLT 519.

[16] Sir Gerald Gordon, in his commentary to the case, suggests that in practice it may well be that the jury will be obliged to convict if they indicate to the trial judge that they think that the accused does not fall within an extant defence to murder but that his intention to kill was not wicked.

[17] 2001 SCCR 583, 591.

[18] See also Christie, n 14 above.

[19] See *Thomson v HMA*, 1986 SLT 281. See below.

[20] It should be noted that in *Parr v HMA* 1991 SCCR 180, the defence attempted to use quasi-provocation evidence in order to establish that the jury should have been invited to consider a verdict of culpable homicide in a case where the accused struck the victim several times with a hammer. It was held that the nature of the acts themselves was such that the judge was correct to withdraw the issue of culpable homicide from the jury. Perhaps that approach is questionable, given *Drury*.

although it has been suggested that coercion is not a defence to murder,[21] there now seems little rationale for excluding evidence of coercion in murder cases. For such evidence is surely a way of showing that the accused lacked wicked intent even if he killed intentionally in response to the coercion. Finally, there is a rule in Scots law that, in cases of mistaken self-defence, the defence will only be available if the accused makes a reasonable mistake as to the necessity of defending himself.[22] But, unless it can be shown that such an accused was wickedly reckless in defending himself in that way, it may be that a conviction of murder is no longer competent where the defendant honestly but unreasonably believes that he is being attacked.[23]

This aspect of the decision in *Drury* is undesirable. Changes in the law of murder indicated above may be desirable in substance, but to allow the jury to consider such evidence in a way unconstrained by any set of rules or principles is unlikely to produce consistent or otherwise just results. Whilst I do not think that decisions regarding categorisation of crime by degree can ultimately be captured in neat and precise rules, *Drury* potentially opens up flexibility too far and fails to recognise the proper role and status of defences.

The attempt to close the door which was blown open in *Drury* has begun in *Gillon v HMA*.[24] There it was decided that one could separate the underlying theory of mens rea adopted and the criteria required to satisfy it. The criteria, it is suggested, are those that are laid out in specific defences. In other words, *Drury* was read in the more conservative way outlined in (a) above. The passages cited from *Drury* were selective to say the least, presumably to avoid direct criticism of Lord Rodger's appreciation of the structure of criminal responsibility. However, it is still not clear what the response of the courts should be if the accused, in a quasi-provocation case, pleads lack of mens rea even though he clearly intended to kill. The jury should be directed to investigate whether the intent of the accused was wicked, and presumably the evidence of provocation must be admitted to help the jury to determine whether that is the case.

5. Wicked Recklessness

As noted above, the mens rea of murder may be complete even if the accused did not intend to kill, if he displayed 'such wicked recklessness as to imply a

---

[21] This was suggested by the trial judge in *Collins v HMA*, 1993 SLT 101, although the comments may be regarded as obiter, as coercion was not raised as a defence in the case. The issue was not commented on by the High Court in the appeal despite the defence being mentioned, which seems to imply that the possibility of coercion in a murder case was not being ruled out.

[22] *Owens v HMA* 1946 JC 119. For further discussion see F Leverick, 'Mistake in Defence after *Drury*' (2002) *Juridical Review* 35.

[23] See also J Chalmers, 'Collapsing the Structure of Criminal Law', 2001 *SLT (News)* 241, at 242–3.

[24] (2006) HCJAC 61. The case has, like *Drury*, the authority of having been decided by a court of five judges.

disposition depraved enough to be regardless of the consequences'. This phrase is hardly crystal clear, although it is regarded by some Scots lawyers as satisfactory.[25] Subsequent case law has failed to clarify matters.

(i) Objectivity

It is often commented that wicked recklessness is to be interpreted objectively. That is, it is suggested that one looks at the acts of the accused rather than attempting to discover what is in his mind. This is so, it has been suggested, because one cannot assess what was in the mind of the accused, so one must infer that from his acts. However, that explanation is problematic. First, the definition of wicked recklessness itself implicitly refers to a state of mind, for states of mind are surely central to establishing the 'depraved disposition' of the accused. Secondly, the inference of such a disposition is to be made from the violent acts of the accused, but those violent acts must themselves be intentional. So, for example, Lord Cameron, in *Cawthorne* suggests that 'such reckless conduct, *intentionally* perpetrated, is in law the equivalent of a deliberate intent to kill' (his emphasis).[26] It is not so much that the mens rea of murder is defined objectively, then. Perhaps there is a constructive element to the mens rea of murder, where the mens rea need not correspond precisely with the actus reus, although decisions are insufficiently clear to establish whether this is the case.[27] Finally, if the explanation of the alternative mens rea of murder is that it is difficult to prove an intention to kill, that seems contrary to the spirit of the presumption of innocence.[28]

Whilst the term 'objective' tends to be used by criminal lawyers to denote standards to be applied to the defendant's behaviour regardless of his or her state of mind, it is not clear that this captures what the courts intend when they use the term 'objective'. For example in *Broadley v HMA*[29] the accused was charged with the murder of his wife by stabbing her several times with a knife. He sought to rely on factors which might have motivated the attack, such as that his wife had left him, as well as factors which might be called 'quasi-excuses', such as that he was a weak man and that he had argued with his father in law, to argue that he

---

[25] See *Report of the House of Lords Select Committee on Murder and Life Imprisonment* (London, 1989). The Draft Criminal Code for Scotland suggests the alternative 'callous recklessness' in s 37. It is not entirely clear that this has the advantages of clarification that are suggested in the commentary.

[26] 1968 JC 32, 38.

[27] See below.

[28] How *that* is to be interpreted, of course, is contested. See, eg, P Roberts, 'The Presumption of Innocence Brought Home: *Kebilene* Deconstructed' (2002) 118 *LQR* 41, and 'Drug Dealing and the Presumption of Innocence: the Human Rights Act (Almost) Bites' (2002) 6 *International Journal of Evidence and Proof* 20; V Tadros and S Tierney, 'The Presumption of Innocence and the Human Rights Act' (2004) 67 *MLR* 402; RA Duff, 'Strict Liability, Legal Presumptions, and the Presumption of Innocence', and P Roberts, 'Strict Liability and the Presumption of Innocence: An Exposé of Functionalist Assumptions', both in AP Simester, *Appraising Strict Liability* (Oxford, 2005).

[29] 1991 SCCR 416.

did not kill in a wickedly reckless manner. These contextual factors were excluded on the ground that the mens rea of murder is to be determined objectively. But the factors were not raised by the accused to suggest that he lacked the state of mind necessary for murder. Furthermore, as has already been noted, surely it would be central to justifying a conviction that the attack with the knife was intentional. An accidental stabbing would not constitute murder.

(ii) Murder and the Intention to Assault

The question of objectivity is related to the question whether an intention seriously to assault the victim is sufficient to constitute the mens rea of murder. English law has been criticised by some for adopting such a 'constructive' approach to the offence of murder.[30] In Scots law the authorities are not entirely clear whether murder is a constructive crime. Juries have sometimes been directed that an intention to assault the victim is a third alternative to an intention to kill or wicked recklessness outlined by Macdonald.[31] However, the status of an intention to assault, in the context of murder, is now probably only that it is a way of establishing wicked recklessness.[32] If a third limb of the mens rea of murder remains, it only remains in the context of violent robbery.[33] However, the relationship between an intention to assault and the relevant disposition of the accused in Scots law is unclear.

The central question is the status of the disposition of the accused. The prosecution is required to prove that the accused displayed such wicked reckless-ness *as to imply* a disposition regardless of the consequences. This might suggest that the prosecution does not need to prove that the accused *had* such a disposition. It need only prove that the accused attacked the victim in a wickedly reckless way, such that the relevant disposition *could* be implied. In other words, a conviction may be competent even if the jury do not think that the relevant disposition has been proved by the prosecution to the criminal standard.

This is important for, if the prosecution is not required to prove the relevant disposition, it is also not required to prove that the defendant had any particular attitude toward the death of the victim. Consider two hypothetical cases in which

---

[30] It might be thought to depart from the correspondence principle, if indeed that is a proper principle of criminal law, on which there is a developing literature. See A Ashworth, *Principles of Criminal Law*, 4th edn (Oxford, 2003) at 88; J Horder, 'A Critique of the Correspondence Principle in Criminal Law' [1995] *Crim LR* 759; B Mitchell, 'In Defence of the Correspondence Principle' [1999] *Crim LR* 195 (and Horder's following reply, 'Questioning the Correspondence Principle—A Reply' [1999] *Crim LR* 206); V Tadros, *Criminal Responsibility* (Oxford, 2005) at 90–9.

[31] See, eg, the direction of Lord Avonside in *Cawthorne v HMA* 1968 JC 32, which did not receive criticism on appeal.

[32] See *Arthur v HMA* 2002 SCCR 796.

[33] If, as I will suggest, *Broadley* 1991 SCCR 416 is to be treated with suspicion in the light of *Arthur* 2002 SCCR 796 and *Halliday* [1998] SCCR 509, perhaps the authority concerning killing in the course of a robbery discussed in GH Gordon, *Criminal Law*, 3rd edn (Edinburgh, 2001) ii, at 302–5 should be treated with the same suspicion.

the defendant severely beat the victim in an identical manner, but did not hit him on the head, and the victim died of his injuries. A1 claims that he purposefully avoided the head to lessen the risk of death, and that claim is substantiated by some evidence (perhaps, for example, he can show that he had been advised to avoid the head just before the beating to diminish the risk of death). A2 gave no particular thought to the issue. He recognised the risk of death in the assault. If the jury are unsure about whether A1 is telling the truth, is a conviction of murder nevertheless competent? Perhaps one thing that the courts are attempting to convey by using the language of objectivity, for example in *Broadley v HMA*, is that A1 and A2 are to be treated in the same manner. Once the prosecution has proved an intentional violent assault where death is an obvious and serious risk, nothing more need be established.

Perhaps, on the other hand, evidence that the accused lacked the relevant attitude to the consequences of his actions is relevant to determining whether the accused is to be convicted of murder. So, for example, in *Arthur v HMA*[34] it was suggested that the use of violence, even life-threatening violence, is 'only the basis on which the relevant mental state, namely utter and wicked disregard for the consequences to the victim, could be inferred'.[35] In that case, it appears that even the intent to use 'life-threatening' violence is insufficient for the mens rea of murder if the accused does not disregard the consequences to his victim. This seems to suggest that using very serious violence against the victim, hoping that the victim survives it, is insufficient for a conviction of murder if the victim dies of his injuries. Consequently, the jury ought to acquit in A1's case.

Probably this is the view most consistent with other authorities. For example, it is consistent with the decision in *Halliday v HMA*[36] in which it was decided that the failure of the two accused to call an ambulance after the attack on the victim could provide evidence that they displayed wicked recklessness in the attack. It was decided that:

> The evidence that, once the attack was over, the appellants failed to call an ambulance and proceeded instead to see to the washing of their clothes, is again evidence which the jury could properly regard as casting light on the attitude of the appellants at the time of the attack and as tending to show that they had been wickedly indifferent to the consequences of the attack on the deceased.[37]

If evidence which provides the context of the attack, and which tends to show indifference on the part of the accused, is relevant to establishing wicked recklessness then surely contextual evidence which tends to show lack of indifference must be relevant also. From that, the proper conclusion is that the rule in

---

[34] 2002 SCCR 796.
[35] 2002 SCCR 796, 80. Similarly, in *Miller and Denovan v HMA*, High Court, Dec 1960 unreported (see CHW Gane and CN Stoddart, *A Casebook on Scottish Criminal Law* (Edinburgh, 2001), at 404–6), it was suggested that 'it can still be murder *if the jury are satisfied* that there was a wilful act displaying *utter recklessness of the consequences* of the blow delivered' (Gane and Stoddart's emphasis).
[36] 1998 SCCR 509.
[37] 1998 SCCR 509, 513.

Broadley, even if it is correct in its consequences in that case, was poorly formulated. Finally, if the decision in *Halliday* is accepted, there is obviously no room for the idea that wicked recklessness is to be understood objectively, for in that case the jury were explicitly invited to consider the attitude of the accused, surely a subjective issue.

(iii) Withdrawing Culpable Homicide from the Jury

In both *Miller and Denovan* and *Broadley*, as well as *Parr v HMA*,[38] appeals arose because the trial judge did not leave open to the jury the possibility of a conviction of culpable homicide. The issues discussed in this section will obviously be relevant in determining when this is properly done. Both appeals were dismissed on the ground that if the prosecution's case was to be believed regarding the nature of the attack, the only possible offence which the jury could convict of would be murder. This is a warranted conclusion in *Broadley*, but less convincing in *Miller and Denovan*, in which the victim was hit over the head with a large piece of wood by one of the accused to facilitate a robbery.

6. Murder Art and Part

It is worth a brief (and due to constraints of space, incomplete) excursion into the law of art and part, as this is perhaps one of the most controversial aspects of the law of murder in Scotland. Art and part is the Scottish auxiliary offence of assisting the principal to commit an offence, akin to the mode of participation known to English as aiding, counselling or abetting. Recent developments in the law of art and part in the context of homicide re-establish a broad scope of the offence, and those developments can only be regarded as troubling. The central case is *McKinnon v HMA*.[39]

McKinnon decided that murder may be perpetrated art and part by the accused if (a) the principal killed; and (b) the accused, by his words or actions, actively associated himself with a common criminal purpose with the principal which was or included the taking of human life or carried with it the obvious risk that human life would be taken. It is not necessary for the prosecution to prove that the accused was aware that there was any risk that human life would be taken if that risk was obvious.[40] If the common criminal purpose involved the carrying of weapons, and the accused knew this, that would be sufficient to establish the

---

[38]   1991 SCCR 180.
[39]   2003 SCCR 224.
[40]   There are, however, some passages that appear to conflict with that. See J Chalmers, 'Art and Part Liability in Homicide' (2003) 62 *Greens Criminal Law Bulletin* 2.

mens rea of art and part murder, it has been suggested, for if weapons were carried, it would be obvious that they might be used. *McKinnon* seems to suggest that the accused can be convicted of murder art and part even if he has no awareness of any risk of death, or even a risk of injury, whatsoever when joining the common purpose, and that is surely unwarranted.

McKinnon also confirms that if the accused associates himself with some lesser common purpose, which does not carry the obvious risk that murder may be committed, it is open for the jury to convict the accused of culpable homicide even if the principal is convicted of murder. For example, if the accused reasonably believes that all that is intended is some minor injury to the victim, a conviction of culpable homicide may be warranted if the principal murders the victim.[41] However, the case does not make any provision for a conviction of the lesser offence if the accused dissociates himself from that aspect of the common plan at a later date.

It is not clear whether the decision in *McKinnon* applies in circumstances of spontaneous concert. Scots law has tended to distinguish antecedent concert and spontaneous concert. It may be that the more subjective individualised approach of *Brown v HMA*[42] will be used with regard to spontaneous concert. The judgment in *McKinnon* tends to characterise more subjective and individualised approaches to murder art and part that exist in the case law[43] as applying to spontaneous rather than antecedent concert. However, it is not obvious that there is any principled reason to distinguish antecedent concert from spontaneous concert in this way.[44]

7. Partial Defences

As in the law of England and Wales, there are two partial defences to murder: provocation and diminished responsibility. These defences are partial in that they 'reduce' a charge of murder to a conviction of culpable homicide. In contrast with the situation in England and Wales, the defences have been developed in the common law and they have still not been put on a statutory basis.

---

[41] 2003 SCCR 224, 237, following *Mathieson v HMA* 1996 SCCR 388.

[42] 1993 SCCR 382.

[43] See discussion of *Melvin v HMA* 1984 SCCR 113, in *McKinnon v HMA* 2003 SCCR 224, at 236–7.

[44] It is also now difficult to determine the status of the decision in *Kabalu v HMA* 1999 SCCR 348. In that case, the victim was chased by a group of people and beaten to death. The accused arrived on the scene after significant blows had been delivered to the victim. It was decided that he could not be convicted of murder as he had not seen the extent of the earlier violence. But it is not clear that a conviction would be ruled out by the objective approach of *McKinnon*. It is also unclear whether to call this attack an example of spontaneous concert at all. It may be that the appropriate distinction has to do with the adoption of prior injuries rather than future acts of the accused, another distinction which it is difficult to justify in principle. See also *McLaughlan v HMA*, 1991 SLT 660.

(i) Diminished Responsibility

The creation of the defence of diminished responsibility was almost certainly motivated at least in part by the desire to avoid imposing the death penalty. Consequently, the defence was historically fairly broad.[45] Until the recent case of *HMA v Galbraith*[46] the defence had gradually narrowed, primarily to prevent it being used by those suffering from psychopathic personality disorder or equivalents. The burden of proof in establishing the defence of diminished responsibility is on the party seeking to establish it.[47]

Prior to *Galbraith*, the leading case on diminished responsibility was *HMA v Savage*.[48] In that case the jury were charged that murder could be reduced to culpable homicide in the following circumstances: that there was an aberration or weakness of mind; some form of mental unsoundness; a state of mind which is bordering on, though not amounting to, insanity; and some form of mental disease. However, this was put fairly casually by Lord Alness as 'the kind of thing that is necessary' for use of the defence.[49] In *Connelly v HMA*[50] it was decided that this test was required to be read such that the absence of any element would make the defence unavailable to the accused. A consequence was that the defence was unavailable where the accused did not suffer from a mental disorder, mental illness or disease. That, it appeared, excluded those with personality disorder from the defence. Furthermore, in *Williamson v HMA*,[51] which followed the judgment in *Connelly*, it was held that mental disorder, mental illness and mental disease were different ways of referring to the same thing rather than alternatives, hence narrowing the defence further.

These decisions would also have excluded from the defence women who killed their partners after suffering domestic abuse. For, whilst such women have been described as suffering from 'battered woman syndrome',[52] it is not clear that such a syndrome would amount to a disease of the mind. Such circumstances gave rise to a reconsideration of the defence in *Galbraith*.

In *Galbraith*, *Connelly* was overruled, and the defence was broadened in two ways. First, it was decided that the defence might be made available to a

---

[45] See *HMA v Galbraith* 2001 SCCR 551, at 566, which outlines the different kinds of case which grounded the defence.

[46] 2001 SCCR 551.

[47] *Lindsay v HMA* 1997 JC 19.

[48] 1923 JC 49.

[49] *HMA v Savage* 1923 JC 49, 50.

[50] 1990 SCCR 504.

[51] 1994 SCCR 358.

[52] See L Walker, *The Battered Woman Syndrome* (New York, 1984). There is a large body of literature about whether there is such a syndrome and its relationship to criminal defences. See, eg, AM Coughlin, 'Excusing Women' (1994) 82 *California Law Review* 1; R Schopp, B Sturgiss and M Sullivan, 'Battered Woman Syndrome, Expert Testimony, and the Distinction between Justification and Excuse' [1994] *University of Illinois Law Review* 45; J Dressler, 'Battered Women Who Kill Their Sleeping Tormenters: Reflections on Maintaining Respect for Human Life while Killing Moral Monsters', and J Horder, 'Killing the Passive Abuser: A Theoretical Defence', both in S Shute and AP Simester (eds), *Criminal Law Theory: Doctrines of the General Part* (Oxford, 2002).

defendant even if he did not suffer from a mental disease. Other psychological disorders might provide a foundation for the use of the defence. The law is to proceed on a case-by-case basis to determine which disorders have the potential to found a defence of diminished responsibility and which do not. Causes of the disorder that may found the defence include sunstroke, alcoholism, strokes, tumours, disorders of the thyroid or prescribed drugs. If the accused is of low intelligence, suffers from schizophrenia or is depressed, the defence may also be available. Finally, relevant to the facts of *Galbraith*, a recognised mental abnormality that follows from abuse suffered by the accused might also be capable of founding the defence. The mental disorder must be recognised by the 'appropriate science', but that may include psychologists as well as psychiatrists.[53] It may be questioned whether the legal conception of diminished responsibility should be restricted in this way.[54] Personality disorder, on the other hand, is explicitly excluded as a foundation of the defence,[55] as is voluntary intoxication.[56]

Secondly, the degree of mental impairment required for use of the defence was clarified and reduced in *Galbraith*. As noted above, in *Savage* it was suggested that the defence would be available only if the accused had a mental state bordering on insanity. In *Galbraith* it was decided that it is normally neither necessary nor appropriate to direct the jury in these terms, and that, as in English criminal law, substantial impairment would be sufficient. It is only in cases where alternative defences of insanity and diminished responsibility are raised that the jury may be directed that the defence is available if the mental state of the accused was on the border of insanity.[57] However, given that such a degree of impairment is not necessary for use of the defence it is difficult to understand why such a direction would ever be appropriate.

For the defence of diminished responsibility to be available in Scotland, as has been noted, it must be shown that the accused suffered from substantial impairment of his ability to control and determine his actions. There are different kinds of impairment that may ground the defence. In understanding mental disorder defences, one may distinguish cognitive, evaluative and volitional functions of the mind.[58] *Galbraith* suggests that all three kinds of impairment may ground the defence of diminished responsibility.[59] The Scots law of insanity has tended to

---

[53] *Galbraith v HMA* 2001 SCCR 551, 574.

[54] See V Tadros, 'The Structure of Defences in Scots Criminal Law' (2003) 7 *Edinburgh Law Review* 60.

[55] This built on what may, at least, be described as strong scepticism about any plausible distinction to be drawn between those suffering from psychopathic personality disorder and ordinary criminals in *Carraher v HMA* 1946 JC 108.

[56] See *Brennan v HMA* 1977 JC 38, although it appears that voluntary intoxication was regarded as potentially available to found the defence in *Savage*.

[57] *Galbraith v HMA* 2001 SCCR 551, 571.

[58] See V Tadros, *Criminal Responsibility* (Oxford, 2005), ch 12 for discussion.

[59] *Galbraith v HMA* 2001 SCCR 551, at 572–3.

recognise irresistible impulse as a possible basis for the insanity defence[60] (although that may be called into question by *Cardle v Mulrainey*[61]), and *Galbraith* suggests that there may be a similar basis for the defence of diminished responsibility. There is disagreement in the academic literature as to whether irresistible impulse ought to be accommodated in the defence.[62] This account of the kinds of abnormality that may be relevant invites an explanation, which is not forthcoming, of why the defence is not available to those suffering from psychopathic personality disorder.[63] The only explanation that is given is that old fig leaf of 'policy concerns'.[64]

If there is insufficient evidence, when taken at its highest, to found the defence of diminished responsibility, the judge may remove the issue from the jury, inviting them to convict of murder if they are to convict at all. However, it is unclear how this conception of the defence relates to the interpretation of the mens rea of murder developed in *Drury*. Perhaps *Galbraith* provides evidence that the proper interpretation of *Drury* is that it merely incorporates existing rules of defences into the question whether the accused had the wicked intent necessary for murder. But as *Drury* is not mentioned in *Galbraith*, the relationship between the two is open to speculation.

(ii) Provocation

The law of provocation in Scotland is in need of substantial reform. There are a number of respects in which Scots law of provocation differs from the law of

---

[60] This is more or less explicit in *HMA v Kidd* 1960 JC 61: see V Tadros, 'Insanity and the Capacity for Criminal Responsibility' (2001) 5 *Edinburgh Law Review* 325.

[61] (1992) SCCR 658. That case was concerned with involuntary intoxication with amphetamines. It was decided that there was insufficient evidence of a total alienation of reason, which is the standard required for the insanity defence as developed in *Kidd*. However, the judgement considers a very small range of the relevant authorities on irresistible impulse in Scotland, and is consequently probably insufficient to rule it out as within the scope of the defence. Furthermore, it does not overrule *Kidd*, which is the leading case on the insanity defence, and is explicit that the defence may be available even if the accused understands the nature and quality of the act and that it was wrong. Finally, it may be that the case is restricted to the defence of non-insane automatism.

[62] See, eg, A Ashworth, *Principles of Criminal Law*, 4th edn (Oxford, 2003) 211; S Morse, 'Uncontrollable Urges and Irrational People' (2002) 88 *Virginia Law Review* 1025; M Smith, 'Irresistible Impulse' in N Naffine, RJ Owens and J Williams (eds), *Intention in Law and Philosophy* (Aldershot, 2001); V Tadros, *Criminal Responsibility* (Oxford, 2005), ch12. The Scottish Law Commission, in its *Report on Insanity and Diminished Responsibility*, Scot Law Com No.195 (Edinburgh, 2004) oddly suggests that all the relevant volitional questions pose difficult practical problems and, when properly framed, collapse into cognitive questions properly understood in the context of insanity. But in the context of diminished responsibility it suggests that the phrase 'ability to determine or control conduct' is clear and well understood.

[63] James Chalmers suggests that such a path was open to the High Court, as *Carraher* had not explicitly ruled out the use of the defence for cases of psychopathic personality disorder. See J Chalmers, 'Abnormality and Anglicisation: First Thoughts on *Galbraith v H M Advocate (No 2)*' (2002) 6 *Edinburgh Law Review* 108.

[64] *Galbraith v HMA* 2001 SCCR 551, 574.

England and Wales. In almost all respects, the defence is broader in England and Wales than it is in Scotland, though it is arguably too broad there. The irony in this context is that, whereas jury discretion is more tightly constrained in determining the mens rea of murder in England and Wales in contrast with Scotland, it is much less tightly constrained in England and Wales in determining whether the defence of provocation ought to be available.

Given this, it might be argued that the jury have a similar amount of discretion in each system: discretion in the law of provocation in England and Wales compensates for less discretion with respect to the mens rea of the offence. However, whilst this may be true, jury discretion is distributed unevenly across the two systems and it is difficult to find a rational basis on which this should be the case. Hence, these differing degrees of discretion with respect to mens rea and provocation can be considered a ground of criticism of both systems. It is difficult to see how there can be a rational basis for substantially constraining discretion with regard to one question concerning fault (the mens rea in England and Wales and the defence of provocation in Scotland) whilst opening up discretion very substantially in respect of another (the mens rea in Scotland and the defence of provocation in England and Wales).

(a) The Basis of the Defence

Perhaps the most substantial difference to note between Scotland and England and Wales is in relation to the kind of provocation that will satisfy the defence. The Homicide Act 1957 broadened out the basis of the defence in England and Wales to include provocation by words, acts or a combination of the two. In Scots law in contrast, with one exception, the basis of the defence is limited to provocation by physical violence. The exception concerns accused who discover infidelity by their partners.[65]

That there should be restrictions on the basis of the defence ensures that the jury in Scotland have a much more limited role than in England and Wales in determining whether the conditions of the defence are satisfied. And indeed the defence will not be left to the jury unless there is evidence that the provocation falls within one of the two categories on which it can be based. This has the advantage that spurious grounds for the defence such as nagging by one's partner, which have grounded the defence successfully in England and Wales, will not be left for consideration by the jury.

However, there are two problems with this aspect of the defence. First, it may be thought overly restrictive. Other than in the infidelity cases which I will consider in a moment, the only basis of the defence is violent provocation. However, there are arguably other forms of provocation that ought to be available to ground the defence. A position in the middle of that in Scotland and that in

---

[65] The leading case is *HMA v Hill* 1941 JC 59.

England and Wales might be desirable. Allowing the jury complete control over whether the grounds of the defence are sufficient, as is the case in England and Wales, will fail to achieve consistency and will lead to arbitrary decisions or decisions which reflect prejudices of the jury. Restricting the defence as much as is the case in Scotland, on the other hand, fails to accommodate cases in which the provocation, whilst not violent, is extreme, or even where other forms of provocation are accompanied by non-extreme violence.

Secondly, the infidelity exception is itself difficult to understand. It is difficult to see why discovering the infidelity of one's partner is any more provocative than finding out other things about the victim. In fact, it might be thought difficult to understand how such a finding could be sufficiently grave to provoke the defendant to kill in a wickedly reckless manner. Whilst it is no doubt the case that discovery of infidelity still commonly results in very strong feelings, it is difficult to see anything that might justify the exception in modern times. Rather, this form of the defence is probably best thought a remnant of the days in which killing one's spouse or (normally) her lover was seen as having some kind of honour attached to it.

(b) Provocation by Violence

Where the accused kills as a consequence of violent provocation, there are two conditions that need to be fulfilled for the defence of provocation to be available. First, he must react immediately to the provocation.[66] Secondly, the response must not to be grossly disproportionate to the provocative violence.[67]

The immediacy requirement is generally interpreted restrictively in Scots law. First, the immediacy requirement is part of the substantive law. So where in England and Wales lack of immediacy is merely evidence that the defendant did not lose self-control,[68] in Scotland it is a substantive condition of the availability of the defence. Secondly, the gravity of the provocation is determined entirely by the acts immediately prior to the homicide. There is no room in Scots law for cumulative provocation, even as a way of assessing the gravity of the immediate act.[69] Both rules are restrictive, and effectively ensure that the defence will very rarely be available for battered women who kill their abusive partners. This, coupled with the developments in *Galbraith* considered above, ensures that diminished responsibility is the defence most likely to be successful in such cases.

The requirement that the response must not be grossly disproportionate reveals that provocation in Scots law is closely related to self-defence. Most provocation cases involving violence may well be cases of excessive self-defence

---

66 *Thomson v HMA*, 1986 SLT 281.
67 *Robertson v HMA* 1994 SCCR 589, affirmed in *HMA v Gillon* 2006 HCJAC 61.
68 *R v Ahluwalia* [1992] 4 All ER 889.
69 See *Thomson v HMA*, 1986 SLT 281.

resulting in death, where the accused does not fulfil the proportionality require-ment for the full defence. For the expanding group of scholars who are sceptical about the defence of provocation, such cases may be thought the most deserving of the partial defence.

The requirement that the reaction must not be grossly disproportionate to the provocation may at first sight seem difficult to understand. In *Gillon v HMA*,[70] counsel for the appellant argued that the test ought to be replaced by an ordinary man test so that there would be a single and unified test for provocation. One ground of argument was that the language of proportionality was difficult to understand in this context, as provocation is primarily a defence to murder and killing will always be disproportionate to any provocative violence. This argu-ment, the High Court claimed, is fallacious on the ground that it made 'a comparison involving the consequences of the violence used in retaliation, as opposed to its nature and extent'.[71] That is no answer, however, for it is not at all obvious that the 'nature and extent' of the violence can be neatly distinguished from its consequence. For example, if A beats B to death with a baseball bat, what is the nature of the violence and what is its consequence? Is the nature of the violence *swinging* the bat, or *hitting* B with the bat, or *fracturing B's skull* with the bat, or *killing* B?

(c) Provocation by Infidelity

The requirements of provocation by infidelity are much the same as provocation by violence except that the proportionality requirement is replaced by the English-inspired test that the ordinary man would have done what the accused did. In *Drury* it was established that the jury would not be required to consider whether the accused responded in a way that was proportionate to the infidelity on the ground that violence and infidelity were incommensurable.[72] Hence, whether there was sufficient provocation is to be determined purely by the immediacy question and the question whether the ordinary person might have done what the defendant did in response to the provocation.

The category of infidelity has gone through substantial expansion in recent years. It now includes not only married couples, but anyone in a relationship where there is an expectation of infidelity, including same-sex relationships. Furthermore, the accused need not have discovered his partner 'in the act'; mere disclosure of infidelity is sufficient. Finally, disclosure of a more persistent course of unfaithful conduct is sufficient to ground the defence even if the accused was

[70] *HMA v Gillon* 2006 HCJAC 61.
[71] *Ibid*, para 22.
[72] Of course, one need not accept that incommensurability entails incomparability. For further discussion and references to the extensive literature see V Tadros, 'Conflicts about Conflicts' (2002) 4 *Juridical Review* 183.

aware that his partner had been unfaithful. This process of expansion is an ironically modern and politically correct evolution in an arguably anachronistic and perhaps even sexist context.

As in the law of England and Wales, it must be shown that the accused did as the ordinary person might have done. The move from the reasonable person standard to the ordinary person standard occurred in *Drury v HMA*, and mirrors the move made in *R v (Morgan) Smith*.[73] It is equally difficult to understand. If the defendant has shown himself to be *ethically* ordinary (and what else could the test refer to?) why is he deserving of a criminal conviction? Furthermore, it is difficult to imagine an ethically ordinary person killing in response to provocation at all.[74]

The question whether accommodation should be made in Scots law for defendants who cannot be expected to meet the standards of ordinariness in respect of responding to provocation was left open in *Drury*. However, given the collapse of the distinction between offence and defence discussed above, it may well only be consistent with that decision to adjust standards in this way, for surely there are features of the defendant which make him more susceptible to responding violently to provocation but which are not evidence of 'wickedness', such as some mental disorders or involuntary intoxication. That being said, in the recent case of *Gillon v HMA*,[75] English law and New Zealand law on that issue were characterised as 'in a state of confusion',[76] strongly indicating that the High Court will be unsympathetic to arguments of that kind.

8. Conclusions: Proposals for Reform[77]

Perhaps the central question when considering reform of the substantive criminal law concerns the relationship between trials and sentencing. It is common for those thinking about criminal justice to say about a particular circumstance which determines how we should treat the defendant, be it a feature of the crime or of the defendant himself, that its moral significance is best reflected in the sentence rather than in categorisation in the criminal law. Often statements of that kind are made without reference to any obvious set of general principles, let alone any deep normative theory, about what it is appropriate for trials to consider and the degree of constraint that decisions at trial ought to have over sentencing.

---

[73] [1999] QB 1079.
[74] See V Tadros, *Criminal Responsibility* (Oxford, 2005), ch 13 for more developed analysis.
[75] *HMA v Gillon* 2006 HCJAC 61.
[76] *Ibid*, para 11.
[77] For my more developed views of reform of the law of homicide in the context of England and Wales see V Tadros, 'The Homicide Ladder' (2006) 69 *MLR* 601.

The main definition of murder in Scots law was, I suggest, broadly along the right lines prior to *Drury*. Things have gone awry in *Drury* which needs correction, a process which has been partially achieved in *Gillon v HMA*. If interpreted correctly, the law prior to *Drury* captured the appropriate range of cases. Critics primarily worry about the vagueness of the term 'wicked recklessness', even given its 'definition' by Macdonald.[78] Beyond that, more needs to be done to ensure consistency between decisions regarding the content of wicked recklessness. Ideally the phrase needs to be replaced with something a little more focussed, although as I have suggested, there is a limited amount that can be done to constrain discretion without excluding relevant considerations in determining the gravity of killing. These are matters, I suggest, which ought to be considered at trial rather than at the sentencing stage. Criminal convictions make public declarations about the kind and degree of wrongfulness of the conduct of the accused. Where crimes are differentiated by degree, it is important that those declarations reflect morally significant features of the killing. An overly strict set of rules distinguishing between murder and culpable homicide will inevitably fail to achieve that.

There is good reason to include within the mens rea of murder some form of extreme recklessness. Cases in which the accused takes a substantial risk with the life of the victim and the victim dies are appropriately categorised as murders. However, mere reckless conduct ought not to be sufficient. Scots law already recognises that it is required for a conviction of murder that the accused is at least reckless with respect to the *death* of the victim. Recklessness with regard to other kinds of harm is insufficient to ground a conviction. And, as is true in Scots law, it ought to be required that the jury, in determining whether the accused fulfilled the mens rea of the offence, consider whether the recklessness of the defendant was sufficiently grave. So, for example, reckless drivers may be reckless in respect of death given the number of deaths on the road. But it is surely inappropriate that all reckless drivers who kill ought to be convicted of murder.

However, the way in which this is achieved in Scots law is problematic. The term 'wicked' in itself does little to guide the jury in their decision-making and the 'definition' of wicked recklessness is confusing and ragged, leading to evidential problems considered above. It should not be imagined that it would be appropriate to constrain too much the discretion of the jury in determining the question. There are a number of factors that may be relevant in determining whether a killing ought to be classified as a murder or as a culpable homicide. More precision in the law of England and Wales leads to the offence of murder being both under- and over-inclusive. But if the terms to be used are vague, they should at least allude to the appropriate kinds of grounds on which the question should be determined.

Here I suggest two possibilities. One is that the accused should be guilty of murder if he acts 'believing that he was exposing another to mortal danger'.

---

[78] See the text at n 9 above.

Another is that he would be guilty of murder if he *heinously* exposed another to the risk of death. Each of these possibilities includes reference to the risk of death, which is appropriate for the law of murder, and respects the correspondence principle, which is appropriate for an offence as serious as murder. Both attempt to retain the focus on recklessness whilst making clear that merely acting in a way that creates a higher than normal risk of death would be insufficient. Furthermore, both are clearly focussed on the nature of the risk-taking in a way that the term 'wicked recklessness' is not. Hence, some of the questions of motive that seem to have created confusion in Scots law are excluded. Of course, the terms are by no means precise and the jury would retain a relatively high degree of discretion. But, given the range of considerations that affect the gravity of a killing, it is difficult to avoid that without warranting inappropriate categorisation in some cases.

Whatever the mens rea of murder, a proper palette of partial defences is necessary to ensure that the distinction between murder and culpable homicide reflects the gravity of killing in a just fashion. At present there are only two partial defences to murder with little momentum for reform. In contrast the Law Commission of England and Wales has recommended a broader range of partial defences,[79] and even that might be argued to be too narrow to do the job.[80] At least a partial defence of duress needs to be added to the current provisions, and perhaps a partial defence of involuntary intoxication as well for cases where the accused retains the mens rea of murder but is less culpable due to the intoxication. As suggested above, it should be recalled that the offence of murder includes those accused persons found guilty art and part, which is currently problematically broad and includes accused persons who are significantly less culpable than most of those convicted as principals, and perhaps not even sufficiently culpable to warrant a criminal conviction at all. At any rate, a conviction of murder for all those involved, no matter their degree of involvement or their mental state, is harsh, especially given the mandatory life sentence that is reserved for the offence.

A more substantial reform project would be to alter the range of homicide offences. As with English and Welsh law, there is some good reason to increase the number of homicide offences that are available. The Law Commission of England and Wales has suggested dividing murder into two categories: first and second degree murder. Another possibility is to divide culpable homicide into two degrees of culpable homicide and manslaughter. Culpable homicide at present includes a wide range of conduct from intentional killing in response to discovering the infidelity of one's partner to a very minor assault which causes death.[81] Killings in this range are very different both in kind and in degree of gravity. The

---

[79] *A New Homicide Act for England and Wales?*, Consultation Paper No 177 (London, 2005); although see *Murder, Manslaughter and Infanticide*, Law Com 304 (London, 2006).

[80] See Tadros, n 77 above.

[81] See *Bird v HMA* 1952 JC 23.

category of manslaughter could, for example, include cases in which a charge of murder is reduced by a partial defence as well as killings where the accused intended serious harm but did not contemplate the possibility of death. Culpable homicide would then be reserved for killing where the accused intended or was reckless with regard to less serious injury or was reckless with respect to serious injury.

My tentative view is that, were it not for the mandatory sentence, an extra rung to the homicide ladder in Scots law might be added within the category of culpable homicide rather than the category of murder. The main reason to divide up murder, I suggest, is to restrict the worst effects of the mandatory life penalty. Culpable homicide is perhaps more problematic with respect to its breadth than murder. Perhaps the central virtue of the Scots law of homicide is the broad outline of the definition of murder, then, or at least it was until *Drury*. Even this definition needs clarification and refinement. The partial defences and the offence of culpable homicide need substantial reform, as does the law regarding art and part with respect to murder.

9

Fault for Homicide in Singapore

STANLEY YEO

1. Introduction

THIS CHAPTER WILL examine the treatment of fault required for homicide under Singaporean criminal law. The law is contained in the Singaporean Penal Code[1] which is borrowed from the Indian Penal Code 1860.[2] The provisions on homicide are virtually identical in both codes save for the addition to the Singaporean code of the plea of diminished responsibility. As might be expected, the Singaporean courts have generally looked to Indian case law when interpreting the provisions. Sometimes, the Singaporean courts have referred to English developments, but only by way of comparison, being mindful that the law is governed by the Code. Additionally, the Singaporean courts have, at least until the 1990s, worked closely with the Malaysian courts in interpreting and applying the provisions.[3]

The discussion commences with an overview of the structure of fault for homicide under the Singaporean Penal Code (henceforth, the 'Code'). There follows a description of the various types of fault for culpable homicide amounting to murder, and thereafter of the types of fault for culpable homicide not amounting to murder. Next comes a description of rash or negligent conduct causing death which the Code treats as falling outside the label 'culpable homicide'. Finally, aspects of selected partial defences to murder under the Code will be considered.

---

[1] Cap 224, 1985 Rev Ed (Singapore).

[2] For a brief historical account see Chan Wing Cheong and A Phang, 'The Development of Criminal Law and Criminal Justice' in K Tan (ed), *Essays in Singapore Legal History* (Singapore, 2005), at 247–50.

[3] The Malaysian Penal Code Revd 1997, reprint 2002, has also been borrowed from the Indian Penal Code.

2. The Code's Structure of Fault for Homicide

The Code uses the term 'culpable homicide' to describe killings involving a very high degree of fault. There are two types of culpable homicide, namely, murder and culpable homicide not amounting to murder. The Code commences with a definition of culpable homicide (section 299) which is followed by a definition of murder (section 300). Under this structure, culpable homicide not amounting to murder is what is left of section 299 which does not overlap with murder. Where killings are accompanied by a degree of fault falling below that prescribed for culpable homicide, the Code accommodates them under a different offence (section 304A). Penalty provisions have been designed to reflect the varying degrees of fault for murder (section 302), culpable homicide not amounting to murder (section 304), and causing death by a rash or negligent act (section 304A). The main provisions read, in part, as follows:

Culpable homicide

299. Whoever causes death by doing an act with the (1) intention of causing death, or (2) with the intention of causing such bodily injury as is likely to cause death, or (3) with the knowledge that he is likely by such act to cause death, commits the offence of culpable homicide.

Murder

300. Except in the cases hereinafter excepted culpable homicide is murder —

(a) if the act by which the death is caused is done with the intention of causing death;

(b) if it is done with the intention of causing such bodily injury as the offender knows to be likely to cause the death of the person to whom the harm is caused;

(c) if it is done with the intention of causing bodily injury to any person, and the bodily injury intended to be inflicted is sufficient in the ordinary course of nature to cause death; or

(d) if the person committing the act knows that it is so imminently dangerous that it must in all probability cause death, or such bodily injury as is likely to cause death, and commits such act without any excuse for incurring the risk of causing death, or such injury as aforesaid.

Punishment for murder

302. Whoever commits murder shall be punished with death.

Punishment for culpable homicide not amounting to murder

304. Whoever commits culpable homicide not amounting to murder shall be punished —

(a) with imprisonment for life, or imprisonment for a term which may extend to 10 years, and shall also be liable to fine or to caning, if the act by which death is caused is done with the intention of causing death, or of causing such bodily injury as is likely to cause death; or

(b) with imprisonment for a term which may extend to 10 years, or with fine, or with both, if the act is done with the knowledge that it is likely to cause death, but without any intention to cause death, or to cause such bodily injury as is likely to cause death.

Causing death by rash or negligent act

304A. Whoever causes the death of any person by doing any rash or negligent act not amounting to culpable homicide, shall be punished with imprisonment for a term which may extend to 2 years, or with fine, or with both.

Table 9.1 spells out the various degrees of fault contained in sections 299, 300 and 304A, commencing with the most culpable and gradually descending to the least. The diagram also categorises the types of fault into intention-based fault, knowledge-based fault and negligence-based fault, with intention regarded as the most culpable and negligence the least.

Table 9.1: Scheme of Fault Elements and Penalties for Homicide

Type of Offence	Fault elements in descending order of culpability	Penalty
Intention-based fault		
Murder	Intention of causing death (s 300(a)).	Mandatory death penalty (s 302)
Murder	Intention of causing such bodily injury as the offender knows to be likely to cause death (s 300(b)).	Mandatory death penalty (s 302)
Murder	Intention of causing bodily injury which is sufficient in the ordinary course of nature to cause death (s 300(c))	Mandatory death penalty (s 302)
Culpable homicide not amounting to murder	Intention of causing such bodily injury as is likely to cause death (s 299(2))	Maximum life imprisonment (s 304 (a))
Knowledge-based fault		
Murder	Knowledge that act is so imminently dangerous that it must in all probability cause death, and without excuse for incurring such a risk (s 300(d))	Mandatory death penalty (s 302)

Culpable homicide not amounting to murder	Knowledge that act is likely to cause death (s 299(3))	Maximum 10 years' imprisonment (s 304(b))
Causing death by rash act	Knowledge that act might possibly cause death (s 304A)	Maximum 2 years' imprisonment (s 304A)
Negligence-based fault		
Causing death by negligent act	Falling short of the standard of care expected of a reasonable person in the same circumstances as the accused (s 304A)	Maximum 2 years' imprisonment (s 304A)

Each of these types of fault will be described in detail below. However, it would be useful here briefly to highlight where they each fit within the overall structure of the Code provisions on homicide noting, in particular, the careful gradations of fault between murder, culpable homicide not amounting to murder, and the offence of causing of death by rash or negligent act.

In relation to intention-based fault, the Code structure places at the apex the paradigm fault element of murder, namely, an intention to cause death: section 300(a). Below this is an intention to cause such bodily injury as the offender knows to be likely to cause the death of the person to whom the harm is caused: section 300(b). This comes very close to the paradigm fault for murder, given that the offender intended the bodily harm knowing that it was likely to cause death. Consequently, he or she deserves to be convicted of murder. Next in order of degree of culpability is an intention to cause bodily injury to any person and the injury intended is sufficient in the ordinary course of nature to cause death: section 300(c). This is a hybrid subjective/objective form of fault, with the offender intending to cause the bodily injury which is objectively appraised 'most probably'[4] to cause death. As such, it is not as culpable as section 300(b), but nevertheless comes close to it and therefore warrants liability for murder. Where an offender intends to cause the bodily injury which is objectively appraised to be 'likely' (that is, 'probably' as opposed to 'most probably') to cause death, he or she is regarded as not displaying the fault required for murder but for culpable homicide not amounting to murder: section 299(2).

With regard to knowledge-based fault, an offender who does an act knowing that it is so imminently dangerous that it must in all probability cause death or such bodily injury as is likely to cause death and without any excuse for incurring the risk is regarded by the Code as displaying the fault for murder: section 300(d). Although knowledge is generally not in the same league as intention,

[4] Paraphrasing the words 'sufficient in the ordinary course of nature to cause death' appearing in s 300(c).

knowledge of the virtual certainty[5] of causing death or bodily injury likely to cause death is comparable in degree of culpability to the forms of intentional murder under section 300(c). Where an offender does an act knowing that it is 'likely' (that is, 'probable' as opposed to virtually certain) to cause death, this lesser degree of knowledge compared to section 300(d) warrants him or her being convicted of culpable homicide not amounting to murder: section 299(3). Where an offender has done an act knowing that it could possibly (as opposed to 'be likely to/probably') cause death, he or she has not displayed the fault required for culpable homicide under the Code. Consequently, such an offender is guilty of the crime of causing death by a rash act: section 304A.

As far as negligence-based fault is concerned, the legislature has regarded this as insufficient for culpable homicide. Accordingly, it has devised a separate offence of causing death by a negligent act: section 304A. This is a notable difference from the English common law, which recognises negligence-based fault as capable of attracting liability for the serious offence of manslaughter which is the Code equivalent of culpable homicide not amounting to murder.

The penalty provisions for murder, culpable homicide not amounting to murder, and causing death by rash or negligent act directly reflect the gradations of fault for these offences. Commencing with murder, all the four types of fault specified in section 300 attract the mandatory death penalty: section 302.[6] This shows the legislature's stance that the degree of blameworthiness for all these types of fault are so closely comparable to one another that they are deserving of the same penalty. In relation to culpable homicide not amounting to murder, the replacement of the mandatory death penalty with a maximum of life imprisonment clearly reflects the lower degree of culpability for this form of offence compared to murder. Interestingly, the penalty provision imposes a more severe penalty for intention-based culpable homicide not amounting to murder (maximum of life imprisonment: section 304(a)), compared to knowledge-based culpable homicide not amounting to murder (maximum of 10 years' imprisonment: section 304(b)). Regarding the offence of causing death by a rash or negligent act, a maximum penalty of two years' imprisonment is prescribed: section 304A. This may be unacceptably low, and calls have been made to increase it substantially.[7] However, the point remains that the low penalty reflects the legislature's view that the fault accompanying these cases of killings falls far short of the degree of fault required for culpable homicide under the Code.

In summary, the Code's structure of fault for homicide displays the following positive features:

---

[5] Paraphrasing the words 'so imminently dangerous that it must in all probability cause death' etc appearing in s 300(d).

[6] The debate over whether the mandatory death penalty should be imposed for murder or whether it should be replaced by, say, life imprisonment does not form part of this discussion.

[7] See Chan Wing Cheong, 'What's Wrong with Section 300(c) Murder?' [2005] *Singapore Journal of Legal Studies* 462 at 469, who proposes that it be raised to 10 years' imprisonment. The Penal Code (Amendment) Bill 2006 will, if enacted, raise the maximum penalty for rash act causing death to 5 years' imprisonment but leave intact the 2-year maximum term for negligent act causing death.

1. comparable degrees of culpability for the various types of fault recognised for murder;
2. a full expression of the interconnectedness between the fault elements for murder and culpable homicide not amounting to murder;
3. the imposition of a very high degree of culpability in murder cases involving the intentional causing of bodily injury short of an intention to cause death;
4. the imposition of a very high degree of culpability in murder cases involving the fault element of knowledge;
5. the imposition of a relatively high degree of culpability in cases of culpable homicide not amounting to murder;
6. the strict maintenance of subjectivity for the fault elements for all forms of culpable homicide so as to exclude negligence;
7. a penalty structure which seeks to reflect the varying degrees of culpability of fault for murder, culpable homicide not amounting to murder and causing death by a rash or negligent act.

More generally, the Code's structure of fault for homicide promotes the important criminal law principle of maximum certainty in the definitions of offences. It does so by spelling out the fault elements for murder and for culpable homicide not amounting to murder with as much precision as possible. The structure also promotes the significant principle of fair labelling the aim of which is to ensure that offences are appropriately categorised and labelled so as to represent the nature and magnitude of the particular form of law-breaking.

The Code's efforts at achieving maximum certainty have attracted the criticism that, in practice, too fine distinctions are made between the fault elements for murder and those for culpable homicide not amounting to murder.[8] As against this is the view of the Indian Supreme Court that the differences between the various clauses of sections 299 and 300 are fine but real and, if overlooked, might result in miscarriages of justice.[9] The Court warned against interpreting the differences according to 'minute abstractions' and suggested that the safest approach was to keep in focus the key words used in the various clauses of sections 299 and 300.[10]

Admittedly, there will be borderline cases occasioned by the fine distinctions made by the Code between the fault elements for murder and for culpable homicide not amounting to murder. It is submitted that the benefits of maximum certainty and fair labelling to be gained by having these distinctions far outweigh the problems of uncertainty in the few borderline cases. A practical and

---

[8] See Koh Kheng Lian, CMV Clarkson and N Morgan, *Criminal Law in Singapore and Malaysia: Text and Materials* (Singapore, 1989), 407; M Govindarajulu, 'Some Aspects of the Law of Homicide' [1941] *Madras Law Journal* 91 at 94. For a judicial observation see the Malaysian Federal Court case of *Tham Kai Yau v PP* [1977] 1 *MLJ* 174 at 176, per Raja Azlan Shah FJ.

[9] *State of Andhra Pradesh v Punnayya* AIR 1977 SC 45 at 50, per Sarkaria J.

[10] *Ibid*, at 49. In Singapore, this issue may be less of a concern since the jury system was abolished for capital cases in 1970.

just solution to such cases is to convict the accused of the lesser offence on the ground that '[a]ll provisions of the penal law must be interpreted, if there is room for doubt, in favour of the subject, and most of all the provisions relating to the offence of murder'.[11]

3. Murder

(i) Intention to Cause Death: Section 300(a)

This is the paradigm form of fault for murder.[12] The meaning of 'intention' is left undefined by the Code. However, since the Code differentiates 'intention' from 'knowledge' when spelling out the fault for murder in section 300, 'intention' is restricted to its purposive sense, leaving 'knowledge' of the risk of death to be recognised as a separate type of fault for murder under section 300(d). The following observation by the Indian Supreme Court bears this out:

> The framers of the Code designedly used the words 'intention' and 'knowledge' and it is accepted that the knowledge of the consequences which may result in doing an act is not the same thing as the intention that such consequences should ensue ... As compared to 'knowledge', 'intention' requires something more than the mere foresight of the consequences, namely, the purposeful doing of a thing to achieve a particular end ...[13]

The intention to cause death need not be premeditated but could be formed at the spur of the moment.[14] The Singaporean courts have held that such intention is to be inferred from the facts of the case, in particular, the nature, place and number of injuries and the type of weapon used.[15] However, the courts have steered away from the one-time English common law maxim that a person is 'deemed to intend the natural and probable consequences of his acts'.[16] Thus, it has been held that 'the introduction of the maxim ... is seldom helpful and always dangerous' and that 'judges in this country should avoid using this maxim in their summings up to the jury when dealing with the question of intention in murder trials'.[17]

---

[11] *Emperor v Aung Nyun* AIR 1940 Rang 259 at 265, per Mosely J.

[12] It is replicated in s 299(1) on account of the structure of ss 299 and 300 making the latter a subset of the former. This form of fault amounts to 'first degree murder' under the scheme proposed by the Law Commission in its Consultation Paper No 177, *A New Homicide Act for England and Wales? An Overview* (London, 2005), para 5.26.

[13] *Jai Prakash v State (Delhi Administration)* 1991 2 SCC 32 T 42, per Jayachandra Reddy J.

[14] *Ismail bin Hussain v PP* (1953) 19 *MLJ* 48.

[15] For a good case example see *Tan Buck Tee v PP* [1961] 1 *MLJ* 176.

[16] *DPP v Smith* [1961] AC 290.

[17] *Yeo Ah Seng v PP* [1967] 1 *MLJ* 231 at 234, per Barakbah LP.

(ii) Intention to Cause Bodily Injury Known by the Accused to be Likely to Cause Death: Section 300(b)

This type of fault for murder involves a combination of two subjective mental states, with the first being an intention to cause bodily injury and the second being knowledge that the intended injury was likely to cause death. It is noteworthy that the seriousness of the injury is not assessed objectively but on the basis of the accused's particular knowledge that such injury is likely to cause death. This feature is borne out in cases where section 300(b) has resulted in a murder conviction against the accused who knew that death from the injury was likely only because, to his or her knowledge, the victim suffered from some physical infirmity.[18]

The justification for recognising this form of fault for murder under the Code lies in a comparison with the fault elements of culpable homicide under section 299. Section 300(b) requires proof of the subjective mental states of two clauses of section 299. The accused must not only intend to cause bodily injury (the subjective component of section 299(2)) but must also know that such bodily injury is likely to cause death (the subjective component of section 299(3)). Consequently, section 300(b) is much narrower than the generic offence of culpable homicide, thereby making this form of fault closely comparable in degree of culpability with an intention to cause death.

Section 300(b) has the advantage of dealing with the issue of a victim's unusual physical susceptibility under the fault element for murder rather than under the concept of causation. This is a much clearer approach to the determination of criminal responsibility as it avoids having to rely on the contentious causal principle that an accused must take the victim as the accused finds him or her.[19]

(iii) Intention to Cause Bodily Injury which is Sufficient in the Ordinary Course of Nature to Cause Death: Section 300(c)

This type of fault for murder comprises a subjective and an objective component. The former is an intention to cause the bodily injury which had caused death. The latter requires the bodily injury intended to be one which was, in the ordinary course of nature, sufficient to cause death. The courts have paraphrased the words 'in the ordinary course of nature' as 'in the usual course if left alone',[20] which practically means that the inquiry is whether the injury intended to be inflicted by the accused was one which would 'most probably'[21] result in death if

---

[18] For a case example see *Anda v State of Rajasthan* AIR 1966 SC 148. See further M Sornarajah, 'The Definition of Murder under the Penal Code' [1994] *Singapore Journal of Legal Studies* 1 at 9–10.

[19] This principle is subscribed to by the English law: eg, see *R v Blaue* [1975] 3 All ER 446.

[20] *State v Ghana Padhan* (1979) 47 *Cut LT* 575.

[21] *State v Behari* AIR 1953 All 203.

there was no medical or surgical intervention.[22] Section 300(c) differs from the other types of fault for murder recognised under section 300 in that the accused may be convicted of murder where death was neither intended nor known to be highly probable.[23] In practice, section 300(c) is the type of fault for murder most frequently relied upon by the prosecution.

For several years, the Singaporean courts have been plagued with controversy over the correct interpretation of section 300(c).[24] One line of case authorities held that, once it is proved that the accused intended to cause some bodily injury, the remainder of the injury is objective, namely, whether or not the injury in fact inflicted was sufficient to cause death. Indeed, the Singapore Court of Appeal had gone so far as to rule that an intention to cause a minor injury is sufficient to attract a murder conviction if the injury actually inflicted was sufficient in the ordinary course of nature to cause death.[25] The opposing line of case authorities is that section 300(c) requires the prosecution to prove that the accused intended to inflict the particular injury which was in fact inflicted on the victim, and which injury is objectively assessed to be sufficient in the ordinary course of nature to cause death.[26] Lately, the Singapore Court of Appeal has come down in favour of this second view.[27] This is to be greatly preferred because it renders the accused's blameworthiness comparable with the other three forms of fault found in section 300. In support of this view, it has been surmised that section 300(c) was introduced by the Code framers to prevent accused persons, in cases where it may be difficult to prove an intention to kill, from avoiding a murder conviction.[28] The discredited view, by contrast, essentially creates a form of constructive murder by convicting a person who intends only to inflict a minor injury but happens to cause death.[29]

Proof that the accused intended the particular injury which caused death may occasionally pose a practical difficulty. The courts have advocated a broad commonsensical approach, with the Indian Supreme Court advising that:

> In considering whether the intention was to inflict the injury found to have been inflicted, the enquiry necessarily proceeds on the broad lines as, for example, whether there was an intention to strike at a vital or a dangerous spot, and whether with

---

[22] *Mohamed Yasin bin Hussin v PP* [1975–7] SLR 34. See also *Kishore Singh v State of Madhya Pradesh* AIR 1977 SC 2267; *State v Rajasthan v Dhool Singh* AIR 2004 SC 1264.

[23] S 300(a), (b) and (d) all require a connection between the accused's mental state and the consequence of death being caused.

[24] For a detailed discussion see A Tan, 'Revisiting Section 300(c) Murder in Singapore' (2005) 17 *Singapore Academy of Law Journal* 693; Chan Wing Cheong, 'What's Wrong with Section 300(c) Murder?' [2005] *Singapore Journal of Legal Studies* 462.

[25] *Ong Chee Hoe v PP* [1998] 4 SLR 688. See also *Tan Joo Cheng v PP* [1992] 1 SLR 620.

[26] For an early case example see *Mohamed Yasin bin Hussin v PP* [1975–7] SLR 34.

[27] *Tan Chee Wee v PP* [2004] 1 SLR 479; *PP v Lim Poh Lye* [2005] 4 SLR 582.

[28] See P Ratan, 'Culpable Homicide' (1958) cited in *Essays on the Indian Penal Code* (New Delhi, 1962), 153.

[29] The Code framers' aversion to constructive crime is borne out by their refusal to include felony (or constructive) murder in s 300.

sufficient force to cause the kind of injury found to have been inflicted. It is, of course, not necessary to enquire into every last detail as, for instance, whether the prisoner intended to have the bowels fall out or whether he intended to penetrate the liver or kidneys or the heart.[30]

It may be observed that section 300(c) is the Code equivalent of the English common law fault for murder of an intention to cause grievous bodily harm.[31] The Indian formulation comes closer to the paradigm fault element for murder because of the more severe type of bodily injury required. For instance, knee-capping may constitute 'grievous bodily harm' but would not satisfy the description of 'bodily injury sufficient in the ordinary course of nature to cause death'. A further positive feature of section 300(c) not found in its English counterpart is that it provides the courts with greater guidance over the determination of the type of injury required. Unlike the English law, which unhelpfully stipulates that 'grievous bodily harm' means 'really serious bodily harm,'[32] section 300(c) provides for the injury to be measured according to the high probability of death resulting to a normally healthy person in the absence of medical intervention.

(iv) Knowledge that the Act is so Imminently Dangerous that It Must in All Probability Cause Death without Excuse for Incurring the Risk: Section 300(d)

This type of fault for murder is premised on knowledge of the risk of causing bodily injury, and therefore differs from the previous ones which are based on intention to cause bodily injury. Since intention is a generally more culpable form of fault than knowledge, section 300(d) imposes several requirements which ensure that the requisite knowledge is comparable in degree of culpability with the types of intentional murder recognised under section 300. The first of these requirements is that the accused must have known that his or her conduct would in all probability cause the specified harm. Actual knowledge is needed; negligence is insufficient.[33] The degree of risk that is known must be of the highest level and has been judicially interpreted as 'approximat[ing] a practical certainty'.[34]

The second requirement is that the type of bodily injury risked must be of death or bodily injury which is likely to cause death. The first type of harm of causing death is uncontroversial as it aligns this form of fault with the paradigm

---

[30] *Virsa Singh v State of Punjab* AIR 1958 SC 465 at 467, per Bose J.

[31] It would clearly constitute 'second degree murder' under the scheme proposed by the Law Commission, *A New Homicide Act for England and Wales? An Overview* (London, 2005), para 5.30.

[32] *R v Cunningham* [1982] AC 566 at 574, per Lord Hailsham LC.

[33] *William Tan Cheng Eng v PP* [1970] 2 MLJ 244.

[34] *State of Andhra Pradesh v Punnayya* AIR 1977 SC 45 at 51, per Sarkaria J. Such a case would amount to 'first degree murder' under the scheme proposed by the Law Commission, *A New Homicide Act for England and Wales? An Overview* (London, 2005), para 5.10.

fault for murder of an intention to cause death. However, the second type of harm of causing bodily injury which is likely to cause death is problematic. The courts have yet to resolve the issue of whether to assess this form of injury objectively or subjectively. The objective interpretation stipulates that the accused must know of the high probability of causing some bodily injury; thereafter, whether that bodily injury satisfies the description of 'likely to cause death' is for the trier of fact to decide. This interpretation is objectionable for making section 300(4) wider than its generic equivalent under section 299(3). This is because an objective reading of section 300(4) will only require the accused to have known of the likelihood of causing some bodily injury, whereas section 299(3) is more demanding in requiring the accused to have known that the bodily injury was likely to cause death.

Consequently, it is the subjective interpretation which should be adopted. However, this interpretation suffers from creating too fine a distinction between 'knowledge of causing death' and 'knowledge of causing injury which is likely to cause death'. This may explain why, in practice, the courts have tended to ignore this second type of harm and base their decisions on the first. From a reform perspective, section 300(4) could be improved by limiting the type of harm to death alone. Besides removing the uncertainty posed by the second type of harm, insistence on the harm being one of death alone will bring section 300(4) that much closer to the paradigm for murder of an intention to cause death. The need for the type of harm risked to be of the gravest kind is especially necessary given that the mental state of section 300(4) is the less culpable one of 'knowledge' compared to 'intention'.

A third requirement before a person can be convicted of murder under section 300(4) is that the prosecution must establish that the accused was 'without excuse for incurring the risk' of causing the prescribed injury. The 'excuse' referred to covers extenuating circumstances other than those provided for by the Code as general defences[35] or partial defences[36] to murder. Cases are rare where the accused has avoided a murder conviction on account of having an excuse to take life-endangering risk. One example is the Indian case of *Emperor v Dhirajia* where D was a village woman who had been the subject of domestic violence by her husband.[37] One night, she sought to escape with her infant in her arms but was hotly pursued by her husband. Panic-stricken, she jumped into a well with her baby with the result that it drowned. The court held that D lacked the intention to injure her child but knew that her act was so imminently dangerous

---

[35] These are called 'general exceptions' and appear in Part IV of the Code. They apply to all offences and, if successfully pleaded, result in a complete acquittal. They include the defences of insanity, intoxication, private defence, duress, necessity, consent and mistake of fact.

[36] These are called 'special exceptions' and appear under s 300 of the Code. They apply to murder alone and, if successfully pleaded, result in a conviction of culpable homicide not amounting to murder. They include the defences of provocation, excessive private defence, sudden fight and diminished responsibility which will be discussed below.

[37] (1940) All 647.

that it would in all probability cause death within the purview of section 300(4). However, the homicide did not amount to murder because, considering her circumstances, there was 'excuse for incurring the risk of causing death'.

What constitutes an excuse under section 300(4) is a question of fact and not of law for the court to decide on a case-by-case basis. This requirement has been rightly criticised for being too imprecise. However, the solution does not lie in restricting the term 'excuse' under section 300(4) to the general or partial defences under the Code. Such a measure would deny the courts the opportunity to reflect in their decisions the reality that dangerous conduct is often tolerated by society in situations where the prescribed defences are inapplicable. A possible remedy may be for the courts to adopt the test of whether the accused's risk-taking 'involves a gross deviation from the standard of conduct that a law-abiding person would observe in the accused's position'.[38]

(v) Penalty Structure

The Code imposes the mandatory death penalty on anyone convicted of murder, irrespective of the particular type of fault under section 300 that was proven against him or her.[39] This stands in contrast to the Indian Penal Code which provides the sentencing court with a limited discretion whether to impose the death penalty or imprisonment for life and also with a fine.[40] In practice, the Indian courts have tended to use the capital sentence only where the prisoner intended to cause death. The reasons for not imposing the capital sentence include the youth of the offender, the lack of premeditation, the presence of provocation which was insufficient to reduce the offence to culpable homicide not amounting to murder, and the relatively minor role the offender played in cases where the murder had been committed by more than one person. It is submitted that the Indian position is to be preferred for enabling the court to impose the more lenient sentence in cases where justice deserves it.

4. Culpable Homicide not Amounting to Murder

By eliminating from section 299 what amounts to murder under section 300, it is deduced that the Code recognises two types of fault for culpable homicide not amounting to murder. The first of these is an intention to cause such bodily

---

[38] American Law Institute Model Penal Code, *Proposed Official Draft* (Philadelphia, 1962), s 2.02(2)(c).
[39] S 302.
[40] S 302.

injury as is likely to cause death: section 299(2). The second is knowledge that the act is likely to cause death: section 299(3).

(i) Intention to Cause Such Bodily Injury as is Likely to Cause Death: Section 299(2)

This type of fault is directly related to the fault element for murder under section 300(c) of an intention to cause bodily injury which was sufficient in the ordinary course of nature to cause death. Both these forms of fault have in common the accused's intention to cause bodily injury. The difference lies in the type of injury intended. It has been held that section 300(c) requires the injury 'most probably' to result in death in contrast to section 299(2) which requires death from the injury to be 'probable'.[41] The distinction between 'most probable' and 'probable' is fine but appreciable. In practice, the courts will rely on expert medical opinion to decide which description the particular injury fits. However, since the question is one of fact, the court remains the ultimate decider. Furthermore, where there is uncertainty as to whether the case comes under section 300(c) or section 299(2), the courts have resolved the doubt in favour of the accused by convicting him or her of the lesser offence.

It should be emphasised that the fault element under section 299(2), like that under section 300(c), does not require the prosecution to prove that the accused knew or even considered the likely effect of the injury on the victim. This explains why section 299(2) has no connection with the fault element for murder under section 300(b), which requires proof that the accused had such knowledge.

Where the intended injury falls short of that envisaged by section 299(2), the accused is not guilty of culpable homicide but may be liable for some lesser offence involving the intentional causing of non-fatal bodily injury such as the offences of voluntarily causing hurt or grievous hurt.[42] By way of reform, it is submitted that a new offence be introduced of intentionally causing bodily injury which might (that is, 'possibly') cause death. This offence would cover cases one rung down in terms of culpability from section 299(2) of an intention to cause bodily injury which is likely (that is, 'probably') to cause death. The offence would also better reflect the fact that death has occurred in contrast to the available offences of intentionally causing non-fatal bodily injury.

(ii) Knowledge that the Act is Likely to Cause Death: Section 299(3)

This type of fault is closely connected with the fault element for murder under section 300(d) of knowing that the act is so imminently dangerous that it must in

---

[41] *State v Behari* AIR 1953 All 203.
[42] Defined in ss 321 and 322 of the Code respectively.

all probability cause death. Both these forms of fault have in common the accused's knowledge that his or her act creates the risk of causing death. Where they differ is in the degree of risk known to the accused, with section 300(d) requiring knowledge of the 'highest degree of probability' of death occurring, while section 299(3) requires knowledge that death will probably occur.[43] As with the comparison between section 300(c) and section 299(2), the distinction is fine but appreciable.

Another difference between section 299(3) and section 300(d) lies in the matter of inexcusable risk-taking. Section 299(3) does not require proof, as section 300(d) does, that the accused had committed the act 'without any excuse for incurring the risk of causing death'.[44] A likely explanation for this is that the Code framers were very concerned to ensure that only the most damning form of knowledge would attract liability for murder. Insofar as culpable homicide not amounting to murder was concerned, while it was still a serious offence, justice to the victim and the community dictated that the accused should be liable for this offence once he or she had displayed the fault of persisting with the act knowing that it was likely to cause death.

Where the degree of risk of death known to the accused falls short of 'probable', the accused may be liable for the lesser offence of causing death by a rash act under section 304A of the Code.[45] The fault element of this offence comprises knowing of the possibility of causing death, and therefore falls one rung below, in terms of degree of culpability, the type of fault under section 299(3).

(iii) Transferred Malice

Having studied the fault elements for murder and culpable homicide not amounting to murder, we are in a position to consider the Code's version of the doctrine of transferred malice under English common law. This is expressed in the following provision:

> 301. If a person, by doing anything which he intends or knows to be likely to cause death, commits culpable homicide by causing the death of any person whose death he neither intends nor knows himself to be likely to cause, the culpable homicide committed by the offender is of the description of which it would have been if he had caused the death of the person whose death he intended or knew himself to be likely to cause.

Interestingly, the wording of this provision clearly confines its operation to cases where the accused intended to cause death, thereby excluding cases where the

---

[43] In this regard, s 299(3) is comparable to 'second degree murder' proposed by the Law Commission, *A New Homicide Act for England and Wales? An Overview* (London, 2005), para 5.33.

[44] In contrast, the Law Commission's proposed 'second degree murder' has a requirement of an unjustified risk of causing death: see *ibid*, para 5.31.

[45] This offence will be considered further below.

accused intended to cause only a bodily injury of the kind described in section 299(2) or section 300(c). The reason for this restriction is unclear. It is submitted that these other types of fault should likewise attract the doctrine, given that they are intention-based and therefore generally higher in degree of culpability than the knowledge-based fault covered by the provision.

(iv) Penalty Structure

Section 304 of the Code prescribes a higher penalty for section 299(2) compared to section 299(3). This reflects the Code framers' view that intention is more blameworthy than knowledge in the context of culpable homicide. This penalty arrangement is unusual since the Code does not generally distinguish the penalty according to the fault of the convicted person. Thus, for example, for cases of voluntarily causing hurt[46] or grievous hurt,[47] acting with knowledge as opposed to intention could at most be a mitigating factor in sentencing. The arrangement under section 304 may be criticised on the ground that the culpability for section 299(2) may actually be lower than for section 299(3) rather than the other way round. Arguably, an offender who intends bodily injury which (whether he or she knows it or not) is likely to cause death is less blameworthy than one who knows that he or she is likely to cause death.

5. Causing Death by a Rash or Negligent Act

The schematic approach to the fault elements for murder and culpable homicide not amounting to murder continues into the less serious offence prescribed in section 304A of the Code. As the section number indicates, this offence was introduced at a later stage. It provides for two forms of fault, the first being causing death by a rash act, which is a less culpable form of fault than culpable homicide not amounting to murder under section 299(3). The second is causing death by a negligent act, which has no equivalent under section 299 but which the legislators thought should be criminalised. Regrettably, section 304A suffers from an absence of detail as to what constitutes 'rashness' or 'negligence', leading the courts to interpret them as best as they can.

---

[46] S 321.
[47] S 322.

(i) Rash Act Causing Death: Section 304A

The courts have defined 'rashness' under this provision as amounting to knowing of the possibility of causing death.[48] In doing so, they have been careful to distinguish this form of fault from that under section 299(3) of knowing that death was likely (that is, 'probable').[49] Furthermore, in the Singapore High Court case of *PP v Poh Teck Huat*, Yong Pung How CJ observed that criminal rashness and criminal negligence involve two different types of fault as shown by the disjunctive language used in section 304A.[50]

The Chief Justice went on to observe in *Poh Teck Huat* that, while rashness was more culpable than negligence, 'negligence does not end nicely where rashness begins and there is a certain degree of overlap [so that] it is possible for the culpability of an offender who has committed a rash act to be akin to that of a negligent act'.[51] It is submitted that this blurring of the distinction between rashness and negligence is unfortunate. His Honour should have instead highlighted the distinction by noting that rashness comprises an accused's advertence (that is, actual knowledge) of the risk of death, whereas negligence comprises inadvertence to such risk, with the court measuring the accused's conduct against the standard of a reasonable person.

(ii) Negligent Act Causing Death: Section 304A

At the outset, it is observed that the Code framers were clear that negligence, however gross, does not amount to culpable homicide under section 299. However, this does not answer the question of what degree of negligence is required for the offence under section 304A. The courts have held that it is neither the degree of negligence required for manslaughter under English law[52] nor an intermediate standard between that required for manslaughter and the civil standard of negligence.[53] Rather, the degree of negligence under section 304A is the same as for civil cases.[54] Having so ruled, the courts have acknowledged the need to maintain a distinction between criminal and civil negligence

---

[48] This type of fault is much more culpable than the Law Commission's proposed fault for manslaughter of causing death by a criminal act foreseen as involving a risk of causing physical harm: see *A New Homicide Act for England and Wales? An Overview* (London, 2005), para 5.50.

[49] *PP v Teo Poh Leng* [1992] 1 SLR 15; *PP v Tiyatun* [2002] 2 SLR 246.

[50] [2003] 2 SLR 299 at para [18].

[51] *Ibid*, at [19]–[20].

[52] *PP v Mills* [1971] 1 MLJ 4 at 5, per Williams CJ.

[53] This intermediate standard was pronounced by the Privy Council in *Dabholkar v King* AIR [1948] PC 183 on appeal from Tanganyika which has an identical provision to s 304A.

[54] *Mah Kah Yew v PP* [1969–71] 1 MLJ 1, and reaffirmed recently in *Lim Poh Eng v PP* [1999] 2 SLR 116, and *Ng Keng Yong v PP* [2004] 4 SLR 89.

and have sought to do so by pointing to the differing burdens of proof, and also that section 304A requires the additional element that the accused's negligence must have caused death.[55]

The courts have also held that the standard of care expected cannot be lowered by taking into account the particular accused's lack of knowledge, skill or experience. This is well illustrated in the Singapore High Court case of *Ng Keng Yong v PP*[56] which involved the negligent performance of the accused's duty as an Officer-of-the-Watch (OOW) on board a naval vessel, resulting in the death of several of her fellow crew members when it collided with a merchant vessel. The court rejected the accused's contention that she should be measured against the standard of a trainee OOW and not a reasonably competent and qualified OOW. The court justified its ruling by noting that taking into account a particular accused's experience would make the standard of care so fluctuating as to make the law uncertain and ambiguous; it was much better for an accused to be held to the certainty of a general standard.[57] Another reason given by the court was that societal protection required the standard of care to be that of a competent and qualified reasonable person performing the dangerous activity; to permit a lower standard would unreasonably place the safety of everyone else around the accused at risk.[58] Although there is substance in these reasons, it remains troubling that the law should convict and punish a person for failing to discharge a standard of care which he or she has not yet attained.[59] While it is entirely proper to insist on the general standard of care for civil cases where compensation lies at the heart of the matter, the law should permit the accused's lower standard to be recognised for criminal liability under section 304A. Under this view, in *Lim Poh Eng*, the standard of care expected of the accused would be that of the reasonable trainee OOW.

(iii) Penalty Structure

Section 304A does not distinguish in terms of penalty between cases where death was caused by a rash act as opposed to a negligent act. However, in practice, the courts have regarded negligence as being less culpable than rashness and have accordingly imposed a lesser sentence where the offender was found to have negligently caused death.[60] From a reform perspective, the penalty provided for

---

[55] *Lim Poh Eng v PP* [1999] 2 SLR 116 at para [17]; *Ng Keng Yong v PP* [2004] 4 SLR 89 at para [63].

[56] [2004] 4 SLR 89.

[57] *Ibid*, at paras [76]–[77], citing with approval Megaw LJ in *Nettleship v Weston* [1971] 2 QB 691 at 707.

[58] N 56 above, at para [79].

[59] It is unclear whether lack of training or experience could affect the 'capacity to appreciate the risk of death' component of gross negligence manslaughter proposed by the Law Commission: see *A New Homicide Act for England and Wales? An Overview* (London, 2005), paras 5.44–5.45.

[60] Eg, see *PP v Teo Poh Leng* [1992] 1 SLR 15.

in section 304A of a maximum of two years' imprisonment is extremely low and should be increased. Notably, that same penalty is prescribed for the offence of a rash or negligent act which causes grievous hurt.[61] Additionally, a higher penalty should be prescribed for causing death by a rash act compared to by a negligent act. The Penal Code (Amendment) Bill 2006 will, if passed, improve the law by increasing the maximum penalty for rash act causing death to five years' imprisonment, while retaining the two-year term for negligent act causing death.[62]

6. Partial Defences to Murder

Besides spelling out the fault elements for murder, section 300 of the Code has seven 'special exceptions' or partial defences to murder which, if successfully pleaded, reduces the offence of murder to culpable homicide not amounting to murder. These special exceptions are provocation, exceeding private defence, sudden fight, diminished responsibility, exceeding public powers, consent and infanticide.[63] Due to constraints over length, only the first four of these defences have been selected for discussion and, even then, only to point out certain matters which are likely to be of interest to those seeking a comparison with English law. When considering these defences, it is important to bear in mind that in Singapore, the legal burden is on the accused to prove a defence on a balance of probabilities.[64]

(i) Provocation: Special Exception 1 to Section 300

The main part of this provision reads as follows:

> Culpable homicide is not murder if the offender whilst deprived of the power of self-control by grave and sudden provocation, causes the death of the person who gave the provocation, or causes the death of any other person by mistake or accident.

---

[61] S 338.

[62] The Bill proposes a similar revision to the s 338 offence, with the penalty for rash act causing grievous hurt increased to 4 years' imprisonment while retaining the 2-year term for negligent act causing grievous hurt.

[63] For a detailed discussion of these defences see S Yeo, *Criminal Defences in Malaysia and Singapore* (Singapore, 2005).

[64] By virtue of s 107 of the Evidence Act Cap 97, Reprint 1999, and discussed by the Privy Council in *Jayasena v R* [1970] AC 618. For a critical discourse against placing the burden of proving a defence on the accused see M Hor, 'The Presumption of Innocence—A Constitutional Discourse for Singapore' [1995] *Singapore Journal of Legal Studies* 365 at 369–76.

Although this exception does not refer at all to an objective test, the Singaporean courts have, following the lead of their Indian counterparts, read the test into it.[65] Additionally, the courts have adopted the ruling of the House of Lords in *DPP v Camplin*[66] of partially subjectivising the test by attributing certain personal characteristics of the accused to the ordinary person.[67] Under this ruling, the accused's personal characteristics are categorised according to whether they affect the gravity of the provocation or the power of self-control of an ordinary person.[68]

The Singaporean courts have held that any of the accused's personal characteristics which affect the gravity of the provocation may be attributed to the ordinary person for the purpose of determining whether such a person might have lost self-control and reacted in the way the accused did. Where a characteristic of the accused does not affect the gravity of the provocation, it is unnecessary to refer to it and the courts will ignore it.[69] It follows that the law will recognise only those characteristics of the accused which were the subject of the provocation. This stems from the proposition that, for the provocation to be grave and sudden, it must have been directed at a particular characteristic of the accused.[70]

In respect of the accused's personal characteristics affecting the power of self-control, the courts have followed *Camplin* in recognising youthful immaturity as a relevant characteristic.[71] A case has yet to be decided as to whether the sex of the accused is also to be so recognised, as was done in *Camplin*. There is, however, case authority recognising the power of self-control expected of the social group to which an accused belongs.[72] The level of self-control contemplated here is that of a whole class of normal people of a particular social group. As such, the temperaments of individuals whose powers of self-control are regarded as abnormal within their own class or group will be excluded. It follows that the Singaporean courts would not go so far as the House of Lords in *DPP v*

---

[65] For the leading Indian case on this issue see *Nanavati v State of Maharashtra* AIR [1962] SC 605.

[66] [1978] AC 705.

[67] The Singaporean courts have preferred this term to that of the 'reasonable man' under English law: see *PP v Kwan Cin Cheng* [1998] 2 SLR 345 at para [65].

[68] *Ibid*, at 718 per Lord Diplock, and approved of in *PP v Kwan Cin Cheng* [1998] 2 SLR 345 at paras [48]–[50]; *Lim Chin Chong v PP* [1998] 2 SLR 794 at para [29]; *Lau Lee Peng v PP* [2000] 2 SLR 628 at para [29].

[69] *Ithinin bin Kamari v PP* [1993] 2 SLR 245 at 252.

[70] *PP v Kwan Cin Cheng* [1998] 2 SLR 345.

[71] *PP v Koh Swee Beng* [1990] SLR 462.

[72] *Koh Swee Beng v PP* [1991] SLR 319. See also the Brunei High Court case of *PP v Lim Eng Kiat* [1995] 1 MLJ 625 where the court held that the test to be applied was the self-control 'of the ordinary man of the [Chinese] community in Brunei from which the defendant comes'. The Brunei Penal Code has an identical provision to s 300 of the Singaporean Code.

Smith (Morgan)[73] to permit an accused's particular mental condition or personality trait to affect the power of self-control expected of an ordinary person.[74]

(ii) Exceeding Private Defence: Special Exception 2 to Section 300

This partial defence to murder is available to an offender who is unsuccessful in pleading the general defence of private defence under the Code.[75] For the purposes of this discussion, it will suffice to note that the general defence requires the accused not to have caused 'more harm than it is necessary to inflict for the purpose of defence'.[76] This involves a largely objective appraisal of the necessity of the accused's conduct in the circumstances as reasonably apprehended by him or her.[77] If the court finds that the killing was unnecessary (and therefore that excessive force was used), the court will then consider whether Exception 2 will apply to reduce the offence to culpable homicide not amounting to murder. The exception reads:

> Culpable homicide is not murder if the offender, in the exercise in good faith of the right of private defence of person or property, exceeds the power given to him by law, and causes the death of the person against whom he is exercising such right of defence, without premeditation and without any intention of doing more harm than is necessary for the purpose of such defence.

The term 'good faith' appearing in the exception is defined by the Code as doing or believing in something 'with due care and attention'.[78] On one interpretation, the term requires the accused to have reasonably believed the killing to be necessary for the purpose of defence. However, a competing interpretation is that the word 'exercise' appearing in the exception means to 'invoke' or 'summon' the right of private defence as opposed to acting out that right. Under this interpretation, the purpose of the term 'in good faith' is to require the existence of the circumstances which avail the accused of the right of private defence before the exception can be considered. This latter interpretation has been adopted by the

---

[73] (2001) 1 AC 146. *Smith (Morgan)* was not followed by the Privy Council in *Attorney-General for Jersey v Holley* [2005] UKPC 23; [2005] 3 All ER 371.

[74] See *PP v Kwan Cin Cheng* [1998] 2 SLR 345 at para [65], which held that the defence would be denied 'to those who overreact because they are exceptionally pugnacious, bad-tempered and over-sensitive'.

[75] The general defence is covered in ss 96–106 of the Code. For a detailed discussion see S Yeo, *Criminal Defences in Malaysia and Singapore* (Singapore, 2005), Ch 5.

[76] S 99(4), which reads: '[t]he right of private defence in no case extends to the inflicting of more harm than it is necessary to inflict for the purpose of defence.'

[77] S 100, which reads in part: '[t]he right of private defence of the body extends, under the restrictions mentioned in s 99, to the voluntary causing of death or of any other harm to the assailant, if the offence which occasions the exercise of the right is [in response to] ... such an assault as may reasonably cause the apprehension that death ... [or] grievous hurt ... will otherwise be the consequence of such assault'.

[78] S 52.

Singaporean courts, leading them to hold that the exception will succeed where the accused honestly believed (albeit unreasonably) that the killing was necessary in defence.[79]

(iii) Sudden Fight: Special Exception 4 to Section 300

This defence appears to have been borrowed from the English doctrine of chance medley.[80] The exception reads as follows:

> Culpable homicide is not murder if it is committed without premeditation in a sudden fight in the heat of passion upon a sudden quarrel, and without the offender having taken undue advantage or acted in a cruel or unusual manner.

> *Explanation*

> It is immaterial in such cases which party offers the provocation or commits the first assault.

Several of the elements of the exception are interconnected. The requirement for the quarrel and fight to be 'sudden' aligns with the need for the accused not to have premeditated the causing of death. Similarly, the requirement for the killing to have been done in the heat of passion is consistent with the need for the killing not to have been premeditated. At the same time, the recognition by the exception that the killing had been done in the heat of passion explains why the offender is afforded some leeway in taking advantage (provided it was not excessive) over his or her opponent. The rationale for the exception treating an offender as less blameworthy than a murderer is that his or her 'judgment was clouded by the dust of conflict or inflamed by the heat of passion'.[81]

Sudden fight shares certain common features with provocation and private defence, and it is for this reason that all three defences are often pleaded in the same case.[82] By way of comparison with provocation, a feature of sudden quarrels which escalate into fights is that the parties would have provoked each other to a high degree. The express reference in Exception 4 to 'in the heat of passion upon a sudden quarrel' describes the underlying emotion at play in cases of sudden fight, which is the same as the deprivation of self-control contemplated by the defence of provocation. Also, like the plea of provocation, the defence of sudden fight will fail if it is shown that the accused had premeditated the violent encounter. However, there are two material differences between the two defences.

---

[79] *Soosay v PP* [1993] 3 SLR 272.

[80] The doctrine became obsolete when the Offences against the Person Act 1828 (UK) abolished punishment and forfeiture in any case of killing without felony, so as to remove the distinction which had until then existed between chance medley and other cases of excusable homicide such as a killing under provocation.

[81] *Tan Chee Wee v PP* [2004] 1 SLR 479 at para [53].

[82] The comparative exercise which follows has been extracted from S Yeo, *Criminal Defences in Malaysia and Singapore* (Singapore, 2005), Ch 15, which contains further material and insights.

First, the defence of provocation need not have arisen in the course of a fight. Secondly, for provocation it is the loss of self-control which forms the essence of the defence, whereas for Exception 4 it is the sudden fight. One consequence of this is that a higher level of lost self-control is required for provocation than for sudden fight. Another is that the defence of provocation permits a greater degree of disproportionate retaliation than does the defence of sudden fight.[83]

Comparing sudden fight with private defence reveals that they are similar in that the killing must not have been premeditated. This is especially true for private defence, which envisages situations where the accused is taking defensive action against an initial aggressor. Furthermore, circumstances involving a plea of private defence will invariably involve a fight. However, the two defences differ in material ways. First, for private defence it is necessary to identify who the initial aggressor was for the purpose of determining whether the accused's act of killing was done in the lawful exercise of private defence. In contrast, for sudden fight, according to the explanation accompanying the exception, it is immaterial which party committed the first assault. Another difference is that private defence requires the accused to have sought the protection of the public authorities if there was time to do so,[84] whereas this is not a requirement of sudden fight. A further difference is that private defence requires the harm inflicted to have been necessary for the purpose of defence, whereas sudden fight invokes a different measure over what the accused is permitted to do, namely, without the accused having taken undue advantage or acted in a cruel or unusual manner. Under this measure, the accused could still successfully rely on sudden fight even if the act and manner of killing the deceased was not necessary. The allowance under sudden fight given to the accused to exercise a degree of advantage over his or her opponent effectively means that the accused could have used disproportionate force, which is something that is disallowed under private defence.

Thus far, the comparison has been made between sudden fight and private defence. There is also the plea of exceeding private defence discussed earlier which, like sudden fight, is a partial defence to murder. As might be expected, exceeding private defence is closer in similarity to sudden fight than the complete defence of private defence. The feature shared by the partial defences (but not the complete one) is that they can succeed even where the accused had applied excessive force in killing his or her opponent in a fight. That said, these two defences approach the issue of excessive force differently. In the case of exceeding private defence, the accused is partially exonerated because he or she honestly believed that the force used was necessary when it was objectively excessive. In relation to sudden fight, the accused is permitted to exercise a degree of advantage over his or her opponent, which includes applying excessive force,

---

[83] *PP v Seow Khoon Kwee* [1988] 1 SLR 871 is a case example where provocation failed but sudden fight succeeded.

[84] S 99(3), which reads: '[t]here is no right of private defence in cases in which there is time to have recourse to the protection of the public authorities'.

provided it was not so out of proportion to the harm threatened that it constituted 'undue advantage'. The concession of permitting the accused to take advantage recognises the fact that he or she had killed in a sudden fight in the heat of passion upon a sudden quarrel.

It is debatable whether or not a defence of sudden fight should continue to be recognised under Singaporean law. In favour of its abolition is the view that the law should not be seen to condone fights and that the defences of provocation and exceeding private defence adequately cover cases where an accused deserves to escape a murder conviction. For its retention, the argument may be made that fights do often happen suddenly and people who kill in the course of one are less culpable than, say, those who coolly plan and carry out a murder. Furthermore, as real life cases show, there will be circumstances when the defence of sudden fight is established but where the defences of provocation and exceeding private defence will fail.

(iv) Diminished Responsibility: Special Exception 7 to Section 300

This exception was introduced in 1961 when the Singapore legislature decided to adopt the defence appearing in section 2 of the Homicide Act 1957 (UK).[85] It reads:

> Culpable homicide is not murder if the offender was suffering from such abnormality of mind (whether arising from a condition of arrested or retarded development of mind or any inherent causes or induced by disease or injury) as substantially impaired his mental responsibility for his acts or omissions in causing the death or being a party to causing the death.

A study of Singaporean cases has shown that, while clinical witnesses do provide detailed reports to the courts on the accused's mental condition, these nearly always involve scientific criteria and terminology with little or no reference to the legally formulated prescribed causes listed in the exception.[86] The determination of diminished responsibility cases would be improved considerably were trial judges to require clinical witnesses to identify which prescribed cause, if any, in their opinion gave rise to the accused's abnormality of mind. This is because expert evidence that an accused suffered from a clinically recognised mental disorder may not always establish one of the prescribed causes mentioned in the exception.

---

[85] The Malaysian legislature has not done the same, so that only the defence of unsoundness of mind under s 84 of the Malaysian Penal Code is available to mentally disordered persons charged with murder. The Singaporean Code has an identical provision. It reads:
'Nothing is an offence which is done by a person who, at the time of doing it, by reason of unsoundness of mind, is incapable of knowing the nature of the act, or that he is doing what is either wrong or contrary to law.'

[86] See S Yeo, 'Improving the Determination of Diminished Responsibility Cases' [1999] *Singapore Journal of Legal Studies* 27.

(v) Penalty Structure

Where the offender would otherwise have been convicted of murder but for one of the special exceptions, he or she will be punished under section 304 which comprises two parts. The first part covers cases where the offender's fault was intentional, as described in section 300(a), (b) or (c), while the second part covers cases where the offender's fault comprised knowledge alone, as described in section 300(d). Consequently, where one of the special exceptions applies, the sentencing court must determine whether the offender had acted with intention or with knowledge alone. This may pose problems in cases of diminished responsibility where, on account of an abnormality of mind, it is uncertain whether the offender had killed with intention or just knowledge.

7. Conclusion

The Indian Law Commission has recommended the retention of the substantive law expressed in the Penal Code provisions on culpable homicide, thereby attesting to their soundness.[87] However, the Commission thought that the law could be expressed more clearly by dismantling the generic/specie structure of sections 299 and 300. Under the Commission's proposal, murder would first be defined, followed by a provision defining culpable homicide not amounting to murder which expressly excludes the fault elements for murder. The Commission's draft provisions read as follows:

Section 299. Murder

Whoever causes death by doing an act—

(a) with the intention of causing death, or

(b) with the intention of causing such bodily injury as is sufficient in the ordinary course of nature to cause death, or as the offender knows to be likely to cause death of the person to whom the harm is caused, or

(c) with the knowledge that the act is so imminently dangerous that it must, in all probability, cause death or such bodily injury as is likely to cause death, and without any excuse for incurring such risk,

commits murder.

Section 300. Culpable homicide not amounting to murder

Where a person causes death by doing an act with the intention of causing such bodily injury as is likely to cause death or with the knowledge that by such act he is likely to

---

[87] 42nd Report, *Indian Penal Code* (New Delhi, 1971).

cause death, and such act is not murder under clause (b) or clause (c) of section 299, he commits culpable homicide not amounting to murder.

Overall, the schematic approach taken by the Code towards the fault elements for homicide is to be commended for promoting maximum certainty and fair labelling, two important hallmarks of a sound criminal law and criminal justice system. If there is any lesson to be gained by law reformers from a study of the Singaporean (and Indian) law of homicide, it is the need to formulate the fault elements for murder not in isolation but alongside the fault elements for other homicide offences, such as manslaughter and special homicide offences.[88]

---

[88] Eg, culpable driving, the administration of drugs, or engaging in other forms of highly dangerous activities which cause death.

Index